THE YORK
FACTORY
EXPRESS

OTHER BOOKS BY
NANCY MARGUERITE ANDERSON

*The Pathfinder: A.C. Anderson's Journeys
in the West* (Heritage House, 2011)

THE YORK FACTORY

EXPRESS

Fort Vancouver to Hudson Bay, 1826–1849

Nancy Marguerite Anderson

RONSDALE PRESS

RONSDALE PRESS
3350 West 21st Avenue, Vancouver, B.C. Canada V6S 1G7
www.ronsdalepress.com

Typesetting: Julie Cochrane, in Caslon 11.5 pt on 15
Cover Design: Julie Cochrane
Cover Image: York Factory Express boats on their way from Norway House to Oxford House. Courtesy of HBC Archives, 1985/44/34.
Maps: Eric Leinberger
Paper: Ancient Forest Friendly Enviro 100 edition, 60 lb. Husky (FSC), 100% post-consumer waste, totally chlorine-free and acid-free.

Ronsdale Press wishes to thank the following for their support of its publishing program: the Canada Council for the Arts, the Government of Canada, the British Columbia Arts Council, and the Province of British Columbia through the British Columbia Book Publishing Tax Credit program.

Library and Archives Canada Cataloguing in Publication

Title: The York Factory Express / Nancy Marguerite Anderson.

Names: Anderson, Nancy Marguerite, 1946– author.

Description: Includes bibliographical references and index.

Identifiers: Canadiana (print) 2019007180X | Canadiana (ebook) 20190071818 | ISBN 9781553805786 (softcover) | ISBN 9781553805793 (HTML) | ISBN 9781553805809 (PDF)

Subjects: LCSH: Hudson's Bay Company — History — 19th century. | LCSH: Fur trade — Northwest, Canadian — History — 19th century. | LCSH: Fur trade — Northwest, Pacific — History — 19th century. | LCSH: Trade routes — Northwest, Canadian — History — 19th century. | LCSH: Trade routes — Northwest, Pacific — History — 19th century. | LCSH: Fur traders — Northwest, Canadian — History — 19th century. | LCSH: Fur traders — Northwest, Pacific — History — 19th century.

Classification: LCC FC3213.9.F7 A53 2021 | DDC 971.2/01 — dc23

At Ronsdale Press we are committed to protecting the environment. To this end we are working with Canopy and printers to phase out our use of paper produced from ancient forests. This book is one step towards that goal.

Printed in Canada by Island Blue, Victoria, B.C.

This book is dedicated to
Robert James Harvey, Q.C., 1927–2013.
He would have loved these stories.

༄༅

It is also dedicated to my
great-great-grandfather James Birnie,
who travelled out and in with the
1826 York Factory Express.

ACKNOWLEDGEMENTS

Many of the York Factory Express journals have been preserved in the British Columbia Archives, and I thank the Royal British Columbia Museum and the BC Archives for making them accessible to me. Another set of journals came from the University of Alberta Libraries online, "Peel's Prairie Provinces," and I also thank them for their generosity and accessibility.

I give special thanks to the Hudson's Bay Company Archives, who preserved Lieutenant Aemilius Simpson's 1826 journal in its Fort Vancouver records, where I found James Birnie in it. This journal was the inspiration for this book.

I thank my readers, Michael Kennedy, and Susan Smith-Josephy, who both encouraged and criticized me. I also thank Daniel Kyba, who researched John Charles's full story and generously shared his findings with me. Thanks also go to Caroline Gurney, who told me how Paul Kane met Thomas Lowe at Boat Encampment.

More than anyone else I have to thank my editor, Audrey McClellan of West Coast Editorial Associates (www.westcoasteditors.com), whose work has, as always, immensely improved my writing and story-telling.

CONTENTS

THE YORK
FACTORY
EXPRESS

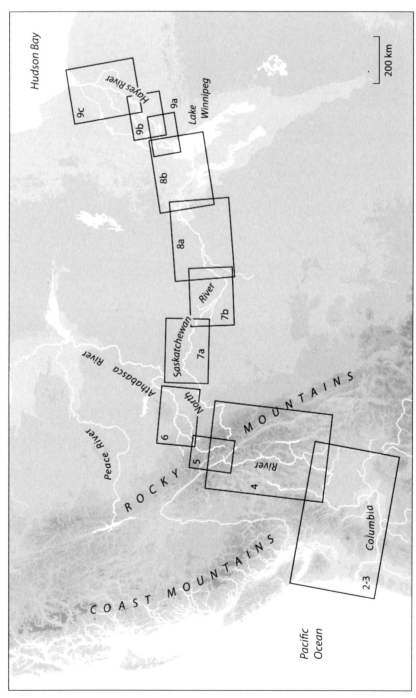

This series of 11 maps will bring the reader from Fort Vancouver, on the Pacific coast, to York Factory, on Hudson Bay, and the return trip.

York Factory Express

ᔑᒷ

LOUIS MARINEAU SPENT most of his adult life in the New Caledonia District west of the Rocky Mountains. From the district's early days, he was there and constantly on the move, a horseman riding from one Hudson's Bay Company (HBC) trading post to another, from one First Nations village to another, throughout the year. Everyone knew him by sight, but no one knew him well.

For the most part he rode alone, but every spring, when the snow lay on the ground, Louis Marineau rode away from Fort Alexandria at the head of the New Caledonia "spring express," taking men and mail to the Columbia River post of Fort Colvile in time to meet the men and boats making their way up the river from the HBC headquarters at Fort Vancouver, near the mouth of the Columbia River. The men from Fort Vancouver, and those who joined them along the way, made up the annual York Factory Express, which crossed the Rocky Mountains on its way to Hudson Bay. Marineau also met the incoming Columbia Express every September at the same post, and he delivered the men new to the territory to Fort Alexandria, on the Fraser River. Marineau's delivery system functioned because he was so reliable: he never failed in his duty. In his quiet way he was an important but unacknowledged part of the York Factory Express, the New Caledonia man who kept the lines of communication open and the men moving.

Almost nothing is known about Louis Marineau. Although he was always called Marineau in the fur trade journals, his full name was Louis Desasten (Martineau). He was French Canadian ("Canadien"), born in Lower Canada (Quebec) about 1800. He arrived in New Caledonia as early as 1826 and may have gone out to Hudson Bay with the early York Factory Expresses in 1827 and 1828. By 1840, he was stationed at Fort Alexandria. He took a First Nations woman as his wife, and if he had children he raised them there. His descendants, if any, are still here, although we do not know who they are.

In the early years of the North West Company, the Canadiens crossed to the west side of the Rocky Mountains in such numbers that they ruled the fur trade. Even after the Hudson's Bay Company took control of the territory in 1821, the Canadiens were the most conspicuous members of the early canoe brigades and the York Factory Express that followed.

They were, however, not the only voyageurs west of the Rockies. The Iroquois were here too, in large numbers. They were the tough guys, the "bullies" of the York Factory Express, who maintained order with their fists. Michel Kaonassé was one of these men. He had arrived at Fort Vancouver by 1834 and served in New Caledonia the following year, where he was steersman in the brigades from Fort St. James to Fort Vancouver. In January 1843, he squared wood for the saws at Fort Alexandria, which meant he acted as carpenter and, probably, boat-builder.

His Indigenous wife died later that year, and he moved on to Fort Colvile after her burial. In 1848, after the death of Joe Tayentas, the long-time guide for the York Factory Express, Michel Kaonassé took over that important position and led out both Thomas Lowe's 1848 express and that of John Charles a year later. In 1849, Kaonassé's inattention led to two boats colliding in the middle of a fierce set of rapids on the Columbia River. The men from one of those wrecked boats were stranded on a rocky islet in the middle of the river until the second boat was repaired and sent out to rescue them. All reached Fort Vancouver in safety.

This accident did not mean the end of Kaonassé's career as guide for the York Factory Express. He continued in that position for a few more years, until 1852, when he injured himself to the point of disability and was replaced by another man. Unable to work, Kaonassé retired from the HBC and disappeared.

Scots and Orkneymen also worked on the west side of the Rocky Mountains, although they rarely made it into the stories of the York Factory Express. They were known to be good agriculturists at the inland posts, but indifferent voyageurs. One of them might be Norman Smith, who travelled west in Thomas Lowe's 1848 Columbia Express. On the Athabasca River, the voyageurs, who were tracking the boats along the riverbank, startled a bear, which ran up the bank in its surprise and attacked Smith. Before it could be driven off, the bear bit Smith's forehead and face, although Lowe said the damage was not serious. Common as the name Smith might be in the East, there are no men of that name in any of the journals from the west side of the Rocky Mountains. It is sometimes difficult to track the men who worked in the HBC trade west of the Rockies, but Norman Smith seems more invisible than most.

This is not true of others: for example, John Greig. He was born about 1825 in the Orkney Islands and joined the HBC in 1844. From York Factory, Greig was sent across the country to Fort Colvile where he worked as a farm labourer. He retired in 1851 and rode to Fort Langley in the outgoing brigade led by Alexander Caulfield Anderson. At Fort Victoria he quarried limestone at "Lime Bay," and burning it in a small kiln, produced lime which he sold to the HBC for use on its farmlands.[1] Eventually he purchased land on Tod Inlet, in central Saanich, where he farmed, manufactured lime, and entertained his neighbours with food, drink, music, and stories of his crossing of the continent with the York Factory Express. After Greig's death, his sons sold the property to the Saanich Lime Company, and eventually the Portland Cement Company, run by Robert Pim Butchart, took it over. Today his farm and lime quarry is part of the world-famous Butchart Gardens.

Many early Canadiens and Orkneymen spent their voyaging career on the east side of the Rocky Mountains, on the Saskatchewan River or in the Red River Colony. There they raised the mixed-blood children they had with their Indigenous wives. When the Canadiens in Lower Canada no longer chose voyaging as their career, the mixed-blood youths from the Saskatchewan District and Red River joined the HBC and were sent to the west side of the Rocky Mountains. They are now known as the Métis (may-tea), from a French word that means "mixed."[2] Michel Fallardeau was one of these Métis. He joined the HBC in 1827, and in the autumn came west over the Rocky Mountains in Edward Ermatinger's Columbia Express.

For the next twenty years, Fallardeau lived and worked in New Caledonia, travelling to Fort Vancouver with the New Caledonia Brigades most years. In 1847, when Chief Trader A.C. Anderson made one of two cross-country expeditions in search of a new brigade trail to Fort Langley from Kamloops, Michel Fallardeau was one of five men who accompanied him.

The following year, Fallardeau suffered a stroke or heart attack while guarding the Fort Alexandria horses, and although he recovered, the attack frightened him. He returned to his family at Kamloops and died there of a supposed beating by Chief Trader Paul Fraser in or before spring 1855. Fraser argued that rough boards were good enough for the coffin of "the rascal," Fallardeau, but the Iroquois who built Fallardeau's coffin objected. Fraser himself was killed in summer 1855 when a tree dropped on the tent he occupied. The suspicion lingers that a voyageur killed Fraser for the beating death of Fallardeau, but no records remain to prove this. It is just a story, but Métis history is recorded in its stories, even on the west side of the Rocky Mountains.

— • —

Canadien, Iroquois, and Métis histories are told in the stories of the York Factory Express, the annual journey from Fort Vancouver to Hudson Bay and return. The main party, often twenty or thirty strong, departed Fort Vancouver (today's Vancouver, Washington), on the lower Columbia River, in late March. They worked their way to the upper river posts, forts Okanogan and Colvile, where in later years they picked up the outgoing New Caledonia and Thompson River men. From those western posts the York Factory Express made its way over the Rocky Mountains via Boat Encampment (at the Big Bend of the Columbia River), Athabasca Pass, and the Jasper Valley. At Fort Assiniboine and Edmonton House, the express-men joined the men of the Lesser Slave Lake Brigades and those of the Saskatchewan District, who were also on their way to York Factory, on Hudson Bay.

The York Factory Express was one of three transportation systems west of the Rocky Mountains. The first transportation system, on which everything else depended, consisted of the London ships that sailed into Fort Vancouver every summer, and also into Hudson Bay. These ships carried the trade goods to the headquarters on the Pacific coast, and on Hudson Bay, where they were picked up by the brigades. They also brought the HBC reports and letters, and passengers who were picked up by the expresses and the brigades. The journey to and from Fort Vancouver, around the southern tip of South America, took the London ships two years, so to save time, many papers and passengers were delivered to York Factory, on Hudson Bay. From York Factory they were transported across the continent to the Columbia District by the incoming express on its return journey to Fort Vancouver.

The second transportation system consisted of the larger, slow-moving brigades, which carried the winter catch of furs from the interior posts to the London ships, then carried the trade goods back to the posts. When the Columbia District men, who travelled in the York Factory Express, reached Edmonton House, they joined the Saskatchewan Brigades that were carrying furs to the London ships at York Factory. The Saskatchewan District's express-men, who were attending the HBC council meeting at Red River (now part of Winnipeg) or Norway House, travelled out with the brigades and were indistinguishable from them.

West of the Rocky Mountains, however, the brigades operated entirely separately from the express. The brigades left their New Caledonia headquarters of Fort St. James in May of every year, carrying out their winter-trapped furs. The brigade men travelled south and east by boat and pack horse to Fort Okanogan, reaching that place in early June — two months after the York Factory Express men had passed the post on their way up the Columbia River.

The brigade boats arrived at Fort Vancouver in late June and delivered their packs of furs to the storehouse, to be shipped to London with the departing London ship.

The brigade men then left Fort Vancouver in July, carrying heavy loads of tobacco, firearms, and trade goods for their winter business of trading with First Nations men for furs. They were at Fort Okanogan by August, a full two months before the incoming express was expected. By early September, they had reached their headquarters at Fort St. James and were distributing the newly imported trade goods throughout the surrounding districts.

The third transportation system was the York Factory Express, which left its headquarters of Fort Vancouver every year, carrying out papers and reports for the annual HBC council meeting in the East. Any passengers who travelled out with the express were either attending the meeting, transferring to different posts east of the Rocky Mountains, or retiring. The York Factory Express was all about fast communication of information to the governor and council, and to London via the ships that sailed into Hudson Bay.

However, when the express-men from the west side of the Rocky Mountains reached Edmonton House, they became part of the Saskatchewan Brigades, helping the men in those brigades make their way to York Factory with their winter furs. The presence of the express-men strengthened the Saskatchewan Brigades, making it safer for all the HBC men travelling down the North Saskatchewan River through the territory of the Blackfoot, Blood, and Peigan, who were, in theory, always ready to attack a weak party of travellers.

— • —

This book tells the stories of the York Factory Express and of the Saskatchewan Brigades. These stories are told in the words of the gentlemen, the educated, usually Scottish traders, clerks, and other administrators who wrote the journals. However, the men who made the express journey possible are the invisible, unnamed Canadiens and their Métis descendants who powered the boats across the continent every year between 1826 and 1854. The gentlemen were the passengers. The Canadiens, Orkneymen, and Iroquois, and their Métis children and grandchildren did all the heavy work and were almost entirely responsible for the success of the 5,400-mile journey. But their history was oral. If the gentlemen had not preserved the stories the voyageurs told them, we would not have a written record of this history today.

The York Factory Express journey to Hudson Bay, and its return as the Columbia Express, was unique to the Hudson's Bay Company's fur trade west of the Rocky Mountains after 1825. The earlier North West Company ran canoe brigades across the country from Lachine (now part of Montreal) to the Columbia River, but the HBC's York Factory Express was a different animal altogether. The NWC brigades carried heavy loads of furs or goods; the express carried papers and passengers out of the territory, and papers and passengers in — very little more.

The thirty or so men who travelled out in the York Factory Express began their journey at Fort Vancouver, the HBC's Columbia River headquarters, 100 miles east of the rugged points of land where the Columbia River rumbled into the Pacific Ocean. The express-men paddled their clinker-built boats up the rock- and rapids-filled Columbia to the base of the Rocky Mountains at Boat Encampment, 900 miles east and north of Fort Vancouver. The men literally pulled their boats upriver, for their camp at Boat Encampment was more than 1,500 feet above sea level. They then climbed over the Rocky Mountains on foot. At Jasper's House, on the east side of the Rockies, they were 3,000 feet above sea level. Their river route eastward would return them to salt water once more, at York Factory on the shores of Hudson Bay. It was an amazing climb and an amazing descent, and they would do another climb and descent on their journey home.

But the York Factory Express was more complicated than a difficult climb over the Rocky Mountains, followed by a relatively easy drift down the Athabasca and North Saskatchewan rivers. It was also a carefully timed journey, as the gentlemen were to attend the annual meeting at Red River or Norway House, where they delivered their district accounts to the governor and council of the Hudson's Bay Company. They left Fort Vancouver in time to cross Athabasca Pass in the early spring, while the snow underfoot was solid and the weather generally good. They reached the Athabasca River when its ice was mostly melted. At the point where the Athabasca flowed as far south as it would go, they abandoned their canoes and boats and crossed the land portage to Edmonton House, on the North Saskatchewan River.

More transformations occurred as they reached Edmonton House. At that prairie headquarters the fast-travelling, lightly laden express party joined the Saskatchewan District's slow-moving brigades that lumbered down the North Saskatchewan River, passing through rolling grasslands. The express-men had feasted on biscuits, potatoes, and salmon west of the Rockies; now they gorged on pemmican, bison steaks, and whitefish on the east side of the mountains. On the prairies they hunted "buffalo" (more accurately called bison), moose deer (moose), and bear, and sometimes those creatures hunted them. They gave aid to tattered remnants of Indian bands who had battled their enemies and lost; at times they met the victors of those endless Indigenous wars. As time passed, they met the missionaries who established missions among the First Nations peoples along the Saskatchewan River and at Norway House. On their return to the west side of the

Rockies, they ran into Americans who flooded west over the Oregon Trail to claim lands in the territory the fur traders had opened up.

Changes happened everywhere over these years, but for the Canadien voyageurs and their Métis descendants, life remained much the same as it had been for their seventeenth-century French ancestors, who came from Normandy, Perche, and Île-de-France in the north of France, and Saintonge, Nantes, and La Rochelle to the south. These Canadiens had a long history of settlement in Quebec, and many had long histories of service in the fur trade of the Hudson's Bay Company and its predecessor, the North West Company.

The Canadiens also had a long history of getting along with the First Nations people who lived in villages close to their own in Quebec. Many of their French ancestors had arrived in Quebec with Samuel de Champlain, and, like Champlain, they had a natural ability to get along with others. They were historically a warm, amiable people who called each other friends, brothers, and cousins. They got along with everyone they respected, and quietly resisted those who offended or mistreated them.

The Canadiens brought their French language into the fur trade, and all who worked with them had to speak their tongue. They brought their beloved birchbark canoes to the fur trade as well, but traditions changed and over the years they gave up their canoes for the more practical wooden boats built by the Orkneymen. The Canadiens were adaptable people, always willing to adjust their traditions when it suited them. They sang their traditional songs from France and Quebec, and changed them. They celebrated variations of their Catholic-based ceremonies mixed with the traditions of their First Nations or Métis wives or mothers. When a companion died, as sometimes happened, they mourned his death with a song they called a "complainte." In their world, they were all friends and companions, and they understood and supported each other.

Those who were chosen for the express were strong young men whose overabundance of testosterone was the engine that powered their boats. They brought many and varied skills to the trade: their long-time familiarity with boats, canoes, and water travel gave them the ability to quickly repair the damaged boats and canoes. They were river smart, and when the wind blew in the right direction they put up their sails and relaxed.

They taught newcomers to the trade how to paddle the canoe and carry the loads over the portages, with the tumpline perfectly adjusted to take the weight. These young men were proud of their vocation. Before they arrived at each post they paused to wash their faces and don fresh shirts and ribbons so they could paddle around the final corner in the river as energetically as if they had just started the voyage.

Like all young men, they partied hard, and they drank their regales of rum, given to them by the gentlemen, with gusto. They consumed enormous amounts of meat when it was available, but starved if it was not. They scorned sleep and paddled long hours every day when the going was good and the river safe. They took many risks, knowing they might not survive them, but they also listened to the advice of their elders.

They trusted their respected guide, following his instructions through dangerous passages, and surviving. They teased each other out of bad moods and made jokes of the unbelievable difficulties they endured. In this way, they accomplished the impossible, and they were always careful to make the impossible appear to be only a few days' casual journey.

This was their life, and they were happy in it. They were young men, and flaunting their manliness was a part of the voyageur culture, just as their ability to hunt for food was a part of their manliness. Like their ancestors, who had left France two centuries earlier and made their homes in the wilderness of Quebec, these men chose to live in a new wilderness. They spurned the gentlemen's idea of civilization. They loved their freedoms and believed that they were free. Many times, Canadien and Métis men who arrived on the west side of the Rocky Mountains never returned home, but married and died in the west.

Their many descendants are still here. We are still here.

CHAPTER 1

The First York Factory Express Journeys

ॐ

THE FIRST OFFICIAL York Factory Express journeys took place in 1826, when two groups of men travelled by two different routes to meet and merge at Edmonton House. The main express party departed Fort Vancouver, on the lower Columbia River, in March. The second party, which left Fort St. James, New Caledonia, in May, had a shorter journey to make, and easier rivers with fewer portages and rapids to contend with.

The York Factory Express that left Fort Vancouver in 1826 was a little different from the expresses that came after it and had difficulties that none of the others experienced. Ensuring the York Factory Express ran efficiently was a learning experience for John McLoughlin, the chief factor (head trader) in charge of Fort Vancouver in 1826, and McLoughlin made some choices that placed stress on the men who had to make the journey. For one thing, he ordered the express-men to deliver calves and piglets to Spokane House for the farms at the new post of Fort Colvile that would be constructed over the summer.

Chief Trader John McLeod, recently in charge of the Thompson's River post, had come down to Fort Vancouver and was leaving the territory. HBC Governor George Simpson was moving him to the east side of the Rocky Mountains, where he would take charge of Norway House.[1] McLoughlin gave McLeod the task of leading out the first York Factory Express. His most important duty was to reach Edmonton House in time to join the Saskatchewan Brigades.

The HBC men travelled across the Rocky Mountains regularly, but until 1826 they had taken the old North West Company route down the Athabasca River from Jasper's House to the Clearwater River, then over the Methye Portage to a system of rivers that led them to Cumberland House, on the Saskatchewan River. This year they would cross to the North Saskatchewan River by way of the new Athabasca Portage (sometimes called the "Assiniboine Portage"). No one knew what this new route might hold for them. It turned out, however, that the most difficult part of the 1826 voyage was the more familiar section through the Columbia District to Boat Encampment at the base of Athabasca Pass. John McLeod described the trip in his journal of the first York Factory Express from Fort Vancouver to Edmonton House:[2]

> March 1826 Monday 20th. Started from Ft. Vancouver at 4 p.m. with 2 Boats accompanied by Messrs. [James] Douglas & [Francis] Ermatinger, passengers, 3 Calves & 3 Pigs. Raining very heavy. Encamped early & gave the men time to take their [regale] at the upper end of the [Plain] before the fort.
>
> Tuesday 21st . . . Proceeded and breakfasted at the upper end of Johnston Island. Proceeded and encamped at a little stream opposite [line illegible]. Rained all day and cold. I am much afraid that the calves will not be got up safe.
>
> Wednesday 22nd. Started at half past 5, put the calves ashore at the foot of the Cascades. Breakfasted in the middle of the Portage. Very disagreeable weather since left Ft. Vancouver.

Thursday 23. Raining all Day. Proceeded about 4 a.m. Put the Calves ashore at the Lower end of Thompsons Portage, gave them in charge to the little Chief and Mr. McKay's guide & one Owhyhee [Hawaiian]. Proceeded with the Boats and encamped at the little Rivière Dalles. Great many Indians assembled and Remained all night. Kept watch all night.[3]

He continued his journey on March 24, making his way through The Dalles and the Chûtes. Many First Nations people who lived on the grasslands on the east side of the Cascade Mountains raised cattle, and some coveted the calves that travelled in the express boats. His journal continues:

Got above the big Dalles by 1 p.m. & arrived at the little Dalles and passed them by at 2 and at 3 arrived at the Chûtes where met with a greater Concourse of Indians than I ever saw. Here they volunteered to Carry the Boats which I permitted as I did not wish to encamp here for fear they might injure the Cattle. After we got everything to the upper end of the portage the Indians began to be rather troublesome and pushing forward towards the Baggage and in putting back from it one of them put an arrow in his Bow and as he was taking an aim at me. Mr. Douglas (as he was paying attention all the time) uncovered his gun and backed it. Two of the Owhyhees took the muskets immediately when Mr. Ermatinger and myself joined and advanced with our gun[s] cocked toward the crowd and pushed them back. A Cayouse [Indian] joined us and spoke to the rascals for their bad Conduct. Got the Boats loaded & Mr. Douglas and myself ran along the shore to protect the Calves till were got a Board which being soon accomplished and proceeded a little piece further and encamped for the night.

Saturday 25th. Raining Weather continuing. Proceeded at 8 o'clock having lost some time in gumming the Boats, went on all Day and encamped at 10 Miles above John Days River where a large Band of Indians visited us. Gave them a smoke and the most part of them went off.

Sunday 26th. The weather fair which is the first fair day since we left Vancouver. Proceeded with a fair wind after breakfast and continued all night, when we encamped below the [Big] Island. One of the Calves from being confined in the Boat all day was lame.[4]

The express arrived at Fort Nez Percés (now Walla Walla) on Tuesday, March 28, and departed two days later. On Saturday, it reached Priest's Rapids, and on Tuesday the men camped at the Piscouhoose (Wenatchie) River. The headwinds they had experienced since they left Fort Nez Percés continued to slow their passage, and on Wednesday, April 5, McLeod noted:

> Snow is only beginning to melt in this quarter consequently Rises the main River much higher than it was about this time last year. Continued our Route and encamped above the Great Eddy below the Whirlpool Rapids [possibly Entiat Rapids].
>
> Thursday 6th. Fine weather. Proceeded three quarters past 4 last night having put up very late, the Calves were immediately landed as usual and their being very hungry they went out without stopping in quest of a spot to feed. I went after them and seeing them safe near the camp I did not tie them . . . I never saw so much snow at this season of the year at this place as there is now for it is still in some places on the Hills down to the water side and the main River very high for the Season. Arrived at Okanagan some time after dark.[5]

Ermatinger remained at Fort Okanogan, where he would greet the incoming express some seven months later. Douglas returned to Fort Vancouver once the boats had safely passed the Chûtes. McLeod and his express-men continued to make their way up the swollen Columbia River, arriving at the forks of the Spokane River on April 11. The HBC's Spokane House was located sixty miles up the Spokane River. McLeod made the journey to the post, where he handed over the calves and piglets he had escorted up the river. He also consulted with the free-trader, Jaco Finlay, who occupied the earlier house three miles distant. All this took time, and it was not until a week had passed that McLeod's party continued their journey up the Columbia River. On April 19:

Encamped about 10 miles below the Pend-d'Oreille River.

Thursday 20th. Started half Past 4 a.m. and Breakfasted 6 miles above Pend-d'Oreille River. Cloudy weather. Passed McGillivray [Kootenay] River about 7 p.m. and encamped at the entrance of the [Lower Arrow] Lake.

Friday 21st. Started half an hour before Daylight. Raining all the morning. Breakfasted about 1/3 the Lake. Cold Raining weather continued on till night and encamped about 5 Leagues from the upper end of the first Lake. Rained all this day.

Saturday 22nd. Started before Daylight & Breakfasted upon an Island in the narrows between the two Lakes. Continued on through the Upper Lake and encamped within 4 or 5 Leagues of the Upper end of the Lake. We did not see an Indian all day.

Sunday 23rd. Started as usual before Daylight but we did not go far before we found the Lake Covered with Ice from side to side. Broke our way through with axe and poles and breakfasted at the Upper end of the Lakes where found about 6 Indians from whom we traded a few [snowshoes] called Bear's Paws. The snow is laying thick yet along the River down to the water edge. Came a long Piece up the River and encamped 12 miles below the Dalles [Steamboat Rapid].

Monday 24th. Rained last night but clear weather this morning. Started at Daybreak. Met two Indians below the Dalles from whom we traded 1 Pair snow shoes and a little Bear Meat. Breakfasted below the Dalles. Continued. The Snow & ice is pounded over the water edge along the River which makes it Difficult for the men to haul upon the line. Encamped half way between both the Dalles [between Steamboat Rapid and Dalles des Morts].[6]

On Wednesday, the express party breakfasted below Crooked Rapid, and McLeod recorded that the men who travelled with him, who were used to going up the Columbia River in the springtime, said they had never seen so much snow as there was this year. McLeod listened to these experienced men and carefully recorded their opinions on the difficulty of travelling up the river that year. His men were familiar with the river and all its moods. They knew what was normal, and what was not. They were the experts and McLeod was the amateur — and like all the gentlemen who travelled this river and others, he knew he was the amateur. He put his faith in his voyageurs and depended upon them to get the whole party across the mountains. And his voyageurs responded: they knew their job and took pride in its difficulty and pleasure in accomplishing the impossible.

The weather continued cold, with six feet of snow along the water's edge, and John McLeod's journal continues with a description of the journey's never-ending difficulties, which continued even after they reached Boat Encampment:

> Arrived at the Rocky Mountain [Boat Encampment] on the 27th inst & the boat in security and started on the 28th but the Snow is so deep that we were obliged to Cut our leather Trowsers to make snow shoes of. We arrived on the East side the mountains the 5 May. Ten to 12 feet [snow] at the Columbia (Great Bend) [Boat Encampment] & 30 feet under foot at the summit of the Pass (6,025 feet above sea) on 2nd May.[7]

The express party reached Jasper's House and found it buried to its eaves in snow. McLeod mentions no difficulties on the journey down the Athabasca River or across the Athabasca Portage. He simply notes he arrived at Edmonton House in safety on May 17. This is an earlier date than many later York Factory Expresses reached that North Saskatchewan River headquarters. Against all odds, the first express from Fort Vancouver made it over the Rocky Mountains in time to avoid causing delays to the Saskatchewan Brigades.

The New Caledonia party of the 1826 York Factory Express left Fort St. James in May, two months after the Fort Vancouver men had set out. They always left their post at a later date, as the Peace River remained ice-bound until early May. Chief Factor James McDougall, who led out the New Caledonia group, kept no journal.

But Chief Factor William Connolly, who set out with the brigade to Fort Vancouver at the same time McDougall took out the express, noted the latter's departure and the route it was to take in his Journal of Occurrences:

May 5th Friday. Every arrangement being completed both for the voyage to York Factory & to Fort Vancouver, at 8 o'clock this Morning Mr. James McDougall with 8 Men took their departure from Stuarts Lake for Fort Simpson, McLeod's Lake, where they will Join Messr. [William] Brown & [William] McBean with the people already there with whom they will proceed, under the command of Mr. Brown, for York Factory. The party going by that route consists of the three above-mentioned Gentlemen & 13 Men. As detailed in the last Journal, they are to convey to Hudson's Bay about 44 pieces of Furs & Castoreum, and in order to accelerate their passage from hence to the East end of the Rocky Mountain Portage, and to add strength to the party in case of an attack from the Beaver Indians, four additional Men accompany them as far as the last Mentioned place, from whence they will return, & bring up whatever Leathers may be procured from the Siccanies, and also the Arms taken out for defence, and what property may remain of what I send to Trade with those Indians.[8]

McDougall's route took his men overland to McLeod Lake on horseback with pack horses. At Fort Simpson (McLeod Lake) the men transferred their goods into canoes and paddled north, via the Pack River, to the junction of the Parsnip and the Peace. The latter river brought them through the northern Rocky Mountain Pass, with its short portage at Finlay Rapids, to Dunvegan House, 150 miles from the eastern edge of the Rockies and on the most southerly bend of the Peace River. From Dunvegan they followed the river north to Athabasca Lake, then pushed up the northward-flowing Athabasca River to the point where Fort Assiniboine had been built in 1823 — a two-day canoe-trip up the Athabasca River from the mouth of the Clearwater. From Fort Assiniboine, the Athabasca Portage led them across country to Edmonton House. The overall route was convoluted, but familiar and relatively easy to travel. Before 1826, every man who entered or left New Caledonia travelled in and out by the Peace, Athabasca, and Clearwater rivers to the Methye Portage and Cumberland House.

James McDougall likely travelled across the Athabasca Portage with the Lesser Slave Lake Brigade, arriving at Edmonton House two days after McLeod and the Fort Vancouver party. On May 24, McLeod and McDougall clambered into York Boats with John Rowand (Chief Factor, Edmonton House) and James McMillan (Chief Trader, Columbia District), beginning their journey down the North Saskatchewan River on their way to York Factory. They reached the HBC headquarters one month later, on June 27, 1826.

James McDougall returned with the incoming express that year, leaving his wife at Carlton House. His instructions were to come into the territory by the Rocky Mountain Portage, which would lead him from Jasper Valley to the headwaters of the Fraser River. Aemilius Simpson, who came into the Columbia District with the returning express that year, kept a detailed journal of his trip, which makes it clear that this route had not often been used by the HBC men who worked in the New Caledonia District. In his journal, Simpson wrote:

> This day has been occupied in making arrangements for our journey across the portage & the separation of the brigade for the Columbia & New Caledonia, the latter pursue a route that has thitherto been passed by few, report says it is a good one which soon leads them to the head waters of Fraser's River.[9]

The incoming route through the Rocky Mountain Portage (today's Yellowhead Pass) worked so well in 1826 that James McDougall, now in charge at Fort St. James, decided it should be used as the outgoing route in 1827. James instructed his brother, George, to lead a party of six men from Fort St. James up the still-frozen Fraser River to Tête Jaune Cache, 200 miles to the east. From that small storehouse in the wilderness, George McDougall would cross the Rocky Mountains via the Rocky Mountain Portage that his brother had used a year earlier. George McDougall's final destination was Carlton House on the North Saskatchewan River, 400 miles downstream from Edmonton House. From there, the forty-year-old clerk would return to Fort St. James with the chief factor's wife and children, who had been left behind at that post eight months earlier. The date of his departure from Fort St. James was April 17. If his party caught up to the York

Factory Express at Edmonton House, he and his men would arrive at Carlton House in mid-June.

The first stage of George McDougall's journey was a challenge in itself. This was the first time that the New Caledonia men had crossed the Rocky Mountain Portage from the headwaters of the Fraser River so early in the year. McDougall and his men walked up the frozen Fraser River north of Fort George (today's Prince George) on snow-shoes, carrying enough provisions to last thirty days. (They would reach their first provisioning post in the Jasper Valley.) For the first while they made good headway on the ice, until the sun emerged from behind clouds and melted the snow. "This caused the snow-shoes to become heavy with snow sticking to them,"[10] McDougall noted in his journal.

The seven men arrived at Tête Jaune Cache exhausted after two weeks of heavy walking. One man died there "of a vile disease" that McDougall did not identify (probably venereal disease). The remain-ing men rested and repaired their damaged snowshoes. Then the clerk's most trusted employee reported that some of their provisions were missing. There was little food remaining, and their situation was precarious. The anxious clerk searched his men's packs and discovered that one Canadien employee had thrown away his share of provisions to lighten his own load.

The section of journal that has been published does not tell how the clerk punished the guilty voyageur; it only says that he crossed the mountain portage with his four remaining men:

Fallen timber, deep snow covered the way and we could make but small progress, and the men were so tired each night that I could not get them to make proper shelter for themselves and was in great dread that they would not live out the night.[11]

On May 1, 1827, the five men reached Henry's House in the Jasper Valley and rested for two days. They were delayed at Jasper's House because the Athabasca River was still ice-covered. Once on the Atha-basca they were joined by Edward Ermatinger's outgoing express from Fort Vancouver. In his own journal, Ermatinger noted, "come up with Mr. McDougall and 4 men from N. Caledonia who have been following the ice these 9 days past from Jasper's House."[12]

McDougall reached Carlton House on June 4, and spent the summer there.[13] His duty done, he returned with the Columbia Express in September and once again passed over the Rocky Mountain Portage to the Fraser River and Fort St. James. The New Caledonia men abandoned the spring crossing of their mountain portage the following year and, instead, joined the York Factory Express at Fort Okanogan. However, they continued to cross the Rocky Mountain Portage every fall, heading into their New Caledonia District from the Jasper Valley. As far as the records show, there was no difficulty experienced by any other New Caledonia man until 1835, when an early winter snowstorm forced the party to turn back to Jasper's House.

— • —

Only a few gentlemen who travelled with the York Factory Express kept journals of their experience; it did not seem to be a requirement of their job. Unlike the voyageurs, who tended to be undifferentiated, the five gentlemen who preserved the stories of the express are a varied group, and we know only a few details of their individual pasts and futures.

Edward Ermatinger led the express in 1827 and 1828, and kept excellent journals that have been published. Unlike many of the other gentlemen in the trade, who were Scottish, Ermatinger was born in Italy of Swiss parents. Because of his father's connection with the fur trade, he and his brother, Francis, joined the Hudson's Bay Company, and both ended up on the west side of the Rocky Mountains. After a decade in the business, however, Edward was bored and returned to Montreal. He loved music and culture, and was an accomplished musician who taught other traders to play musical instruments. Fortunately for us, he was as interested in the voyageurs' songs as in other music, and he wrote down the words and music of many of the songs he heard the voyageurs sing.

George Traill Allan was a tiny man, hardly built for the rough-and-tumble life of the fur trade. Because of his small size he spent most of his time clerking at various posts in the Columbia District and in the Sandwich Islands (Hawaii). His 1841 journal, although sporadically kept, is a delight to read as he tells many stories that other gentlemen did not mention — perhaps because the stories were so familiar to those who spent time working away from the various headquarters of the fur trade.

James Douglas took out the York Factory Express three times over his career as clerk and accountant at Fort Vancouver. However, only one transcript of three possible journals survives (the original is lost). Born in British Guiana to a Scottish father and Creole mother, Douglas was educated in Scotland and joined the fur trade in 1819. By 1825, he worked west of the Rocky Mountains in New Caledonia, and in 1827 he came down to Fort Vancouver. He was a stiff, self-controlled man but an excellent manager. His journal was not a business journal, but a personal one that gives a glimpse into the character of the man who would be named governor of the Colony of British Columbia in November 1858.

Thomas Lowe joined the HBC in Scotland in 1841 and spent a year at fearsome Fort Taku on the Northwest Coast. In 1843, he helped build Fort Victoria, and he spent the next decade as clerk at Fort Vancouver. He took out the York Factory Express in 1847 and 1848, and his journals are especially valuable as they record the rapidly changing history of the Oregon Territory in the 1840s.

John Charles was a very young man when he replaced Thomas Lowe as leader of the York Factory Express in 1849. He was the Métis son of HBC Chief Factor John Charles of Red River and Oxford House. Because of his past and his upbringing, his story differs markedly from those of the other clerks. No one in the HBC thought less of him because he carried Indian blood: no one but Governor Simpson, that is. Because John Charles was Métis, he was listed as postmaster in the HBC books, and although Charles had the same responsibilities as Thomas Lowe, he was paid at a considerably lower scale.[14]

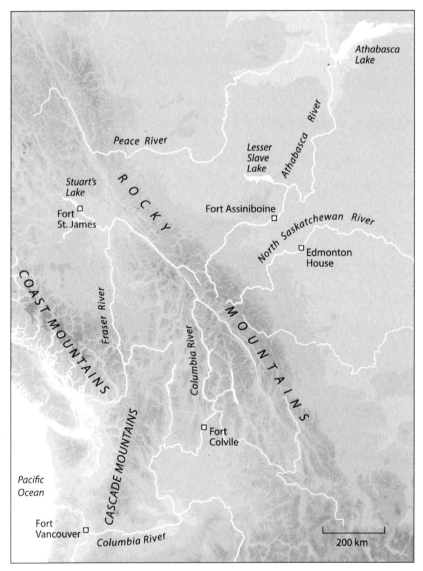

Both the Columbia River and the Peace River led the men from
west of the Rockies to the Athabasca River and Fort Assiniboine.

These are the five gentlemen whose accounts of their journeys
leading the York Factory Express from Fort Vancouver in the years
between 1827 and 1849 have survived. Occasionally other passengers
of the express wrote about some part of the voyage: they might be

gentlemen who joined the group at York Factory for the return passage across the continent to Fort Vancouver, or traders who were travelling from one post to another with the express. Like the gentlemen leading the express, these other journal writers recounted events that happened on the voyage and wrote down the stories they heard — our fur trade history. They learned the names of old places we no longer remember, they camped near the ruins of old posts and heard stories of battles and murders that had happened half a century earlier. Many of the stories recorded in these journals would have been told by the voyageurs. Many more stories were not recorded and have been lost to us.

— • —

Now, however, we are on the banks of the Columbia River, waiting for departure. Because of the Canadien employees (who carried on an ancient maritime tradition of never starting a journey on a Friday), it had become a tradition in the fur trade never to start a long voyage on that weekday — nor would the gentlemen have wished to miss their day of worship on Sunday. The traditional start date for the express was March 20, and most York Factory Express boats paddled away from Fort Vancouver on the first Monday following that date.

The men took up their paddles, and the clerks and passengers settled into the boats. Then the guide — the man who was actually in charge of the express — gave the order to depart.

"*Embarquez!*"

The paddles hit the water and the men raised their voices in song. The gentlemen and their voyageurs had begun their 2,700-mile journey to Hudson Bay.

CHAPTER 2

Fort Vancouver to Fort Nez Percés

৯৫

WHEN THE YORK FACTORY EXPRESS departed from the Columbia River headquarters at Fort Vancouver, the tradition was for every man, woman, and child to come down to the riverbank to wish the express-men *bon voyage*. The men would be gone a long time — a full seven months. Their journey was carefully timed so the men would cross the Rocky Mountains in early spring, when there was little chance of snowfall. They reached Edmonton House, the Saskatchewan District headquarters, in time to join the brigades from Lesser Slave Lake and Edmonton House on their way to Hudson Bay. They would reach York Factory in late June, and leave a few weeks later on their return journey. In September, they returned to Edmonton House. In early October, they crossed the Rocky Mountains for the second time that year. Sometime in early November, if all went well, after a total journey of 5,200 miles, they beached their boats in front of Fort Vancouver. Amazingly, all usually did go well.

Edward Ermatinger is the first of our journal keepers, following in the footsteps of John McLeod, who wrote of his experiences as he crossed the mountains in 1826. Ermatinger led the York Factory Express in 1827 and 1828. The distance from headquarters to Fort Nez Percés was 208 miles, and it took an average of eight days to make the upriver journey. The first of Ermatinger's two journals begins with these words: "March 1827. Tuesday 20th. Fair weather. The Express Boat leaves Fort Vancouver at quarter before 6 o'clock p.m. A second Boat accompanies us as far as the Chûtes to assist in carrying our Boat over them and to strengthen the party."[1]

His party camped three miles east of Fort Vancouver. Traditionally the voyageurs received their regale of rum the first night out,[2] but the express-men also camped close to headquarters so a man could be sent back to pick up anything they had forgotten. The next day they breakfasted at the upper end of Prairie du Thé, 28 miles east of headquarters. (Breakfast generally took place about five hours after they had set off in the morning.) In the evening, Ermatinger's men camped at Portage Neuf, where they wolfed down their second large meal of the day.

There were two portages at Portage Neuf. In 1841, Charles Wilkes, of the United States Exploring Expedition, made an upriver journey to Fort Nez Percés:

> There are two portages here, under the names of the new and the old. At the first, only half of the load is landed and the boats are tracked up for half a mile further, when the load is again shipped. The boats are then tracked to the old portage. A strong eddy occurs at this place, which runs in an opposite direction; and here it is necessary to land the whole of the cargo; after which the empty boats are again tracked three quarters of a mile beyond.[3]

On the following day, the express-men pushed their way up the 20-mile section of river that Lt. Aemilius Simpson described in his 1826 journal as he came downriver on his way to Fort Vancouver:

> For about a League below the Cascades there is a very strong Current
> with rapids. The River branches off into several channels formed by
> Islands; for about 6 leagues below the Cascades the River is bounded
> by a range of High Hills densely wooded, their faces in some places
> being perpendicular with pretty cascades descending some hundred
> feet.[4]

This is the beginning of the gorge of the Columbia River. As they
pushed their way into that fast-flowing section of river, Ermatinger's
men viewed the massive barrier that was the Cascade Range. On
their right loomed triangular Mount Hood, standing 11,000 feet
high. To their left the range of mountains continued north in a
straight line as far as they could see. Straight ahead of them was "the
Cascades," the first of three major hurdles they must overcome as
they made their way through the mountain range. This foaming chain
of rapids tumbled toward them around a sharp bend in the river.[5]

At the Cascades' lower falls, the men emptied their boats. Provisions and trade goods they portaged over the narrow, slippery, four-
mile trail that ran along the riverbank. The boats, however, they
tracked upriver with lines. Ermatinger's journal continues:

> 22nd. Rain most of the day. Clear the Cascades Portage by half past
> 11 o'clock. Sail and paddle the rest of the day. Encamp a little below
> Cape Horn at 6 p.m.[6]

Edward Ermatinger's Cape Horn, which got its name because the
wind blew as fiercely here as the wind around its namesake, stood on
the Columbia's south bank, 72 miles above the fort and across the
river from the mouth of Klickitat River.[7] In all other journals, Cape
Horn was west of the lower Cascades rapids, near Phoca Rock.[8]

At a certain point as they passed through the Cascades, the lush
forestland of the coast gave way to the dry desert of the interior. The
change was so abrupt it was as if a line was drawn in the dust. Rattle-
snakes sunned themselves on the rocks, and the men watched where
they stepped.

The Dalles was the next major hurdle, and in 1827 Ermatinger's men breakfasted below this canyon and falls at about 6 a.m. A year earlier Aemilius Simpson had described The Dalles as "a long & intricate chain [of rapids] rushing with great force through a number of narrow & Crooked Channels, bounded by huge Masses of perpendicular Rock, the faces very much fractured."[9] To pass these rapids, the men carried their loads over a nine-mile portage, which took them a full day to cross.

The Dalles was immediately followed by the Chûtes, which forced the rushing river into a narrow rocky passage. The water fell 20 feet almost immediately and continued to tumble down rocky rapids toward them as it carved its way to the Pacific. These men avoided the Chûtes' hazards by portaging boat and loads on their shoulders over a narrow trail along the riverbanks. (As always, one boat returned to Fort Vancouver after its crew saw the other boats safely across this portage.) Six hours later, at Ceililo Falls, on the Chûtes' eastern edge, they would again place their boats in the water.

The names "Cascades," "Dalles," and "Chûtes" are all French words that came from the language of the Canadien and Métis voyageurs who worked the boats. As has been seen earlier, French was the language of the fur trade. "Cascades" and "Chûtes" translate as "waterfalls," but "Dalles" means "paving stone" or "slab," and The Dalles was named for its slab-like rock walls.

While the term "dalles" was often applied to smaller rapids up and down the Columbia River, it was rarely used on the softer, sandier Saskatchewan River. "Batture," however, was used on both sides of the Rocky Mountains and denoted a sand or gravel bar that lay in the bed of the river. "Bas-fond," a term in constant use on the east side of the Rockies, indicated a shallow or weedy part of the river. "Trou" was the word for "hole" and generally referred to an especially deep piece of water — for example, the deep water at the junction of Whirlpool River (Rivière du Trou) and the Athabasca on the east side of the Rocky Mountains. The "hole" had only to be deep enough that the men's poles no longer touched bottom and they lost control of their boats or rafts.

Other objects or practices were also usually referred to by French terms: "varangue" referred to the boats' ribs; "pacton" described a pack or bundle, most likely made up with carrying straps for portaging; "demi-charge" meant the boats were half unloaded when tracked up-river with ropes or run downriver through shallow rapids. "Boutes" were men more experienced than the others in their own boat; because of their experience they were placed at the head and stern of every boat, where they could wield their larger paddles to better effect.

The guide was the most experienced of all. He gave the orders to all boutes under him and assisted the clerk-in-charge with decisions in regard to the route. As often happened in these journals, the name of Ermatinger's guide remains unmentioned. However, the guides were almost always Iroquois (Mohawk) from Kahnawà:ke (Kanawake), near Montreal. All were wonderful watermen and tough negotiators, unafraid to take on leadership roles. Strong and outspoken, they ruled with their fists.

Edward Ermatinger's journal continues, with Chief Factor John McLoughlin and Chief Trader Alexander Roderick McLeod, both passengers on their way to Fort Colvile, being unable to hire horses from the Coastal (Chinookan) and Interior (Sahaptan-speaking) Indians, who gathered by the hundreds to fish at Ceililo Falls. The negotiations over the horses delayed Ermatinger, who was forced to wait, and his party camped three miles above John Day's River at 5 p.m. They had left Jean-Baptiste Ouvré behind with Sahaptan-speaking Indians who had sent for horses. Ouvré returned after dark. He had been attacked by four other First Nations men who wanted his horses and property. Ermatinger reported that he "cut them off and took their arrows away from them, which Ouvré brought with him as the spoils of war":[10]

> Sunday 25th. Fine weather. We are unable to agree with the Indians for the loan of their horses, therefore the gentlemen walk by turns to lighten the boat which is insufficient to carry all the baggage and 6 passengers besides an extra man and the Indian Slave.[11] Proceed at half past 5. Hoist sail with a light breeze which continues all day.

Assist with the Poles and Paddles. Encamp about 6 miles below the Gros Isle [Blalock Island].

Monday 26th. Some light rain at noon — rest of the day fine.[12]

On March 26th, they were able to hire three Indian horses, and some of the gentlemen rode on to Fort Nez Percés. But Ermatinger was still delayed. "Ouvré returns to our breakfast place in search of a gun left there by mistake. Encamp at 3 o'clock to wait his return."[13] His journal continues:

27th. Fine weather. Two men who went with Ouvré return early this morning and inform us that he has gone in pursuit of an Indian who had watched our departure and made off with the gun. . . . Encamp above the Grand Rapids.[14]

This was the Umatilla Rapid, a long and dangerous piece of water that ran through a narrow canyon with perpendicular walls, 18 miles below Fort Nez Percés and a few miles above the mouth of the Umatilla River.[15] The next morning:

[March] 28th. The Boat arrives at Walla Walla [Fort Nez Percés] by 11 o'clock a.m. Ouvré also arrives on foot having recovered the gun with the aid of Tomas Tuppuri's (the Walla Walla chief) wife.[16]

At Fort Nez Percés, the voyageurs would once again gum their boats to waterproof them. From early years the fur traders had travelled the Columbia River in clinker-built boats rather than birchbark canoes.[17] Their boats had flat bottoms and narrow beams, and were lighter in weight than the York Boats the HBC men used on the other side of the Rocky Mountains. These lighter craft were easier to carry up and down the long, steep portages of the Columbia River.

They were also both rowed and paddled, and their seams, which opened in the heat of the sun or under the strain of the rapids, were stuffed with batten and pitched and gummed frequently to keep them afloat. The gum the men used was a mixture of sawpit resin and tallow. They melted the pitch into the seams of the boat by drawing two pieces of burning firewood along each seam, "blowing at the same time between the sticks, this melts the gum, and a small spatula is used to smooth it off."[18] To a stranger, it appeared as if the voyageurs were "burning their boats behind them."[19]

— • —

By the next year, 1828, thirty-one-year-old Edward Ermatinger had worked in the HBC fur trade for a decade, spending three years in the Columbia District. He had decided to leave the Company, and from York Factory would make his way out to Montreal. His 1828 journal begins on March 22, with the words:

> Two boats with the express take their departure from Fort Vancouver about 10 a.m. . . . Messrs. [Donald] Manson[20] and [Michel] Laframboise with 2 men go with us as far as the Chûtes in case the Indians should be numerous — continues raining all day. Encamp a few miles below the Cascades.[21]

It rained incessantly the following day too, and he and his men were detained a full half day at the Cascades Portage because of low water. They gummed their boats at their camp above the portage. On March 24, the men awoke to fine weather:

> Start at 5 a.m. Sail all day with a fresh breeze and encamp about half way up the Grand Dalles. Indians not numerous about us — however we find it necessary to keep watch all night. Prepare and load our muskets.[22]

Ermatinger's list of supplies shows that each boat was provided with a crate of flintlock guns for defence. His journal continues:

> 25th. Tolerable weather. Got over the Grand Dalles by a little after eight a.m. having carried our baggage from our last night's encampment. Lighten at the little Dalles Portage.[23]

Within The Dalles itself were three narrow points in the canyon, and two "dalles" — one the Grande, and the second the Little or Petite Dalles. Once past The Dalles, his men

Proceed to the Chûtes which we clear by 5 p.m. but few Indians on the Portage. Here Mr. Manson and party take leave of us to return to Fort Vancouver. Leaving the Chûtes hoist sail with a strong breeze and proceed till 7 o'clock when we encamp some distance below John Day's River.[24]

On March 26, Ermatinger's party experienced fine weather and a sailing wind that pushed them upriver all day. Two days later the boats reached Fort Nez Percés early in the morning, and Ermatinger delivered potatoes, butter, and a Fort Vancouver ham to Samuel Black. Black was also short of rum, so Ermatinger supplied a gallon out of the voyage stores. The voyageurs would be short of rum for their regales until such time as Ermatinger was able to secure a new supply.

— • —

In early March 1835, 32-year-old James Douglas led out the York Factory Express, leaving Fort Vancouver two weeks earlier than others had done. The long-time clerk at Fort Vancouver was heading east to the annual meeting of the governor and council of the Hudson's Bay Company, held that year at Red River. His journal is more of a personal record than most. His journal begins:

> Tuesday 3rd March 1835. Left Fort Vancouver today at 9 o'clock with three boats manned with 29 Canadian and Iroquois, part of whom are to be left at Fort Colvile in order to assist the summer Brigade in its ascent [descent] to Vancouver with the annual returns of furs, an object which cannot be accomplished by the servants remaining in the interior.[25]

The brigade Douglas refers to was the long-established horse and boat brigade that brought furs from New Caledonia and Fort Colvile every spring, and returned with trade goods. In the Columbia District, the brigades ran quite separately from the express; in territories east of the Rocky Mountains, they often did not.[26]

The express stopped for an hour's rest at the Fort Vancouver saw-mill. Douglas noted:

> Proceeding from the mill the progress of the boats was greatly retarded by a violent South East wind accompanied with slight showers of rain which induced us to encamp for the night a short distance above the Prairie du Thé. The water of the river is exceedingly muddy making it quite impossible to perceive either stick or stone even tho' nearly on a level with its surface. Owing to this cause chiefly the boats received some hard shocks during the day's journey, and they are in consequence in a very leaky state. . . .
>
> Wednesday 4. The wind still continuing to blow with great violence we could not leave our encampment until broad daylight. And even then we left it uncertain of being able to pass the lofty basaltic rocks which were at a short distance above us [Cape Horn]. As we advanced the gale appeared to freshen, but on reaching the spot where the difficulties had been anticipated we found things nearly in a state of calm, and during the remainder of the day we proceeded onwards at a good steady rate. At 3 o'clock reached the lower end of the Cascades Portage and after transporting all cargoes to the upper end we stopped for the night. The boats will be brought up tomorrow morning. . . .
>
> Thursday 5. At dawn of day the men were on the alert and returned to the lower end of the portage for the boats which have passed the night there. The water being low considerable difficulty was experienced in passing the boats; this was done by dragging them along shore, sometimes in deep water, at others over the stones by means of wooden rollers collected from the Indian fishing stages. On reaching the upper end they were turned up and pitched anew. This operation and that of reloading were not finished before 11 o'clock when all being ready we left the Cascades behind. . . .[27]

In 1836, botanist John Kirk Townsend travelled up the Columbia River as passenger in the New Caledonia Brigade boats, leaving Fort Vancouver on June 26. Of the Cascades, he wrote:

> We arrived yesterday at the upper cascades, and made in the course of the day three portages. As is usual in this place, it rained almost

constantly, and the poor men engaged in carrying the goods were completely drenched.[28]

According to Douglas's journal, his 1835 express also experienced a heavy rainfall at the Cascades:

Friday 6, March. During the night our repose was disagreeably interrupted by a violent storm of rain accompanied by slight showers. The boats being in a very exposed and insecure situation it required our unremitting attention to guard them from injury. At dawn of day we left our encampment with the wind favourable but still rather violent and squally. We proceeded onward at a great rate. No snow in the vicinity of the river; vegetation begins to appear on the sloping hills, and the face of nature is everywhere undergoing a rapid change, and the eye of the spectator is continually delighted with her varied beauties just bursting into existence.[29]

Townsend also enjoyed this part of the river, where he was free to do some botanizing and hunting:

We were engaged almost the whole of this day in making portages, and I had, in consequence, some opportunity of prosecuting my researches on the land. We have now passed the range of vegetation; there are no trees or even shrubs; nothing but huge, jagged rocks of basalt, and interminable sand heaps. I found here a large and beautiful species of marmot (the *Arctomys Richardsonii*) several of which I shot.[30]

James Douglas's journal continues:

In ascending the Great Dalles one boat received a slight injury by coming in contact with another. Passed the smaller Dalles without accident, and gained the [Ceililo] Falls at 4 o'clock with the assistance of a considerable concourse of natives. The whole property was transported over the carrying place before we encamped; the boats remain at the lower end. . . .

Saturday 7. At dawn of day all the men proceeded to the place where the boats were left yesterday evening and with the aid of nearly 70 Indians they were soon carried over; and after making some

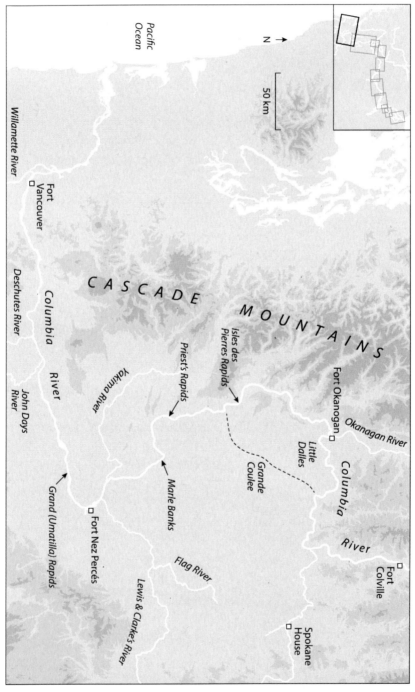

Fort Nez Percés was 200 miles east of Fort Vancouver on the
Columbia River, and Fort Colvile was 600 miles east.

necessary repairs they were loaded and we proceeded on our journey at half past 10 a.m. A gentle breeze aided our ascent considerably and we succeeded in gaining a point covered with willows a few miles above Day's River before encamping. The hills on both sides of the River rise to the height of several hundred feet and are very broken and irregular. They are not uniformly covered with vegetation, and the numerous strata of volcanic rock which project abruptly from their sides gives them a rugged & sterile appearance. During this day's march we passed the entrance of the Falls [Deschutes] and John Day's River both deriving their sources from the Blue Mountains. Beaver was at one time found abundantly on these streams but is now nearly extirpated, being incessantly exposed to the ravages of the hunters. . . .[31]

On March 8, the sky threatened rain and the river ran against them more rapidly than was normal. That afternoon the breeze freshened into a wind that drove the boats before it at a great rate. Douglas, like all the other gentlemen who did none of the heavy work of paddling the boats upstream, watched as the country changed around him. He was surrounded by a dry and sterile desert. Nothing grew here but sparse tufts of grass, and a cactus he called wormwood. His journal continues:

Monday 9 March. We had last night the Company of a few Indians who visited our encampment with the hopes of obtaining a supply of tobacco, a gratification to which they appear to be passionately addicted. Their wishes were easily satisfied, and they soon left us to return to their homes. The wind still in our favour during some hours after our departure. It afterwards ceased and we continued moving slowly at times, with the poles [and] others paddling until the afternoon when the sails were again hoisted, and we proceeded upwards very rapidly. Encamped at the commencement of the Grand [Umatilla] Rapid.

Tuesday 10. A very stormy night which rendered unremitting attention to the boats necessary. Ascended the Grand Rapids with some difficulty but without accident. The river is exceedingly low, and the boats were forced to keep very far out in order to avoid the shoals which everywhere obstructed their progress nearer shore. At 2 o'clock arrived at Fort Nez Percés where an immense concourse of Indians are assembled from all quarters, consisting of various tribes, namely, Nez Percés under which general name may be included the Pellouches, Walla Wallas, Yakemas, and the scattered inhabitants of the River who possess [a] common language and derive their different appellations from their places of residence or some other important cause, rather than from any striking national dissimilarity; and another tribe called Cayuses whose language is entirely distinct from the others.[32]

— • —

The next journal was kept by George Traill Allan, who by March 1841 had been in the fur trade for ten years. He kept his journal for no one but himself. At times it is filled with personal stories that describe common occurrences of every express that no one else recorded:

I left Fort Vancouver on the 22d of March 1841, by the express, accompanied by the following gentlemen — Messrs. [Francis] Ermatinger,[33] [Archibald] McKinlay, [François] Payette, and Dr. [William F.] Tolmie — in four boats — and twenty eight men chiefly Canadians: all the gentlemen of the Establishment, as usual upon such occasions, accompanying us to the River to see us start. Mr. Ermatinger, being the oldest Clerk of the party in the Company's service, the command of conducting the party, so far as he went, of course, devolved upon him. After a voyage of nine days, during which nothing worth recording took place, we reached Fort Walla Walla [Nez Percés], situated in the midst of a sandy plain upon the Banks of the Columbia & in charge of my friend, Mr. Chief Trader [Pierre Chrysologue] Pambrun, who received us most kindly, and presented us to dinner a couple of fine roast Turkies — a rather unexpected sight in this quarter of the world.[34]

— • —

By the early 1840s, the fur trade of the Columbia District was threatened by many changes, none of them unexpected. Americans on the east coast of the continent knew the district as the Oregon Territory, and in their minds it belonged to them. The first Americans arrived at Fort Vancouver in 1832 and did not stay. But missionaries followed, American "immigrants" came next, and by the mid-1840s thousands of American men and women had made their way into the fur traders' Columbia District via the Oregon Trail. By 1847, Methodist missionaries had established missions in several parts of the interior: among them were Reverends Lee and Perkins at Wascopam (The Dalles), the Spaldings at Lapwai, and Reverends Walker and Eells at Tshimakain near old Spokane House.

Missionary Marcus Whitman set up his mission at Waiilatpu, 25 miles from Fort Nez Percés, among the independent Cayuse already noted by James Douglas. Over the years Dr. Whitman offended the Cayuse, and some grew to hate him. Many HBC men saw what was happening and warned Whitman to abandon Waiilatpu. Although he knew his mission was failing, he stubbornly refused to do so.

When Thomas Lowe started off from Fort Vancouver in March 1847, he was aware that the previous winter had been long and cold, with "an awful destruction in Horses, Cows & Sheep at Vancouver & in the Willamette."[35] He did not know, however, that this difficult winter had set in motion a disaster in the area around Whitman's Waiilatpu Mission that would change the district forever. Lowe's journal reads:

> Wednesday, 24th March 1847. Started from Vancouver at noon with two boats, under a salute from the Fort. Had 9 men in each Boat, and about 30 pieces principally Provisions for the voyage. Passengers Mr. [John Lee] Lewes, who goes up as far as Colvile, and Mr. Joe Burke who is on his way to England intending to go home by way of Hudson's Bay. Dined at the Saw Mill, and pushed on five miles beyond, where we encamped for the night, being under the necessity of having one of the Boats gummed, as the Boutes had not been able to gum it before starting. Beautiful weather, and light air down the River.[36]

On March 25, Lowe's party breakfasted at Prairie du Thé and, as the day was windy, took the inner channel of the river below Cape Horn, where they had to make a portage because of low water at the upper end. Beyond that point a light breeze carried them upriver, and they camped that night at the lower end of the first rapid of the Cascades. Shallow water forced his men to drag the boats over the rocks as they pushed their way up the Cascades, and the boats were so strained that they had to be gummed afresh. On March 27, the express started at daylight, making "a good days run and encamped in the evening below the [Wascopam] Mission at The Dalles."[37] Their journey continued the next morning:

> Sunday 28th March. Showery. Passed The Dalles with the assistance of the Indians whom we engaged to haul on the line, and having reached the lower end of the Chûtes in the afternoon the pieces were crossed on horseback and the boats dragged or rather carried across the Portage by the Indians. Encamped at the upper end of the Chûtes, and had the Boats gummed.[38]

On Monday, they had fine weather until noon and set up camp ten miles above John Day's River. On Tuesday, the men paddled against a strong headwind all day, making slow progress. Lowe noted:

> The boats were a good deal scraped in coming up the rapids, and had to be gummed. Encamped a few miles below the lower end of the Big [Blalock] Island.
> Wednesday 31st. Remarkably hot. Had a light head wind. Encamped at the lower end of the Grand Rapids. The Indians whom we passed assisted us a good deal in tracking the boat with their horses.
> Thursday 1st April. Beautiful warm day, but wind still against us. Passed the Grand Rapid before breakfast, and had to gum the boats at the head of the Rapids. Hard work tracking and poling the remainder of the day. Arrived at Fort Nez Percés about 7 o'clock in the evening.[39]

Over the summer of 1847, while Thomas Lowe's express made its way across the continent to York Factory and returned, a deadly combination of measles and dysentery spread through the Columbia District. In the fall, Lowe's incoming party reached Fort Nez Percés, where they "found the Measles very prevalent, the Indians were dying in great numbers."[40] The seeds of this infection had been sown a year earlier, over the long hard winter of 1846–47, when thousands of Indian horses and cattle died, and First Nations peoples starved.

Then measles came north from Sutter's Fort with Walla Walla Chief Peu-Peu-Mox-Mox's men, who were returning from a California trading expedition. This infectious illness spread quickly among the First Nations peoples, who had no resistance to it. Thousands died. Some Cayuse chiefs, who lived near Waillatpu Mission, blamed Dr. Marcus Whitman for the many deaths in their tribe — they believed he was poisoning them. At the end of November, two weeks after Thomas Lowe's express left Fort Nez Percés, the angered Cayuse invaded the mission house, killing the missionary, his wife, and a dozen other Americans.

On hearing of the massacre, Fort Vancouver's Chief Factor Peter Skene Ogden put together a group of well-armed employees and paddled upriver to rescue the American women now being held hostage by the Cayuse. After a month of tense negotiations, Ogden succeeded in securing the release of the women and brought them downriver to Fort Vancouver.

The massacre of the missionaries inflamed the thousands of Americans who had by this time travelled over the Oregon Trail to settle in the Willamette Valley south of Fort Vancouver. They declared war on the First Nations people and formed volunteer armies that marched into the interior to deal with the Cayuse, who retreated eastward to the area around Spokane House and Fort Colvile.

The end result of the massacre and American retribution was the Cayuse War, which turned the entire Columbia basin into a war zone and threatened to close the Columbia River to the HBC men. The brigades from New Caledonia and Fort Colvile were diverted to a newly explored but unimproved route via Kamloops and Fort Langley, but the York Factory Express had no other route out of the territory. When Thomas Lowe led the express away from Fort Vancouver in 1848, Chief Factor Peter Skene Ogden worried he might not make it to Fort Colvile. In March 1848, Ogden wrote to HBC Governor Sir

George Simpson, "I hope Lowe will escape all points by land and enter and reach you in safety."[41]

Lowe began his 1848 journal with these words:

1848, March 20, Monday. About 3 p.m. I started from Fort Vancouver with three boats in charge of the express, but one of these boats is to return from the Chûtes, and accompanies us merely to assist in carrying our boats & property across the Portages, and to make a stronger party in case of any danger from the Indians. When we started the Fort fired a Salute of 7 guns, as did also the Brig *Mary Dare*.[42] Mrs. Ermatinger & daughter, Bishop [Modeste] Demers,[43] and Mr. Robert Logan cross the Mountains, and Mr. [Henry Newsham] Peers accompanies us as far as Colvile, from whence he is to proceed to New Caledonia, Narcisse Raymond likewise goes up as a passenger as far as Walla Walla.... Encamped about 5 miles above the Saw Mill. It has been showery all day. We have got 3 tents to pitch every night.[44]

As was usual, the women and gentlemen passengers occupied the canvas tents, while voyageurs slept out on the ground. Lowe's journal continued:

March 21, Tuesday. Rained a little in the morning, but kept fair the rest of the day.... Had a fair breeze after passing Prairie du Thé, which took us up to the Cascades. Encamped on the South side of the River nearly opposite Portage Neuve [Neuf].[45]

On March 22, the men carried the pieces across the Cascades Portage and brought the boats up. They breakfasted at the portage's upper end and camped that night ten miles farther on. On Thursday, they took advantage of the westerly breeze and reached the Wascopam Mission, below The Dalles, where they camped. On Friday, Lowe's men "got through The Dalles without much trouble, and on arriving at the Chûtes had all the pieces taken across, but the boats are left until tomorrow. Encamped at the Upper end of the Portage."[46]

25, Saturday. Had two of the boats carried across this morning, the other one returns from this place to Vancouver in charge of Charles

Proulx. Marc Charles deserted at the Portage, and we had to push on without him. As it came on to blow a perfect gale, were obliged to put ashore in the afternoon about 10 miles above the Chûtes.[47]

Desertions were common at Fort Vancouver in these years, as employees abandoned the fur trade for the California gold rush, which was now in full swing.

On Sunday, the express was wind-bound until the afternoon, but made it past John Day's River. On Monday, they again enjoyed a good sail wind, but lost time at a rapid where one of the voyageurs broke his boat. Within hours the boat was repaired, and both vessels were gummed, and they made a good distance before camping for the night. On Tuesday, they were ten miles west of Grand (Umatilla) Rapids. The next day, "Joe injured his boat again . . . in the Grand Rapids, and we had to camp rather earlier than usual to have it gummed. In the afternoon had a sail wind, attended with rain. Encamped about 6 miles below the Fort."[48] The next morning:

> March 30, Thursday. Fine weather, but blowing strong. Reached Walla Walla [Fort Nez Percés] about noon, delivered 11 pieces of Goods to Mr. [William] McBean, and had the boats hauled up and gummed.[49]

Thomas Lowe's express had experienced little trouble coming upriver so far, but the dangerous part of his journey was ahead. The Cayuse murderers and their sympathizers had retreated to the east and now skulked around old Spokane House, southeast of Fort Colvile. In the next stage of his journey, Lowe's party would take unprecedented precautions to avoid confrontations with the tribes involved in the wars with the Americans.

— • —

By 1849, so many fur trade employees had deserted Fort Vancouver for the excitement of the California goldfield that there was an extreme shortage of experienced men at the district's headquarters. In addition to this, Thomas Lowe had given notice that he would leave the HBC's employ at the end of June, so twenty-two-year-old John Charles was entrusted with the leadership of the York Factory Express. His journal begins with the words:

> Tuesday, 20th March 1849. I, John Charles in company with Mr. [Thomas] Lowe, in charge of the express as far as Fort Colvile, started from Fort Vancouver with two boats laden with the Fort Nez Percés Outfit and provisions etc. per party, amounting in all to about 45 pieces and manned by five Iroquois, nine Indians one Kanaka [Hawaiian] and 1 Canadian. Mr. Menetrez passenger. Encamped at the Saw Mill. Wet weather.[50]

They left the Fort Vancouver sawmill early the next morning, and that night camped a little below the Cascades. On Thursday, the men

> embarked in the boats at peep of day and put ashore at the lower end of the Cascade portage where we discharged the boat and breakfasted. After breakfast the pieces were carried over to the Upper end; one of the boats was also taken up to the same point where we passed the night. Weather, unpleasant. Water unusually low. Snow, knee deep on the portage.
>
> Friday 23rd. Had the other boat taken up the Rapids. Gummed the boats as well as the unfavourable state of the weather would permit. Remained at the Cascades all day and night. Allowed the men an extra allowance of Rum, according to promise made to them by the Board.[51]

On Saturday, they had beautiful weather and sailed upriver to their encampment five miles below the Wascopam Mission at The Dalles. They breakfasted the next morning immediately below the Grand Dalles, and borrowed horses from First Nations men so they could ride to the Chûtes. "Here we found upwards of one hundred Indians with their horses waiting the arrival of the boats which were, as also the cargoes, with their assistance carried over to the Upper end of the Chûtes Portage where we camped."[52] The Cayuse War had settled down by now, and the First Nations men, who had always helped the express-men upriver at this point, had returned to aid them again.

After the men repaired the broken boats, they continued upriver. Two days later the party camped at the lower end of the Umatilla Rapid. They breakfasted at the head of the rapid on March 28, and reached Fort Nez Percés about 5 p.m.

This fort was one of the earliest posts in this territory, having been constructed in 1818 by Donald McKenzie of the North West Company (NWC). It stood on the east bank of the Columbia, half a mile south of the Walla Walla River. Over its long history, Fort Nez Percés had never proven to be a productive fur trade post, but First Nations peoples who surrounded the post provided the fur traders with horses that travelled many thousands of miles over the brigade trails from Fort Okanogan (American spelling), Thompson's River, and Fort Alexandria far to the north.

In 1849, John Charles and Thomas Lowe discovered that Chief Trader William McBean had traded for twelve horses that would carry the gentlemen on the next leg of their journey east to Fort Colvile, while the boats continued their journey upriver under the charge of a single clerk. For the men in the boats, it was a 378-mile journey, by river, to that upper Columbia River post, and it would take two weeks to make the distance. The gentlemen, however, would ride horses across the scablands of the Columbia plateau, reaching Fort Colvile four days before the boats.

A Revillon Frères party camped on the Athabasca River. They were a French fur trading company that competed against the HBC in the early 1900s. Little is known about this company, but many of the images we now use are theirs. (COURTESY: GLENBOW ARCHIVES, NA-1338-18)

View of the Peace River, Alberta. Before 1826 the HBC men in New Caledonia travelled by the Peace River and the Clearwater, passing over Methye Portage on their way to Cumberland House and York Factory with their furs. (COURTESY: GLENBOW ARCHIVES, NA-1214-4)

Fort Vancouver. By the mid-1830s the original Fort Vancouver had doubled in size to 318 feet by 638 feet. By the time Henry James Warre visited the fort in 1845, new construction had extended its stockaded length to 733 feet. (COURTESY: BCA, PDP05241)

Les Dalles, Columbia River. During the summer freshets, the Columbia River rose sixty feet as it passed through the narrows of the Grande Dalles. The men portaged their boats along the river banks rather than risk their lives in the whirlpools. (COURTESY: LAC, MIKAN 3018243)

In 1818, the NWC men built Fort Nez Percés, also called Fort Walla Walla, from logs they fished out of the Columbia River. The fort was levelled by fire in 1842, and rebuilt of adobe bricks baked in the sun.
(COURTESY: GLENBOW ARCHIVES, NA-1274-18)

Hauling a Boat up a Rapid, probably on the Columbia River. Though they may have changed over the years, these Columbia boats are direct descendants of the wooden canoes that NWC explorer David Thompson constructed at Boat Encampment in January 1811.
(COURTESY: LAC, MIKAN 1834221)

Hauling Up a Rapid, Les Dalles des Morts.
(COURTESY: BCA, PDP00057)

A drawing showing men pushing a boat upriver with poles. It required good balance to propel these boats upriver, as the men stood in the boats with poles touching the gunwales, but slanted toward the rear so as to not lift the bow.
(COURTESY: GLENBOW ARCHIVES, NA-1598-1)

Columbia River Canyon, near Revelstoke. The Little Dalles Canyon contained a series of rapids, four or five miles long, with Steamboat Rapid being the northernmost of them. Today these rapids are drowned behind the Revelstoke Dam. (COURTESY: LAC, MIKAN 3335028)

Rocky Mountains from the Columbia River. As the boats approached Boat Encampment, on the big bend of the Columbia River, the men had a good view of the Rocky Mountains over which they were to climb. (COURTESY: LAC, MIKAN 3018248)

Ascending the Rocky Mountains. In springtime the HBC men had
a hard climb on snowshoes up the steep hill of the Grande Côte. The trail
led from the banks of the Wood River to the top of the plateau that
separated rock-bound Jeffrey Creek from the valley of Pacific Creek.
(COURTESY: LAC, MIKAN 2834212)

In the early years the HBC men used birchbark canoes on the
Athabasca River, but they were easily damaged on this shallow river,
and replaced by boats that resembled York Boats.
(COURTESY: GLENBOW ARCHIVES, NA-843-14)

Revillon York Boat freighting on Lesser Slave River, Alberta.
The HBC men often complained about the clumsy sturgeon-nosed boats
that replaced the birchbark canoes once used on this river.
(COURTESY: GLENBOW ARCHIVES, NA-1338-20)

York Boat Under Sail, Norway House. In this case the beam (side) wind means that the sail is attached front and rear. Note the men sitting on the oars to which the sails are tied. (COURTESY: HBCA, 1987/363-Y-2/56)

York Boat on Split Lake. The rowers are seated on alternate sides of the boat, with their oars passing through simple oarlocks on the opposite side of the boat. When the oarsmen are working, the steersman uses his long sweep to steer the boat. (COURTESY: HBCA, 1987/363-Y-2/65)

CHAPTER 3

Fort Nez Percés to Fort Colvile

୬୧

FROM FORT NEZ PERCÉS the fur traders continued their journey up the Columbia River toward Fort Colvile, which stood a half mile north of Kettle Falls. Again the boats faced numerous barriers in the form of rapids along this twisting stretch of river, although they tended to be less hazardous than those on the lower river. But river travel varied. When the Columbia ran high between its banks in the spring, whirlpools formed; when the water was low, the rapids became more intense. At Priest's Rapids, the steepest rapid on this part of the Columbia, the river climbed 70 feet in only ten miles.[1] Paquin (Buckland's) Rapid followed shortly after, and beyond that was the more dangerous Rocky Island, or Isles de Pierres Rapids. The first (of three) Little Dalles (this one in Nespelem Canyon) blocked the river a few miles east of Fort Okanogan, and finally the express-men negotiated Grand (Rickey) Rapids, seven miles south of Kettle Falls. At the foot of Kettle Falls, they hauled their boats out of the river and carted them over the quarter-mile portage to the fort.

On March 28, 1827, the gentlemen of Edward Ermatinger's express walked away from Fort Nez Percés alongside the boats. "The Boat having been pitched and our business at this place settled, we resume our journey at half past 3 p.m. Encamp at 6 o'clock 4 or 5 miles below Lewis and Clark's river."[2] This was the Snake River.

It rained that evening but the next morning was clear, and they started at 5 a.m. By evening, they had travelled "8 or 9 miles up what is termed the Marle Banks,"[3] where they encamped on an island. Marl is a rich earth of clay mixed with remnants of seashells that the Canadiens called les Terres Jaunes. The clay cliff of the Marle Banks (Hanford Reach) stood on their right-hand side going upriver.

They began their journey next morning at 4 a.m. and camped two miles above the Marle Banks. At 11 o'clock they met Archibald McDonald, who carried letters informing them that the New Caledonia people were going out by their new route, the Rocky Mountain Portage to Jasper's House via the headwaters of Fraser River and Tête Jaune (Yellowhead) Pass. Although this route was soon abandoned as an outgoing express route, it continued to be used by the New Caledonia men on their return from York Factory.[4]

Ermatinger's 1827 journal continues: "Proceed half way up the Priest's Rapid and encamp at quarter past 6 p.m."[5] The next day:

April. Sunday 1st. The Boat continues her progress up the Rapids (which are very bad this year, the water being remarkably low) at half past 6 a.m. Clear the Rapids by 11 o'clock. Proceed up the River and encamp at half past 6 p.m. about 12 or 15 miles above. Hire an Indian canoe to carry some of the passengers.[6]

It rained a little the following day, and they camped that night above Buckland Rapids.

On April 3, the boats cleared the Rocky Island Portage with the gentlemen walking alongside, and the entire party camped above the Piscouhoose (Wenatchie) River. There, Ermatinger traded with First

Nations people for meat and edible bulbs such as camas, probably paying for these food items with tobacco. On the next night, they camped above Chelan River, and Ermatinger reported that the "gentlemen afoot found a good deal of snow on the hills today."[7]

The next morning, they resumed their journey, and reached Fort Okanogan that evening. Fort Okanogan stood on the east bank of the Okanogan River, a little above its junction with the Columbia. Built in 1811 by Pacific Fur Company men, it served the HBC as a transportation depot for the heavily laden New Caledonia Brigades on their way down to Fort Vancouver every summer. On the brigade's return from the Columbia District headquarters in July, the men would switch again from boats to horses, continuing their journey north to Kamloops and beyond.

But Ermatinger's express-men were bound for York Factory, not Kamloops. They stopped for a short time at Fort Okanogan before continuing their journey up the Columbia. On April 7:

> Fine weather. At 10 o'clock Messrs. McLoughlin, McLeod and E. Ermatinger leave Okanogan on horseback in order to join the Boat at the Grosse Roche [Hellgate] whither they arrive at 3 p.m. having met with a great deal of snow the first half of the distance on the hills. The Boat only arrives at 7 p.m. Encamp.[8]

On April 8, the hardworking express-men camped at the north end of the Grande Coulée where it touched the Columbia River. Two days later they poled their boats past the mouth of the Spokane River, and on April 12 they reached the base of Kettle Falls. Crossing the portage, they reached Fort Colvile that afternoon.

At Fort Colvile, the express-men were already 704 miles from the shores of the Pacific Ocean, and 586 miles from Fort Vancouver. They had begun their journey close to sea level; at Fort Colvile they were about 1,800 feet above. They had powered their boats upriver with paddles — but song had been a fuel for their engine. These men sang while they worked. One man (generally a boute) sang the lines while all others joined in the chorus. The singer fashioned his song to suit the method of transportation — fast-paced songs for paddling down-river and slow for pulling up. They sang traditional songs from Quebec and France, old songs about their supposed fear of the wolves ("*J'ai trop grand peur des loups*"), or lonely songs about swimming in a fountain ("*À la claire fontaine*").

Most were based on traditional French songs but others were cre-ated (although never written down) by the voyageurs themselves as they went along: "*Épouser le voyage*" ("To wed the voyage") was one of these, and "*Le six mai de l'année dernière*" ("Last year on the sixth of May") was another.[9]

They began singing as soon as they picked up their paddle or oar and did not stop until the day's work ended. The song's refrain might change every time it was sung and with every new man who led them in song. One thing remained unchanged throughout the journey: the songs regulated the stroke of the paddle or oar, and different songs were sung for canoes that used paddles, and boats that used either paddle or oar.

The men sang of religion or adventure, jealousy or the joys of mar-riage or gathering fruit and flowers. Some were courting songs, some erotic fantasies. All were medieval in form, and their themes the same as those of the seventeenth-century songs brought to Quebec by the original Frenchmen who came from Normandy and elsewhere. These voyageurs sang the same songs their fathers had sung as they paddled up and down the rivers of the interior, and that their grandfathers had also sung. They sang them for the same reason: to distract themselves from the hard work of paddling or rowing their boats upriver or down. And like their fathers and grandfathers before them, they made so much noise with their singing that First Nations hunters com-plained they scared the game away. Perhaps they did, but not always.

— • —

In 1828, Edward Ermatinger's business-like journal tells a great deal about the goods that the express-men carried up and down the river. On March 29, he departed Fort Nez Percés:

We take our departure at 9 a.m. taking with us 1 Roll Tobacco for Colvile. Leave at Walla Walla 10 muskets and 9 [powder] horns and shot bags for the people down coming.[10] Encamp at 6 p.m. [blank] miles below the Marle Banks. A few Indians visit us. Saw a good many geese and ducks to-day very wild. The mountains behind Walla Walla covered with snow.

30th. Embark at half past 4 a.m. and proceed the fore part of the day sailing with a light breeze. Afternoon the wind becomes ahead blowing fresh. Encamp at half past 7 p.m. a short distance above Marle Banks. . . . One of our boats last night half filled, having been hauled up upon a stone which, the boat being very old, opened her seams. Some of our stores got wet.[11]

On March 31, they spent eight hours in their passage up Priest's Rapids, and on April 1 they passed the head of what was called the Grande Coulée. This coulée was, indeed, an extraordinary ravine, rarely used by the men of the express but in regular use by the outgoing brigades as an overland route to the Columbia River near Fort Okanogan. Ermatinger's journal continues:

2nd, Wednesday. Embark about half past 4 a.m. Breakfast below Isle des Pierres. Haul up these Rapids, then hoist sail with a light breeze which continues to assist us occasionally the rest of the day — pole and haul up many rapids. Encamp at half past 6 p.m. above the River Piscouhoose [Wenatchie]. Find ice and snow in many places along the banks of the Columbia. Country begins to assume a more fertile appearance than since we have left the Chûtes. Scattered trees now seen upon the mountains and much snow.[12]

The next night they camped above Chelan River, and on April 4 found "snow and ice very thick along the banks of the River. Met an Indian with a note and horse from Mr. A. McDonald, Okinagan."[13] The horse was provided for his use, and he "Set off to the Fort. Boats arrive at 5 p.m., find Messrs. McGillivray, McDonald, and Ermatinger here."[14] Archibald McDonald served in New Caledonia this year, and Joseph McGillivray was at Fort Alexandria. Francis Ermatinger,

Edward's boisterous younger brother, had spent the previous year at the Thompson's River post of Kamloops.

One year after McDougall's disastrous crossing of the snowbound Rocky Mountain Portage (Yellowhead Pass), the New Caledonia men chose to travel out of the territory via Fort Okanogan. But because the Columbia River beyond Fort Okanogan was so impeded by the rapids that clogged Nespelem Canyon, some of the gentlemen would meet the boats at the Gros Rochers (Hellgate), upriver from the post. In later years, they would await the express at comfortable Fort Colvile.

From Fort Okanogan, the York Factory Express started

with the boats about noon. Our number of men are now increased to 20 — 2 from New Caledonia and 1 from this place. Passengers J. McGillivray, Esq., Messrs. A. McDonald and E.E. . . . Encamp at 7 p.m.

Monday, 7th. Fine weather. Start at half past 4 a.m. Passed the Gros Rocher [Hellgate] at 1 p.m. Here Messrs. McGillivray and McDonald embark, having ridden across from Okanagan. Encamp at 7 p.m.[15]

Two days later they pushed past the mouth of the Spokane River, and on April 11 Ermatinger wrote:

Arrive at the Kettle Falls at 11 o'clock. Find Messrs. [John] Work and [William] Kittson at Fort Colvile. Mr. [John Warren] Dease not yet arrived.[16]

— • —

Over the next few years the route from Fort Nez Percés to Fort Colvile changed. The boats continued upriver to forts Okanogan and Colvile without the gentlemen (except one clerk who supervised). Instead, the gentlemen took to horseback and rode across country to Fort Colvile. This overland route followed the north bank of the Snake River to a place where they cut off to the north, crossing the Palouse River and camping on one of the larger lakes along the route.

Although none of the gentlemen who kept journals gives this route its proper name, it is the historic Shawpatin Road travelled by NWC explorer David Thompson in August 1811. Thompson left the Snake River at a place he called Currant Brook (probably Rock Creek) and, skirting the dusty scablands of the Palouse Hills, touched on the Four Lakes region near modern-day Cheney, Washington State. From there the road crossed a waterless plain to wooded Deep Creek and the banks of the Spokane River. James Douglas's 1835 account is the earliest surviving express journal to describe the Shawpatin route. He begins at Fort Nez Percés:

> 1835, Wed. 11 March. The boats left Fort Nez Percés at 11 o'clock, and I departed soon afterwards with a small party of 3 men on horseback to proceed direct across land to Colvile. During the first 9 miles we followed the banks of the Columbia to the entrance of Lewis and Clarke's [Snake] River which we crossed by means of a wooden canoe borrowed from a native resident there. Our route during the remainder of the day never diverged from the North bank of that river. We encamped at 6 o'clock in the evening. Two of our horses having become fatigued we left them at an Indian camp and procured 2 better ones in their stead.
>
> Fri. 13. Left Lewis & Clarke's River and proceeded direct across the country. Passed Flag [Palouse] River and halted the horses at a small river 2 hours march from the former and encamped at a small lake.
>
> Saturday 14. Favoured by a bright moonlight we continued our march at half past 3 o'clock and after five hours walk halted at a small lake to feed and refresh the horses. They are very poor and require to be managed with the utmost care in order that their strength may hold out to the journey's end. The country through which we are passing is not possessed of many attractions either in point of beauty or utility. . . . Encamped in the Spokan Woods. Between Nez Percés and these woods have not seen a single tree.[17]

His route took him almost due north from the banks of the Snake River, across the scablands to the place where the unique landscape disappeared into the open forests of Spokane Woods south of Spokane River. Douglas took an additional four days to cover the distance between Spokane River and Fort Colvile.

— • —

George Traill Allan's party enjoyed a quicker journey than James Douglas's, although he followed Douglas's route more or less. It becomes clear that Allan had no eye for the beauty of the land he found himself in, but he did not lose his sense of fun, and took pleasure in the ridiculous situations he found himself in. His express party left Fort Nez Percés on April 1, 1841, with a herd of horses purchased from the local Indigenous horsemen:

> As the Country through which I now passed was all much of the same description, I may here mention, that its general appearance was not particularly pleasing, consisting principally of hills without a stick of wood to adorn their summits or relieve the eye from the sameness of the landscape which now presented itself to an immense extent, the surface of the ground over which we rode at no tardy pace was so covered with badger[18] holes that it required the utmost caution to guide our riding horses clear of them. . . . After a ride of four days we reached Fort Spokane, an old establishment, abandoned some years ago. . . . On crossing the River, which we did by the assistance of two Indians in a small Canoe, I was very much surprised, when gaining the opposite bank, to hear my name distinctly pronounced by one of a band of Indians assembled there to greet our arrival; but on looking in the direction from when the voice came I immediately recognized my old friend, a young Indian chief called Garry, who had entered the Columbia with me ten years before. . . . When I had known him he was well clothed and could both read and write: now, however, the march of improvement had apparently retrograded, as he made his appearance wrapped up in a Buffalo Robe à la Sauvage.[19]

The First Nations man who called Allan's name was Spokane Garry (1811–1892). When he was fourteen, his father, a Spokane chief, sent him to be schooled at the missionary school in the Red

River Settlement. His training completed, Spokane Garry travelled home in the 1831 incoming Columbia Express with Allan. Over the years that followed his return, Spokane Garry became an influential leader for his people.

Allan's party reached Fort Colvile on the night of April 7, where he was welcomed by Chief Trader Archibald McDonald with a *feu de joie*, a celebratory firing of guns. Allan's provisions had run out and he was so hungry that he tested a food item he had previously rejected:

> On leaving Fort Vancouver Mr. [Francis] Ermatinger, a veritable John Bull and our caterer for the grub department of the voyage, had prevailed upon Captain [William] Brotchie, whose vessel was then laying at Vancouver, to get made for us, a couple of large plum puddings, & the same puddings upon being tried on the voyage from Vancouver to Walla Walla, had been found wanting, not in quantity but in quality, and until our arrival at the last mentioned post had layen [sic] neglected and almost forgotten — while seeing me equipped for the trip on horseback from Walla Walla to Fort Colvile, Mr. Ermatinger had slipped in amongst my eatables a piece of those identical puddings; being this morning therefore pressed by hunger, I had, I presume, dived deeper than usual into the recesses of my haversack and finding poor Brotchie, I made, sans ceremoni & cannibal-like, a most hearty Breakfast upon his remains.[20]

— • —

In 1847, clerk Thomas Lowe led the York Factory Express away from Fort Nez Percés in the spring that followed a long, hard winter marked by deep snow. Lowe's journal records some of the long-standing traditions of the fur trade, including the salutes fired as men arrived at and departed from the forts. The HBC employees lined up to fire their flintlock guns into the air, one shot at a time but close together so that the "boom" of the guns rolled through the country-side, one after another.

Lowe's account of the journey from Fort Nez Percés begins on Saturday, April 3. While the boats had begun their trip upriver the previous day, the gentlemen began their ride on the following day to Fort Colvile:

Started from Walla Walla at 3 p.m. to proceed overland to Colvile. We have 9 horses, including two light ones, and I have with me Mungo Marouna as guide, Alexis St. Gelin and an Indian, besides Wm. Wentzel from the Fort, to take back the horses when we come to the snow. The Fort fired a salute when we started. Encamped at the Toosha [Touchet] River, having come about 25 miles.

Sunday 4th. Fine warm weather. Got as far as Pelluse [Palouse] River, where it falls into the Nez Percés [Snake], and encamped on the opposite side, having swam our horses, and crossed ourselves & property in a canoe. Found a large camp of Indians at this place, who have small patches of land under cultivation. Days march about 40 miles.

Monday 5th. Pushed on until 9 o'clock at night, and encamped near the lower end of the Big Lake, as there was no intermediate encampment. Made today about 60 miles. Fine in the fore part of the day, but snowing in the afternoon and all night. One of the horses gave out, and had to be left.

Tuesday 6th. Shortly after starting this morning, met with a party from Colvile, consisting of David Finlay[21] and two Indians, on their way to Walla Walla for a Band of horses, as the Horses at Colvile have nearly all died this winter.[22]

This was the same hard winter that had killed the animals at forts Vancouver and Nisqually, and those belonging to the Cayuse and Walla Walla First Nations that lived in this territory. Lowe's party found a good deal of snow on the way, and as there was no good encampment for a long distance, they camped after walking only fifteen miles. The next day was just as difficult:

Wednesday 7th. Fine day. Much snow in the road, and could only proceed with the Horses about 15 miles, when we encamped, and sent the Horses back in charge of Wm. Wentzel. Got the snow shoes ready, and the loads arranged. Slept about a couple of hours, & walked the whole night. Engaged one of D. Finlay's Indians to carry a load to Colvile. The snow was hard, and we walked fast.

Thursday 8th April 1847. Walked the whole day, and arrived at the Spokan River after sundown, having come upwards of 50 miles since we left the Horses. Crossed the River in a canoe, and encamped on the opposite bank, where were several lodges of Indians. Fine day.[23]

In the morning, Lowe's party reached Walker & Eells' mission house near old Spokane House, where they rested until the moon came up and the snow hardened. They walked until morning and began again at dark. "But as it rained much, and the snow was too soft, we had to encamp about midnight."[24] The next day they reached the Colvile mill stream and descended it in a canoe, resting for the night at Alexander Dumond's farm-house.[25] On April 12, the party set off on foot to Fort Colvile, thirty miles away. "The road between the Farm and the Fort was very bad, and we did not reach the Fort until 10 o'clock at night."[26]

Three days later, Marineau (Louis Desasten) and Michel Ogden brought down the accounts and retiring servants from New Caledonia and Thompson's River.[27] The boats that had made their way up-river under John Lee Lewes's supervision arrived on April 17, and by April 24 everything was ready for the next stage of their journey.

— • —

Thomas Lowe also led the express out in 1848, but things were different this year. The changes had begun shortly after he returned to Fort Vancouver with his express the previous year. The Cayuse War, which is mentioned in Chapter 2, was only three months old and nowhere near being won or lost when the time came for the 1848 York Factory Express to set out. Although for the most part First Nations people remained on good terms with the HBC men, in 1848 the express-men played it safe. East of Fort Nez Percés they stuck close to the banks of the Columbia River rather than riding over the Shawpatin Road, which would have put them at risk of meeting hostile Cayuse:

1848, April 1, Saturday. Still blowing very strong but made a start in the afternoon, and encamped within sight of the Fort on the opposite side of the River. We have to take up 30 horses from this place to Colvile, and as no men can be spared from the Fort, and no Indians can be procured, I have been obliged to give one man from each boat, who are to assist Mr. [Henry Newsham] Peers and Robert Logan to drive them. The party with the horses are to encamp every night with the boats, for mutual protection against the Indians.

April 2, Sunday. Strong head wind, so that we could not start until noon. Got about 3 miles above the Nez Percés [Snake] Forks.

3, Monday. Fine weather, and the wind has fallen. Breakfasted at the mouth of the Yackima River, and encamped near the commencement of the Grands écorce.[28]

Lowe's "Grands écorce" is what earlier travellers called the Marle Banks — today the White Bluffs of Hanford Reach.

On April 4, they experienced fine, calm weather and the passengers rode their horses along the riverbank in company with the boats. Although the river was low they made good time and camped ten miles below Priest's Rapids. But the next day the weather worsened, and as they approached that rapid the wind blew "strong ahead, and increased so much, that we only got about half way up, although it was dark before we encamped."[29]

April 6, Thursday. Blew very hard all night, and did not moderate until noon, so that we were unable to leave our encampment until then. During the forenoon were employed drying some Bales for Colvile which had got wet in Joe's boat. Encamped at the head of the Priest's Rapid.

7, Friday. Had a strong aft wind before breakfast, which carried us a good distance, but afterwards it changed, and came right ahead, with a little rain. Got to the Traverse below the Rocher de Bois [Mad River] about noon and crossed the horses there to the South side of the River. There I left the boats to proceed overland to Okanagan with the horses, in company with Mr. Peers and two men, having placed Mr. Robert Logan in charge of the Boats during my absence.

The boats started immediately after we had crossed, but we only went about 5 miles, as there was no other place for the horses.

April 8, Saturday. Fine warm weather. Travelled over rough rocky ground during the fore part of the day, but in the afternoon had a much better road. Made a good distance, and encamped where the road falls into the Grand Coolé [sic].[30]

HBC trader A.C. Anderson, who journeyed through the Grande Coulée on several occasions, described it as a red-rocked ravine that "affords excellent travelling; good encampments are found at regular intervals. After following it for about sixty miles, the trail strokes off for the Columbia, at a point a few miles beyond a small lake, called by the voyageurs Le Lac à l'Eau Bleue."[31]

Thomas Lowe's men arrived at Fort Okanogan on April 10:

Mr. [Henry] Peers and his two men are to remain here until the Boats arrive. Having been about two hours at the Fort, and transacted what little business I had to settle with [Joachim] Lafleur, I started on horseback for Colvile accompanied by an Indian as guide. As the South side of the River is too dangerous at present, party of Cayuses being scattered here and there along the road, I intend following the North bank. Took one horse to carry the Paper Box, bedding &c. Rode hard, and encamped where the path strikes the River.

April 11, Tuesday. Beautiful warm weather. Our road today led through a very uneven Country where there was not a tree to be seen. As there is yet too much snow in the Mountains, we had to follow the River, not being able to take the direct road which strikes inland from our last night's encampment. Considering the nature of the Country, we made a good day's work, and encamped at the mouth of the Sans Poile [Sanpoil] River, where there were 3 lodges of Indians, who were very friendly.

April 12, Wednesday. Remarkably warm. In the forenoon crossed the Spokan Mountains, where there is yet a good quantity of snow, but not enough to retard us much. Having rode so hard from Okanagan, my horse got completely fagged in the afternoon, and we had to proceed very slowly afterwards in consequence. Encamped about 20 miles below Colvile at the crossing place.[32]

This crossing place, used by the Fort Colvile Brigades to Kamloops and Fort Langley after 1848, was near the mouth of the Kettle River. Lowe's journal continues:

> 13, Thursday. Clear warm weather. Crossed over to the South side of the Columbia this morning, having procured a canoe from the Indians. Proceeded very slowly, on account of our horses. It was an excellent road through clear open woods, a delightful contrast to the bare and rocky country through which we passed before coming to the Spokan Mountains. Arrived at Colvile about 4 o'clock in the afternoon. Here I found that C.T. [Paul] Fraser had arrived from New Caledonia with the Accounts and retiring Servants, and Michel Ogden from Thompson's River. The Revd. Messrs. Walker & Eells with their families have likewise been here for the last 6 weeks, having been obliged to abandon their Mission at Tchimakain [Tshimakain] on account of the Indians who were threatening to murder them, as they had done Dr. Whitman & his people.[33]

On April 22, Lowe welcomed the news that bands of Cayuse and Palouse Indians, who had been within a few days' ride of Fort Colvile, had dispersed eastward. He began preparations for his upriver journey to Boat Encampment.

— • —

By March 1849, when John Charles led out the York Factory Express, the Cayuse War was over. However, the express-men took no chances; they were heavily armed, and extra men travelled with them for protection. Thomas Lowe accompanied Charles as far as Fort Colvile. Charles then set off from Fort Nez Percés on Friday, March 30, 1849, after the boats had begun their upriver journey:

> Every thing being ready for our overland journey to Colvile, we started from Walla Walla at 1 p.m. with twelve horses, five of which were loaded, the remaining seven being mounted by Michel, Louis, Indian guide, Mr. [Thomas] Lowe, Mr. Menetrez and myself. We reached the Touchee [Touchet] where we camped about 7 p.m., the distance from Walla Walla is computed at twenty miles.

[March] Saturday 31st. Had breakfast the first thing in the morning. The sun was near about setting when we reached the Nez Percés [Snake] River. Camped on the beach, but soon regretted having done so, for the Wind having suddenly sprung up the sand was blown about in such clouds that we were obliged to hurry to bed for fear of being blinded by it.

Sunday, April 1st. Crossed the Nez Percés River about 10 a.m., Indians assisting us. Encamped at an early hour. Travelled about five and twenty miles today. Had a passing shower of hail towards evening.[34]

Once again the express travelled overland to Spokane House and Fort Colvile by the Shawpatin Road:

Monday 2nd. Had breakfast and started before sunrise. Gave the horses a rest at a small stream. Camped pretty early, in consequence of no firewood had we proceeded further today.

Tuesday 3rd. Traveled about 15 miles to day. The horses being very poor and in a weakly condition we were under the necessity of camping early. Met with a great deal of snow on our route. . . . Passed the night under a large red pine tree.

Wednesday 4th. Left our encampment about two hours after sunrise, but were obliged to return to it almost immediately as the horses were utterly unable to proceed in the great depth of snow, which lay around us.[35]

Deep snow had fallen in the winter of 1846–47, but the winter of 1848–49 also saw deep snows that buried the grasslands and killed hundreds of valuable horses at forts Colvile, Kamloops, and Alexandria:

Thursday 5th. Not being able to proceed to Colvile with horses, Mr. Lowe, Michel [Kaonassé], myself and the Indian started on foot about 10 p.m. We travelled the whole night and a greater part of the following day. Encamped on a hill, in sight of Spokan river. Sent our Indian guide to the Spokan lodges to procure snow shoes for us.

About sunset, three Indians arrived at our fire with the much longed for snowshoes, they slept at our fire.

Friday 6th. Blowing very hard all night. Left our encampment one hour before daylight for the Spokan Lodges which we reached a little after sunrise. . . . We crossed the Spokan River after breakfast, having previously engaged two Indians to accompany us, one to carry the express and the other our provisions, shoes etc. [As always in these journeys, their shoes were Indian shoes, or moccasins that tied around the ankle.] Passed the night at Walker & Eells' deserted mission. Road, tolerably good.[36]

The express, or "paper box," was an actual wooden box, carried with straps like a backpack, which transported important papers and accounts to the annual meeting. The party left the mission house before sunrise, with one man carrying the 70-pound box. They camped when the snow softened, and began again in the evening. In the morning they breakfasted at Dumond's house, and camped that night at Louis Brown's farm, 18 miles from the fort. The party reached Fort Colvile on April 9, at 3:30 in the afternoon.

For five days Charles and Lowe awaited the arrival of the New Caledonia Express. Finally, on April 19, 1849, Joachim Lafleur from Okanogan, and Marineau (Louis Desasten) from Fort Alexandria, arrived with the outgoing men.

The express-men prepared to leave Fort Colvile on the following Monday. Their journey up the Columbia River would bring them to Boat Encampment, 300 miles north of Fort Colvile. After a ten-day upriver journey, they would store their boats and hike across the Rocky Mountains. One express passenger with Aemilius Simpson's express called this immense range of mountains a "Barrier between Separated Friends."[37] A formidable barrier it would prove to be.

CHAPTER 4

Fort Colvile to Boat Encampment

δᴿ

THE COLUMBIA RIVER post of Fort Colvile was constructed in 1825, replacing the much older Spokane House, which was inconveniently located on the Spokane River, three days' travel from the banks of the Columbia. The new post's site had been chosen by HBC Governor George Simpson, and clerk John Work constructed it in its horseshoe-shaped valley on the east bank of the Columbia, just north of Kettle Falls. Within a few years Fort Colvile's farms produced rich crops of wheat, barley, maize, turnips, and potatoes. Herds of cattle and horses surrounded the picketed walls of the post, and its pigs and turkeys provided the New Caledonia posts with fresh meat and livestock. Fort Vancouver clerk George Traill Allan described Fort Colvile as he saw it fourteen years after its founding:

> Fort Colvile is a very neat and compact little establishment and nothing I have yet seen in the Indian Country can equal the bounty of its

situation — placed on a rising ground in the midst of a very pretty plain encircled by an extensive & well cultivated farm — the fields & fences laid out with a neatness which does credit to the taste of their projector — here and there a band of Cattle to enliven the prospect and at a considerable distance surrounded on all sides by high mountains covered from the base to the summit with beautiful pines. Nor does the inside of the establishment yield in any respect to the exterior, for, when seated at table with Mr. and Mrs. [Archibald] McDonald & their family, one cannot help thinking himself once more at home enjoying a tête-a-tête in some domestic circle.[1]

On Tuesday, April 17, 1827, Edward Ermatinger and his express party took their leave of the fledgling fort. While this journal is credited to Edward Ermatinger, there are times when it appears to be written by someone else. The journal begins:

The accounts being completed for York Factory as far as circumstances permit express boat manned by 7 men under charge of Mr. E. Ermatinger leaves Fort Colvile in the evening.

Wednesday, 18th. Light snow this morning. . . . Proceed on our journey at half past 5 a.m. Reach the head of the Dalles by 3 p.m.[2]

In spite of the Little Dalles' ferocious whirlpools, which swallowed the mightiest of trees with ease, Ermatinger "experienced very little difficulty in ascending them."[3] But this was a dangerous place, always. A jutting reef at the upriver end of this narrow rock-walled canyon divided the river into two powerful currents that churned downriver toward the boats.

A hundred feet downstream from the reef and before the express boats reached the canyon itself, the swirling river converged into a massive whirlpool that rose and sank, swallowing anything unfortunate enough to get in its way. But as the whirlpool's massive mouth closed with a gusty burp, the river flattened and the guide yelled at his paddlers to push the boat through the danger zone. As fearful as this rapid appeared, no man hesitated. They were all familiar with the river's dangers. They had traversed this rapid many times, and they knew that if they paused, they would be swallowed by the whirlpool.

Ermatinger's journal continues with the express party camping that night eight miles above this second rapid called the Little Dalles, where it snowed. (The first Little Dalles was in Nespelem Canyon, just east of Fort Okanogan.) The next day they camped a short distance below McGillivray's (Kootenay) River. Explorer David Thompson had given this river its name in 1807, in honour of the NWC's McGillivray family. On April 20, the express-men awoke to a hard frost, but ascended several rapids and entered Lower Arrow Lake in the morning. After stopping for breakfast, they hoisted their sail and continued to the camp at the top end of the lake.

On April 21, Ermatinger reported:

Fine weather, but wind strong ahead. Embark at 5 a.m. Pass the narrows and continue up the River to the entrance of the 2nd lake where we encamp at 7 a.m. Our track this day, with the exception of a short narrow of about 1 mile, may all be said to be Lake way, comparing it with what we really called the Lakes — generally not more than 1 mile wide. Passed several camps of Indians in course of the day and traded 7 pairs of Pas d'ours for our journey across the mountains — gave for them 2 scalpers, 13 ball and powders, and some dried salmon.[4] Country still mountainous and covered with snow on the hills.

Sunday, 22nd. Fine weather. Start at 4 a.m. Paddle thro' the 2nd Lake. Re-enter the river at 4 p.m. — find Indians encamped here.[5] Trade from them a little bears' meat and a pair of snow shoes for ammunition and tobacco. Proceed up the River 6 or 7 miles and encamp half past 6.

23rd. Fine weather. Resume our journey at quarter past 4 a.m. Find the River till toward evening very good and the current slack. We then enter a narrow banked on each side by rugged rocks and ascend a succession of strong rapids at the head of one of which we encamp, having before us a short piece of smooth current.[6]

This abrupt narrowing of the Columbia River, the third rapid along this river to be named Little Dalles, was 30 miles north of Upper Arrow Lake, and just north of present-day Revelstoke, B.C. It was a long rapid, three or four miles in length, and today's Steamboat Rapid is the northernmost rapid in the Little Dalles Canyon. In his journal, botanist David Douglas, a passenger in Ermatinger's express, described this set of rapids:

> Where the river takes a sudden bend, and to all appearance is lost in the mountains, a scene of the most terrific grandeur presents itself; the whole torrent is confined to a breadth of thirty-five yards, and tossed in rapids, whirlpools, and eddies; on both sides are mountains towering to the height of six or eight thousand feet from their base, rising with rugged perpendicular precipices from the very bed of the river, covered with dead timber of enormous growth, the roots of which, laid bare by the torrents, and now hurled by the violence of the wind from their original high places, come hurrying down the stream, bringing enormous fragments of earth attached to their roots, and spreading devastation all before them. The sun feebly tipped the mountain-tops as we passed this place, and, seen through the shadowy pines, imparted a melancholy air to the whole gloomy scene.[7]

Ermatinger's 1827 journal continues: "The banks of the river nearly the whole way we came today are still covered with deep snow as well as the woods."[8] The next day he noted, "The part of the River we have this day passed is full of Rapids and strong current with occasional pieces of smooth current — in mounting the Rapids we sometimes used the Line but more frequently the poles."[9] They saw a beaver, but "our gun being out of order he escaped."[10] On April 25, they reached "the foot of the Rapid below the Dalles des Morts."[11] He continues:

> Carry all our baggage at the lower brink of the Dalles [des Morts],[12] haul up our boat safe, tho' it is rather a dangerous place, clear the Dalles about noon. . . . River becomes more rapidous as we ascend. Encamp about 7 or 8 miles above Dalles des Morts at half past 7 p.m.[13]

On April 26, the express-men breakfasted above Rapides Croches.[14] Ermatinger found the "country very mountainous, snow deep."[15]

They camped at the head of another rapid, and on the next day they reached Boat Encampment at noon:

> The most part of the distance we made up the river this day the current was strong but smooth with several steep Rapids. The remainder of the day we occupied in preparing our baggage for the journey across the mountains. The paper trunk (which is very heavy, say upwards of 70 lbs.) is to be carried by 3 men alternately together with their provisions and private baggage. Our other baggage is divided among the remaining four men. Owing to the liberality of the gentlemen by whose posts we passed along the communication we were enabled nearly every night since we left Fort Vancouver to treat ourselves with potatoes at supper and finished the remains of our stock from Fort Colvile today, probably the first ever eaten at this place. Fruits of attention to gardening.[16]

David Douglas described the Columbia River at Boat Encampment, noting that the bigger channel (60 yards wide) lay on the north side of the islands in the middle of the river's big bend. The 40-yard-wide Canoe River flowed in from the north, and from the east the Wood River tumbled down the mountainside into the Big Bend of the Columbia. The Wood was the smallest of the three rivers, but the most important to these express-men. Almost all HBC men considered the Wood a continuation of the Columbia.

— • —

A year later, on April 20, 1828, Edward Ermatinger again pushed away from Fort Colvile on his way to Boat Encampment, and the party camped at the point above the fort. His express experienced no difficulties ascending the river. On April 21, they camped at the White Sheep River, and the next night below Kootenay River, where they gummed two leaky boats. For the next two days they paddled and poled through the Lower and Upper Arrow Lakes, and camped on the upper Columbia one hour's march beyond his 1827 encampment. On April 27, the party spent the night just below Les Dalles des Morts. On the last day of April, they stepped ashore at Boat

Encampment and spent the remainder of the day caching non-essentials, cooking food, and preparing loads to be packed over the mountains.

— • —

On the morning of April 4, 1835, clerk James Douglas woke up at Fort Colvile with feelings of dismay at the sight of the unusually heavy clouds that surrounded the place:

> Rainy wet morning and the atmosphere so overcharged with vapours as to leave no room for any hopes of a speedy change. . . . All the necessary arrangements being completed we recommenced our journey precisely at nine o'clock a.m. with two boats in which are embarked 4 passengers and 23 working men. The banks of the river on both sides rise in some places quite abruptly; [in] others by successive stages as it were, that is a steep ascent succeeded by a . . . horizontal surface leading to the next ascent, and so on to their greatest elevation varying from 2 to 300 feet above the level of the River. These hills are at no distance and confine the view to the course of the River, a circumstance which with their general sterile and rugged aspect gives a disagreeable appearance to the whole scenery. Some of the lower projecting points have a pretty effect, but assuredly owe most of their attraction to the strong contrast offered by their rugged neighbours. The tree most commonly met with here is the Pin Rouge which grows generally over the whole face of the country. Encamped 5 miles below the Mountain Goat River.
>
> Sunday 5. April. A fine clear morning. Continued our route at 5 o'clock, at 6 half [passed] the Mouton Blanc River, at 11 the Flat Head river [Pend-d'Oreille?], and at 6:30 p.m. we encamped at the river des oreille [Beaver Creek?].[17]

On Monday, they paddled through a dense fog that did not disperse until they reached Kootenay River. They entered Lower Arrow Lake before noon and camped that night on a pretty gravelly point halfway up its length. On Tuesday, they camped at the entrance of Upper Arrow Lake. The next night they set up camp at Chûtes au Bovil, which appears to be on the Columbia River just north of Upper Arrow Lake. On Thursday, they spent the night a few miles above Steamboat Rapid, and on Friday:

> Left our encampment at our usual hour half past four, and proceeded onwards very slowly owing to a succession of strong points and rapids, where the pole or the line were constantly required. In the afternoon we overtook a canoe wherein were five Indians with a Canadien Engagé named [Hypolite] Brissotte and family, who had been sent off from Fort Colvile by Mr. [Francis] Heron previous to my arrival there. This man's intention is to cross the mountains and it seems that Mr. Heron had pledged himself that he should be permitted to do so by the present opportunity. On his mentioning that the Indians are unwilling to proceed Mr. H proposed that himself and family should be embarked in one of the boats. Now it being Dr. McLoughlin's express orders that no women should have a passage in these boats, I felt the impropriety of complying with this proposal; but not being fully authorized to act, and Mr. H being my senior and superior in rank, out of delicacy to him I assented and the man & family were accordingly permitted to embark. Called on Mr. Heron this evening and mentioned Dr. McL[oughlin's] orders against the embarkation of families in the express boats; I at the same time explained the motives which induced me to comply with his wishes, and I requested him to state explicitly whether in the event of my being called to account for this disregard of orders he was willing to bear the whole responsibility. He replied that in every case he would stand between me & the consequences.
>
> Saturday, April 11th. Clear, cold night. Reached the Dalles des Morts at 8 o'clock, and at 7 p.m. encamped at St. Martins Rapid.[18]

Always known to be treacherous, St. Martins Rapid was probably the same as Ermatinger's Rapides Croches, or modern-day Gordon Rapids. In September 1825, the NWC employee Joseph St. Martin drowned in the Columbia River, quite possibly in the rapid that bore his name. Fur traders had long memories, and in the York Factory Express boats there were always a few men who told the old stories.

— • —

Thomas Lowe's voyageurs rowed away from Fort Colvile on Thursday, April 22, 1847. "Beautiful weather. Started from Colvile with the two Boats about 5 o'clock in the afternoon, and reached Dease's Encampment, 6 miles from the Fort."[19] On Friday, Lowe's express pulled against a light headwind, passing the Little Dalles in the afternoon and camping a mile below the Pend-d'Oreille River. On Saturday, they camped above Kootenay River, and by Sunday evening they had encamped at what was almost the upper end of the Lower Arrow Lake. Strong headwinds had delayed them, but on the following day they sailed with favourable winds and "camped late, about ten miles from the [lower] end of the upper Lake. Slept in the Boats."[20] The next day:

> Tuesday 27th. Fine weather. Breakfasted at the end of the upper Lake, and camped a little below the Grande Batture.[21]

To the HBC voyageurs, a "batture" was a sand or gravel bar in a riverbed or a lake. James Douglas indicated in his journal that the Grande Batture was "a few points below the [Little] Dalles"[22] in the upper Columbia River, and just north of his Chûtes au Bovil. The express-men's Grande Batture was almost certainly what British Columbians now call the Big Eddy, located on a sharp river bend some 933 miles from the Pacific Ocean. This confused piece of river marked the beginning of the uncooperative section of the Columbia, where the river flowed downward between high rock walls through narrow channels. From here, the men climbed some 400 feet of rapid-filled river in less than a hundred miles.

On April 28, Lowe's men breakfasted at the foot of the Little Dalles, and "had very hard work all day against rapids and strong currents."[23] It rained, and they camped about fifteen miles above Steamboat Rapid. On April 29, they portaged the pieces past Les Dalles des Morts and hauled the boats up with the line. He reported:

> Camped at the head of the Dalles, made a fire on the rocks & slept in the boats.

Friday 30th. Light showers. Camped about 2 miles above the River of St. Martin, on the snow.[24]

According to A.C. Anderson, River of St. Martin or Rivière St. Martin was also called Gold River, and is probably today's Goldstream River.[25]

On May 2, Lowe's men reached Boat Encampment early in the morning. There was a lot of work to be done to prepare themselves for their journey over the Rocky Mountains. At least one boat was stashed in the woods — out of the sun that dried out the planks and opened the seams. Lowe wrote that they

> got the boat which is to be left hauled up, and secured alongside another which we found there. Set the people to cook provisions to take them across the Mountains and got the loads arranged. Took 4 men from the boats to assist to carry until we meet the horses, and hired two Indians we found here to assist us also in carrying.[26]

Some men, paid a bonus to act as personal servants, carried the gentlemen's cassettes over the steep mountain portage.[27] Cassettes were travelling boxes with compartments to hold cups, cutlery, spices, and other small personal belongings of the traders and clerks. They were built of seasoned pine, and made as strong and light as dovetailing, grooving and iron binding could make them. They were a little more than two feet in length, 15 inches in width, and 15 inches deep. The cassettes were painted, and they had a cover that fit into a lap in the wood.

Nothing that did not have to cross the mountains was carried any farther than Boat Encampment. Tea and sugar were considered essential, as were ammunition, balls, and powder. Everything else, including liquor, was cached in a hole dug in the ground and lined with oilskins to prevent water damage. In the early years, the cache was at Boat Encampment, and the men built a fire to disguise the disturbed earth. In 1827, Ermatinger's hiding place was probably across the Canoe River. A.C. Anderson's map of the Upper Columbia indicated that in 1842 the cache was on the Columbia River's west bank, one or two miles south of Boat Encampment.[28]

— • —

One year later, Thomas Lowe led the York Factory Express from Fort Colvile, beginning his journey on April 24, 1848:

> Very cloudy, but no rain. Started from Colvile about 1 o'clock p.m. with two boats for the Mountains. Five men from the Interior go out with us, but we had to leave two of the men here whom we brought from Vancouver.[29]

They enjoyed a sail wind for some distance, and made good progress. The next day his party breakfasted at the foot of the first of two Little Dalles in this section of the river, and spent the night about ten miles above the Pend-d'Oreille River.

In the afternoon of April 26, they enjoyed a sail wind again, and camped fifteen miles from the bottom of Lower Arrow Lake. On April 27, the boats faced a headwind, and they were able to make it only as far as the upper end of the lake. The headwind persisted the next day, but they "pulled to within 10 miles of the end of [the upper lake], & camped."[30] The next day:

> April 29, Saturday. Fine day. Breakfasted at the end of the Upper Lake, and got a good distance up the River.[31]

On Sunday, they breakfasted at the foot of Steamboat Rapid and worked hard with line and pole to get the boats through that turbulent barrier. Lowe's journal continues:

> [May 1] Cloudy throughout the day, and rained in the evening. Encamped on the snow at the head of the Dalles des Morts.
>
> 2, Tuesday. Raining most of the day. Breakfasted a little above McKenzie's Encampment. Got up to the foot of St. Martins [Gordon] Rapid, and encamped on the snow.
>
> 3, Wednesday. Rained last night, and as the weather was mild the

river rose considerably. Rainy unpleasant weather. Got up to within 10 miles of the Boat Encampment.

4, Thursday. Cloudy, but no rain. Reached the Boat Encampment about 8 o'clock this morning, where we found Capot Blanc with two lodges of Indians. Got one of our boats hauled up to be left here until the Autumn.[32]

The second boat would return to Fort Colvile, as was usual, with the incoming men and letters.

— • —

On Monday, April 23, 1849, John Charles left Fort Colvile without Thomas Lowe, who had accompanied him upriver:

Left Fort Colvile for the Boat Encampment about 5 p.m. with two boats laden with provisions and men's property. We encamped at a small distance below Dease encampment. Cloudy weather.

Tuesday 24th. Encamped about ten miles above the "Rivière de Mouton Blanc." Experienced a very heavy shower of rain towards night.

Wednesday 25th. At breakfast the sky cleared up and the sun shone brilliantly. Traded a beaver from an Indian. About 1 p.m. we put ashore at some Indian lodges encamped on the beach where we were informed that the lakes were still frozen over.

Thursday 26th. Reached the first lake, but encountered no ice. Encamped at sundown.

Friday 27th April. Fine weather. Encamped at the end of the first lake.

Saturday 28th. Entered the second lake. Camped at sunset.

Sunday 29th. Blowing furiously all of last night and this morning. Breakfasted at the end of the Grand Lac [Upper Arrow Lake] and camped a little after sundown.

Monday [April] 30th. Passed the small Dalles an hour after breakfast. Tracking and poling up the Rapids almost all day. Cloudy weather. Great quantities of snow and ice along the shore.

Tuesday 1st May. Raining almost all day. Camped at the lower end of the "Mauvaise Rapide" [Dalles des Mortes].

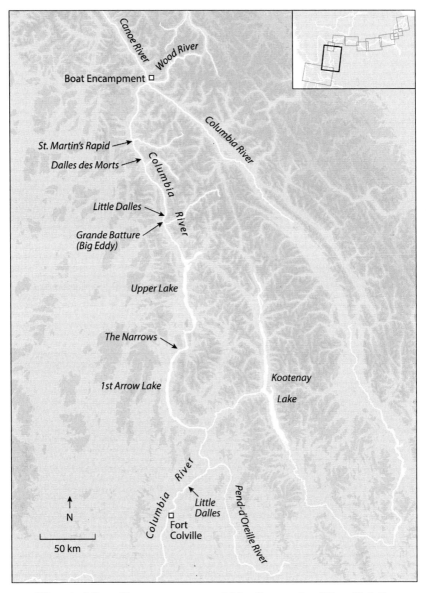

Historical Boat Encampment was 300 miles north of Fort Colvile,
on the Big Bend on the Columbia River.

Wednesday 2nd. After getting safely over the "Bad Rapid" we
breakfasted. Camped at the foot of St. Martin Rapid. Beautiful
weather.[33]

They camped the next night in sight of the Rocky Mountains, and on May 4 "arrived at the Boat Encampment about 8 a.m. Had one of the boats taken up the bank, above high water mark."[34]

Charles's journal is brief and to the point, with no details and apparently without any unusual incidents or problems. But now he and his men prepared for the most difficult part of the journey to Hudson Bay — the passage over the Rocky Mountains via the Grande Côte.

All express-men who arrived at this spot knew they stood at a historic landmark. In the last days of 1810, the warlike Peigan had set up a blockade to prevent NWC explorer David Thompson from crossing to the west side of the Rockies by his regular route via the Blaeberry (Howse) River.

Instead of bluffing his way past the hostiles, Thompson made his way north to cross the mountains via the Athabasca Pass, a route little known to the NWC men at this time. On January 10, 1811, he and his men reached the top of the mountains. A week later they stumbled onto the banks of the Columbia River and set up camp on the Canoe River. There was no good birch bark to be found here, so he designed his canoe of cedar boards, on which design all later Columbia River boats were based.

In mid-April, his boat was finished, and Thompson continued his journey up the Columbia River, toward its source and his trading houses on Pend Oreille Lake and the Spokane River. His route over Athabasca Pass proved so successful that the North West Company adopted it as their annual summer route in and out of the territory. Hundreds and perhaps thousands of men crossed over this steep trail in the nine years that followed. When in 1821 the NWC merged with the HBC, their trail worked so efficiently that there was little reason to search for an alternate route. By the time Ermatinger's express climbed over the pass in 1827, it had been in use seventeen years. When twenty-two-year-old John Charles traversed it in 1849, the trail was seventeen years older than he was.

CHAPTER 5

Boat Encampment to Jasper's House

৯৬

IN 1841, GEORGE TRAILL ALLAN found his journey east to Fort Colvile uneventful (except for Brotchie's plum puddings) and had little to say of his upriver journey to Boat Encampment. But at this place his writing took on a life of its own. Accompanying Allan on this crossing was Doctor William Fraser Tolmie, a deeply religious teetotaller: industrious, reliable, and calm. Allan's story begins on May 5:

> We now started about 10 o'clock am; not finding any snow for the first few miles, we walked in Moccasins, otherwise called Indian Shoes, along the banks of the Columbia [Wood] when we entered the woods & found ourselves in a swamp the water reaching above the Knees, our road leading that way, it was of course unavoidable, we therefore trudged along in no very comfortable trim for about two miles when we again entered the woods and finding deep snow had recourse to the snow shoes — The Doctor and I were light, but the men were

heavily loaded, and many of them having never seen a snow shoe, many and great were the falls they had — The snow shoe has a very admirable and peculiar quality, when one falls down it is no easy matter to get up again, and although I felt for the poor men yet I could not altogether command my risibility though it was however sometimes my misfortune to share the same fate & Dr. Tolmie keeping me in countenance, we did not fail upon such occasions to laugh heartily at each other — The Canadians of all nations possess perhaps the best qualities for voyaging (at least in the Indian Country) where we have to undergo, to use one of their own words, so much misère, however harassing their labour may have been during the day, they no sooner arrive at the encampment for the night than having supplied themselves with an excellent fire and good supper, they commence joking each other — with the greatest good humour upon the mishaps of the past day & having now a tolerable knowledge of their language I really enjoyed them, and now and then put in a word by way of encouragement, to keep up their spirits.[1]

Allan's party set up camp on the banks of the Wood River, in a place that was clear of snow. Their journey began again at 3 o'clock the next morning, when "the voice of our guide an Iroquois, calling out *levez-vous, levez-vous* (get up, get up), put us once more upon our legs."[2] His journal continues:

Everything being now ready and the men loaded we started at 4. It having frozen hard during the night we found that we could travel without the snow shoes, our route laying along the River. We soon found, however, that though enabled to dispense for a time with the snow shoes that we had a more disagreeable task to perform. We had scarcely walked a mile when we were obliged to plunge into the River which we crossed seven times and found the water exceedingly cold.[3]

In 1827, botanist David Douglas described the dangers of crossing the cold and slippery Wood River on its gravel bars:

[The river was] two and a half to three feet deep, clear, and with a powerful current. Though the breadth did not exceed twenty five to fifty yards, the length of time passed in the water was considerable, for the feet cannot with safety be lifted from the bottom, as if once the water gets under the soles of the feet, which should be glided along to prevent this, over goes the whole person. In very powerful currents, it is necessary to pass in a body, and the one supporting the other, in an oblique direction.[4]

Allan's 1841 journal continues:

At last, about 8 a.m. we once more reached the woods and lost no time in consoling ourselves with a substantial breakfast for the hardships of the morning. Having rested the men and ourselves for three hours we again buckled on our armour (the snowshoes) and marched to the attack when we encountered greater disasters than we had done the day before, the snow not being sufficiently shallow to admit of our throwing off the snow shoes, and too deep and soft to permit our walking without them. About 3 o'clock p.m. we got once more clear of the woods & encamped at the foot of a tree which we found free from snow.

Friday 7th. The weather clear and cold at 3 a.m. we started & proceeding along the River without the snow shoes had nearly the same kind of route as the preceding day, only we were obliged to cross the River more frequently and found as we approached the mountain the water still colder, as much so, that upon gaining the bank our leggens [leggings] were stiff with ice, but a smart walk and a good breakfast at the base of the mountain, which we had now reached, soon banished all remembrance of misère.

The Country through which we had travelled for the last three days has nothing in its appearance to recommend it to the eye of the traveler. The River is upon both sides bound in by rather high mountains, wooded to the summits, which confine the view to the River alone. We now betook ourselves to the snow shoes and commenced the ascent which we found very steep. We managed, however, to scramble up about half way, when we encamped.[5]

The steep trail they climbed was called the Grande Côte, and it led to the top of the saddle that separated Wood River and Jeffrey Creek from Pacific Creek and Athabasca Pass.

Another traveller, artist Paul Kane, who came through the pass in 1846, described how the voyageurs prepared their camp on top of the thick layer of Rocky Mountain snow:

> It is necessary to walk repeatedly with snow-shoes over the place chosen for the encampment until it is sufficiently beaten down to bear a man without sinking on its surface. Five or six logs of green timber, from eighteen to twenty feet long, are laid down close together in parallel lines, so as to form a platform. The fire of dry wood is then kindled on it, and pine branches are spread on each side, on which the party, wrapped in their blankets, lie down with the feet towards the fire. The parallel logs rarely burn through in one night, but the dropping coal and heat form a deep chasm immediately under the fire, into which the logs are prevented from falling by their length.[6]

Allan described how, in the morning, "the fire had entirely disappeared, having sunk during the night almost to the ground and the snow was at least ten feet deep."[7]

On May 8, Allan's party continued their ascent of the Grande Côté, "which increased in steepness as we proceeded and obliged us often to crawl upon all fours."[8] His journal continues:

> The Doctor & myself took each our turn in marching ahead not only in the mountain but throughout the whole journey — a task by no means easy as the snow-shoe sinks much deeper before the track is formed & returns upon it a great quantity of snow (when it has as in the present case lately fallen) which forces the foot dreadfully in a long journey & often occasions the mal de racquette or snowshoe sickness which is exceedingly painful. We were both, however, fortunate enough to escape it and about 6 o'clock a.m. we gained the top of the mountain & did not certainly feel regret upon the achievement.[9]

At this point they had reached the saddle at the top of the Côté. Their journey would continue down the saddle's north side to the swampy valley of Pacific Creek, which they would follow up to Athabasca Pass itself. But the toughness of the uphill journey via the

Grande Côté made reaching the saddle an accomplishment to cele-
brate. They did so by building a fire and eating their first meal of the
day. As Allan explained:

> The guide soon joining us we made a large fire long ere the men ar-
> rived almost worn out with their hard journey, which did not however
> prevent them quozzing [sic] each other as usual & many were the
> tales of misfortune recounted.[10]

At the top of the saddle they were 5,000 feet above sea level. Pacific
Creek valley lay about 750 feet below them. At the north end of the
sloping valley, Athabasca Pass loomed 5,700 feet above sea level —
700 feet higher than the saddle.

In those days, the impressive glaciers that crowned the mountains
near Athabasca Pass loomed over the men as they made their way
along the route. In mid-October 1823, John Work noted that "the
little hollows or valleys to the very summits of these mountains are
filled with solid ice."[11] Any man who walked through the narrow pass
under the shining white walls of the fur traders' Mount Hooker (Mc-
Gillivray's Ridge) would feel engulfed by the icefield's frozen grasp.

But in the middle of this barren land of ice and snow, just east of
the summit of Athabasca Pass, were two or three circular lakes called
the Committee's Punch Bowl. Ross Cox gave a clear description of
these lakes:

> They lie on the most level part of the height of land, and are situated
> between an immense cut of the Rocky Mountains. From them two
> rivers take their rise, which pursue different courses, and fall into sep-
> arate oceans. . . . The country round our encampment presented the
> wildest and most terrific appearance of desolation that can be well
> imagined. The sun shining on a range of stupendous glaciers, threw a
> chilling brightness over the chaotic mass of rocks, ice, and snow, by
> which we were surrounded. . . . One of our roughspun unsophisticated
> Canadians, after gazing upwards for some time in silent wonder, ex-
> claimed with much vehemence, "I'll take my oath, my dear friends,
> that God Almighty never made such a place!"[12]

Allan's party encamped by these lakes at 4 p.m. In his journal he notes:

> This place is called the Height of Land, the Columbia River taking its
> rise from one of the Lakes and winding its course to the Pacific; the
> River Athabasca from the other & emptying itself into the Atlantic
> [Arctic] Ocean. The Lakes as I stated, are three, but at the season we
> passed invisible, from the great quantity of snow. We had so far fol-
> lowed the course of the Columbia [Wood River, Jeffrey Creek, and
> Pacific Creek] & had been ascending. We now took that of the Atha-
> basca [Whirlpool] and began to descend.[13]

The number of lakes clustered in this narrow valley at any time of
year varied, but all had a long fur trade history. Before 1821, the lakes
were a favourite camping spot of the Nor'Westers who worked west
of the mountains. In 1825, HBC Governor George Simpson paused
here and, after giving the lake its name, offered everyone in his party
a drink. That tradition remained, but another arose as well, possibly
picked up from the early NWC men. Every tree that surrounded this
cluster of lakes was festooned with the carved names of the gentlemen who had passed through Athabasca Pass — another tradition
rarely mentioned in fur trade journals.

Allan's journal continued on May 9:

> We set out at the usual hour & walked until 7 o'clock when we break-
> fasted, the walk of this morning we found equal to the toil of climbing
> the mountain from the great depth and softness of the snow; & the
> Doctor and myself going ahead as usual to beat the road for the men,
> we found the task anything but an easy one. . . . We now found, as we
> descended, the snow to get less deep, and consequently the walking
> less fagging, our route laying sometimes upon the River & at others
> through the woods.[14]

From the dizzying heights of Athabasca Pass, their trail took them
steadily downhill, past snowbound Campement du Fusil (Kane
Meadow), which was almost 5,200 feet above sea level and five miles
east of the summit. The first obvious landmark was ten miles north of

Athabasca Pass, where the wide gravel flat of the Grande Batture (Scott Gravel Flats), still bounded by mountain and forest, stretched along the Whirlpool River some 4,600 feet above sea level. The express-men had probably reached this place when Allan wrote:

> We fell upon the sands of the River; no snow — to the men a joyful sight; and at the distance of two miles we expected to find the Horses which are always sent from Jasper's House to meet the express and relieve the men of their loads — We now cast off the snow shoes for good & all and bid them good by with pleasure, although they had greatly befriended us. Upon our arrival at the place where we had expected to find the Horses we met with a sad disappointment: none were there! We found the horse Keepers Lodge, or Hut, the remains of the fire, and the fresh tracks of the Horses, so that he must have decamped not two hours previous to our arrival. Upon examining his hut very narrowly we discovered a piece of wood upon which he had managed to draw with charcoal the figure of a Moose Deer and marked sixteen strokes upon which, after various conjectures, we understood that he had been waiting for us sixteen days & there being a scarcity of food for the Horses he was obliged to return to the next encampment which is called the Moose Deer encampment; the men, poor fellows, were rather cast down on arriving, as well they might — but soon recovered their spirits, on my informing them that next morning very early the doctor, the guide & myself would start ahead and send them the Horses; in the mean time we consoled ourselves by taking possession for the night of the hut and found it very comfortable.[15]

Campement d'Orignal, or Moose Deer Encampment, was 14 miles north of Grande Batture on the Whirlpool River, and 28 miles south of Jasper's House. As expected, Allan located the horses at Campement d'Orignal and sent horse-keeper and packhorses south, to meet the men and bring them forward. The next night they camped on the Athabasca River, having crossed over the Whirlpool River at the Grand Traverse. Early the next morning, Allen wrote:

The horse-keeper called me saying it was time to start. I immediately ordered the men to get the Horses ready, a task they set about with great alacrity rejoicing at the idea of their loads being transferred from their own backs to those of the horses. About 8 o'clock we called a halt and had breakfast — our store of eatables being now so much reduced, that having finished that meal, there only remained a few Biscuits & some tea & sugar — & not being able to reach Jasper's house before next day it did not require a great Logician to prove that unless we picked up something betwixt that place and the encampment we should make but a sorry supper of it.[16]

On May 12, Allan set out ahead accompanied by Tolmie and the guide:

After a smart ride of four hours we arrived at the tent of a fisherman and his family, situated in a most romantic spot upon the side of a beautiful lake, its waters so clear that I could see from the hill where I stood, the bottom of the Lake all over. On enquiring at the Fisherman what success, he informed me that the proceeding night he had killed with the spear one hundred white fish, part of which I desired him to send to Jasper's house, now distant only two miles. Upon our arrival there we received a regular Highland welcome from the person in charge, Colin Fraser, formerly Piper to Governor Simpson, but now promoted to the charge of Jasper's House, Colin lost no time in asking us what we would have for breakfast at the same time presenting his bill of fare which consisted of Moose Deers and Sheeps meat & White fish; to travellers like ourselves who had the night before been obliged to hunt for a supper, there could be no choice, the whitefish, however, being just caught, carried the day, and such a hearty breakfast did we make of it as would not have disgraced Richard Coeur de Leon, when he fell foul of the Pantry set before him by the fat Friar.[17]

In every journal written by the gentlemen, the trail up the west side of the Rocky Mountains seems to be gentle and easy. It was not, and it was especially not easy for the voyageurs who did all the work. These men had already spent a month paddling and tracking the heavy boats up the Columbia River to Boat Encampment. They were the ones who packed the loads over the many portages that blocked the river between Fort Vancouver and Boat Encampment, and they also repaired the boats while the gentlemen sat around the campfire.

Once they reached the big bend of the Columbia, they carried the loads. As has been seen, the paper box alone weighed as much as 70 pounds. While it is true that the gentlemen broke the trail, the Canadien voyageurs carried the provisions on their backs. The Canadiens chopped down the trees that made their campsite on the snow, and they maintained the fire and probably made the tea and cooked the shared meals. They were servants.

The voyageurs, although they carried a heavier load, were in far better condition than the gentlemen. They complained about the journey, but they also had the satisfaction of seeing the gentlemen suffer more than a little. In April 1825, HBC Governor George Simpson climbed the Grande Côté on his return to Lachine, and described his experience:

> In the Face of the Hill for about a couple of Miles the Snow was about 18 Inches deep but as we advanced it deepened to 6 feet; the labour of Walking without Snow Shoes was dreadful during the heat of the Day sinking every Step 18 inches to 2 feet we however by great exertion got to the top of the Hill at 5 p.m. having Walked 12 hours with three Indian Shoes on rough Shingle & in deep Snow; every Man in the Camp lame & exhausted. . . . Never did exhausted travelers turn out less disposed to renew a toilsome Journey than we did at 3 o'clock this Morn, every man on the party requiring the aid of a Walking Stick our feet being much blistered and Lacerated by the rough Travel on the Battures and in the Bed of the River; we however improved as we got Warm upon it and continued a Steady pace until 10 O'Clock having by that time forded the River 17 times when the joyful shout was given by one of the people that the Horses were in sight.[18]

In 1847, Thomas Lowe's party climbed the Grande Côté to Athabasca Pass, making their way to Jasper's House on their outgoing journey. They moved quickly and efficiently, covering the 97 miles that separated Boat Encampment from Jasper's House in record time.

The journey could consume anything from five to nine days depending on the condition of the trail. Lowe's party left Boat Encampment on May 2nd, and crossed the swamp to encamp in the woods a little beyond. "There is less snow in the Mountain this year than usual,"[19] Lowe reported:

Monday 3rd. Started at daylight, and walked through the woods on snow shoes until breakfast time, when we reached the Battures, where there was no snow. Walked through the Battures until 3 p.m. then entered the woods, walked on snow shoes about 2 hours, and encamped.

Tuesday 4th. Walked all day through the woods & Battures, and encamped at 4 p.m. half way up the Grand Cote. A fall of snow in the afternoon.

Wednesday 5th. Very cold, and a slight fall of snow in the forenoon. Got to the top of the Grand Cote and breakfasted about 2 miles farther on. Passed the height of land [Athabasca Pass] at noon, and having measured the depth of snow, found only 2 and a half feet on the surface of the Lake. Got as far as the Campement du Fusil.

Thursday 6th May 1847. Started very early and breakfasted at the Grande Batture, where we found the horses that had been sent from Jasper's House for us. There were 14, enough for all hands, so that all were mounted. Sent Michel and [Jean-Baptiste] McKay ahead to Jasper's House to have the boat gummed. . . . I then went on with the remainder of the party, leaving the 4 men and two Indians whom we brought from the Boat Encampment to return with Mr. John Charles and two Scotch Shepherds whom we found here with the Packet for the Columbia.

These Scottish shepherds were on their way to Fort Nisqually (present-day Tacoma), where the HBC raised flocks of sheep. John Charles would clerk at Fort Vancouver and, for a few months, at Fort Victoria. Lowe's journal continues:

The horses had been waiting for us a week. We camped before sundown about 5 hours beyond the Campement d'Orignal [Moose Encampment].

Friday 7th. Passed the Grande Traverse about 11 a.m. and break-fasted at the Campement des Vaches [Buffalo Encampment]. Started again at 2 p.m. and encamped at the Rocher du Bon Homme, about 4 miles beyond Larocque's Prairie. Beautiful day.

Saturday 8th. Started early, and reached Jasper's House at 9 a.m. Mr. Burke arrived yesterday forenoon, but Michel had been able to do but little to the boat. Got it caulked & gummed today, all ready to start tomorrow.[20]

In spite of the difficult climb, every man arrived safely at the HBC post in the Jasper Valley, wherever it might stand over the years, and whatever it was called.

On May 4, 1827, Edward Ermatinger's party arrived at the valley's first Rocky Mountain House, built in 1813 by the NWC's François Decoigne. A few years later its name was changed to Jasper's House. The post stood on the west side of Brule Lake. (The footprints of the buildings remain and can be viewed at the Jasper House National Historic Site, 22 miles east of Jasper townsite.) By the time James Douglas crossed the mountains in April 1835, Michel Klyne had re-built the old post in a new location, west of the junction of the Snake Indian River with the Athabasca.

It was at Jasper's House that the men prepared the boats for their journey down the Athabasca River to Fort Assiniboine, 185 miles downriver. Care of the boats and canoes was essential, as the men depended on them to get safely from one place to another. One jour-nal describes men repairing a canoe whose ties had not been loosened well enough in the autumn to prevent damage by the contraction from freezing temperatures over the winter. Other employees sub-merged a wooden boat in the river to swell the planks and close the gaping seams. This work was done many times over during the jour-ney, but was rarely mentioned by the clerks because it was so familiar.

In May 1849, John Charles reported from Jasper's House, "The Athabasca River appears to be very low and Mr. Colin Fraser is apprehensive that we will meet with ice on our way down to Assini-boine."[21] The express-men who arrived at Jasper's House knew that if the river's water was high, they would enjoy an incredibly fast trip down the river to Fort Assiniboine. If the level was low, however, they would bump their way down to deep water. This western region often suffered from periods of drought, and at times the Athabasca River was too shallow for their boats. Ice could also be a problem; in late, cold winters it broke so late in the season it caused great difficulty for the express. Travellers on this river could guess at the state of the water when they left Jasper's House. They also knew they would be following the floating ice downriver. The only thing they could not know, was when they would meet the ice, and whether it would be solid, or thinly dispersed over the surface of the river.

CHAPTER 6

Jasper's House to Edmonton House

᪗᪘

ON THEIR ANNUAL JOURNEY to Hudson Bay, the York Factory Express men travelled over three major river systems, each of which seeped from under the edges of the glaciers that were part of the massive Columbia Icefield. The Columbia District men had come from territories that were served by the Columbia River. While the Columbia's true source is Columbia Lake in the East Kootenay, about 300 miles south of the icefield, the waters of Pacific Creek flow from Athabasca Glacier, through Athabasca Pass, into the Columbia River at Boat Encampment, via the Wood River. At Jasper's House, on the eastern edge of the same icefield, the Columbia men started the downriver journey to Fort Assiniboine on the Athabasca River, which eventually emptied into the Arctic Ocean. The express abandoned that river at Fort Assiniboine, however, and proceeded overland to the North Saskatchewan River — a silt-laden river that flowed east from the Columbia Icefield's Saskatchewan Glacier.

But the men thought little of geography and were only concerned with getting to Edmonton House as quickly as possible. In 1826, Aemilius Simpson estimated that the length of the river between Fort Assiniboine and the first Jasper's House (on Brule Lake) was "a distance by estimation of 285 miles, the course of the River being particularly Winding, with a very strong current & frequent Rapids occurring."[1]

In May 1827, botanist David Douglas descended the river in one of Edward Ermatinger's canoes. He described it as being "one hundred to one hundred and forty yards wide, shallow and rapid, with low gravelly banks, wooded with Poplars and Pines. Its vicinity abounds with wild fowl, and the Northern Diver [a loon] charmed us with his deep mellow melancholy voice in the evenings."[2]

In 1835, clerk James Douglas was in a hurry to get to Fort Garry (Red River), where he was to be made chief trader. Because of his eagerness to deliver the Fort Vancouver accounts to the council members in an expeditious manner, he descended the Athabasca in April, two weeks earlier than any other party:

> Tues. 21. Left Klyne's House [Jasper's House, which was under the command of Michel Klyne in 1835] this morning at 8 o'clock with one canoe, 4 passengers and 8 men. The other men remain here to mend and prepare the two other canoes for descending the River. They will follow us as soon as they are ready for the journey which will be I suppose tomorrow. The river is very low, and they will be much lumbered with families and baggage, two causes from which much delay may be naturally expected on their way down. Had the case been otherwise I should scarcely have decided on separating the party. But my aim is to reach Edmonton about the 26 current which cannot be accomplished unless the utmost diligence is used. [3]

The families and children Douglas thought would delay him were the two children of Pierre Pambrun of Fort Nez Percés, who were being sent to the Red River school, and the wife and children of retiring Canadien Hypolite Brissotte. Pambrun had sent his children to

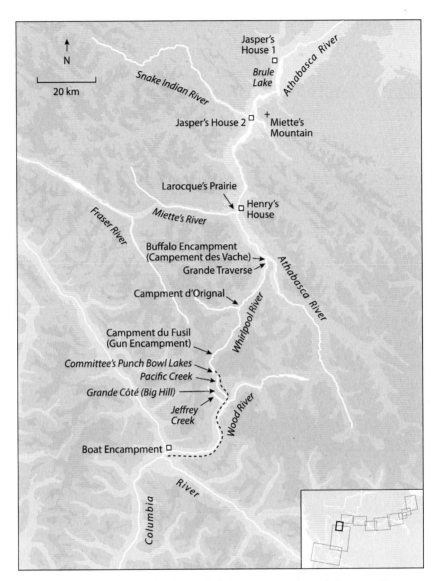

Wood River and Pacific Creek led the men north to Athabasca Pass,
and the Whirlpool River brought them to Jasper's House.

Fort Colvile by the boat that followed Douglas's by a few days. Brissotte, who was retiring, connived with Francis Heron to bring his
family into the boats rather than leave them behind. As we saw in

Chapter 4, McLoughlin (or more likely, Governor Simpson) had issued orders that families were not to travel in the boats. For the most part, everyone ignored the order, but all knew that Douglas was a stickler for the rules. Douglas's journal continues:

> Wed. 22nd April. A very stormy day with snow & rain in abundance. Passed Rapids des Morts [Rapids de Croix] at 12 o'clock, and after proceeding 3 hours more we were compelled to land, the river being entirely filled with ice. After landing I proceeded downwards a few miles on foot to examine the state of the river. In some places the ice does not appear to have moved at all, in others the middle of the channel is open. It being impossible to move at present, we pass the night here to await the event of tomorrow.
>
> Monday 23. Left our encampment of last night but before we had advanced a mile from the place found an accumulation of ice which renders the river impassable at present. At this place we landed and remained stationary for a considerable time to see if the ice would give way. During this state of suspense I walked a short distance down the river and found the ice firm at two places, but beyond these clear water. This circumstance determined me to attempt a passage. Accordingly the canoe and property were carried over the first bridge of ice and launched into the water. We shortly afterwards encountered a second obstruction, then a third which were passed in a similar manner to the first. After proceeding a few miles further we overtook a large body of floating ice near which we encamped. We are now near 15 miles from Baptiste [Berland] River. Distance today 6 miles.[4]

Because Douglas was so impatient to get to Red River, he had now to make his way down the Athabasca before its ice had broken. For the next few days Douglas's party averaged only five miles a day. On April 25, he decided to leave the rest of the party behind. He proceeded downriver with ten men in a lightly-loaded canoe, with plans to portage over the ice:

> Sunday 26. At half past 4 we were on the move, and after gliding smoothly over a few miles of open water we reached a large field of ice, over which all the property was carried. A second soon after appeared

and was passed in the same manner. Soon after we reached Baptiste's River which is exceedingly high and rushes with such impetuous force into the Athabasca River as nearly divides it in two. To our great joy we encountered no more ice during the day, but from the great quantity still adhering to the banks on both sides, it is evident that it has been very recently carried off. Met a canoe from Assiniboine which left that place 5 days ago. They inform us that they were stopped the whole of the 24th & 25th by the ice floating downwards in such quantities as to cover the entire body of the river. Encamped about 40 miles above the Fort.[5]

Douglas's party reached Fort Assiniboine the next morning. This post was located on the north side of the Athabasca River across from a large island, 185 miles from Jasper's House. It existed to serve the Columbia men and was abandoned in the mid-1850s when the men of the York Factory Express discontinued their journeys. By 1859, a few rotting huts stood alone on a beautiful level prairie several miles in extent, 30 feet above the level of the river.[6] Thirty-six years earlier, in October 1823, John Work stumbled on the fort just as it was being constructed:

Embarked at day light and about noon arrived at a new House which Mr. [Ranald] McDonald the gentleman who is superintending the building calls Fort Assiniboyne [Assiniboine], it is situated on the north side of the river. This is the House which was to have been built at McLeod's Branch, the distance of which is four days work up the River, so that we were surprised at understanding that the buildings were here.[7]

In most years, the York Factory Express coming from Jasper's House reached Fort Assiniboine in three days, covering sixty or more miles a day. In 1827, Edward Ermatinger encountered a little ice, and in 1828 he found the river shallow in many places, a common event as its watershed is subject to long periods of drought. In 1847, Thomas Lowe experienced cold, with a day of snow. One year later the river was shallow, and Lowe's boats scraped their way to Baptiste's River (Berland River). But in 1849, everything that could go wrong did go wrong for John Charles's party — low water in the river, float-ing ice that caused delay, showers of rain, and a full day of rain delay at Fort Assiniboine. It took the express nine days to reach Fort As-siniboine from Jasper's House that year.

In May 1841, George Traill Allan had no such troubles. In Sep-tember 1835, the York Factory Express men began to use boats that resembled York Boats for this journey, rather than the canoes they had always used previously. Allan clambered into one of the two boats departing Jasper's House. He and his ten men were four hours into the second day of travel when they stumbled upon a pair of moose about to swim across the river:

> The men immediately stop't pulling & allowed the Boats to drive before the current; in this manner we had approached very near the Deer, who, not perceiving the Boats, took [to] the water and proved to be a Doe with her fawn of a year old. Now the chase commenced in right down earnest, and although there were no scarlet coats amongst us I am sure there could not have been more ardent sportsmen. The Moose finding their retreat cut off from the South side of the River, swam with great speed toward the north, the Doe at this movement received two shots and the Boats coming up a blow from an ax dis-patched her; leaving one of the Boats to secure the prize, we made chase with the other after the fawn, and soon coming up with her, one of the men caught her by the ears and drawing his knife out cut her throat in regular Smithfield fashion. Such was the end of the two moose Deer! — and the excitement of the chase being over, I could not but think of the sanguinary nature of man — & when I perceived the River died [sic] with the blood of the poor Moose, I almost regretted the part I had just taken in their destruction.[8]

Provisioning was an important part of the fur trade, whether the men were at their inland posts or out on the rivers. Becoming the post hunter was an important role for a Canadien employee when he was at home. Once these men were out on the rivers and paddling all day, it was vital they have a good supply of red meat to keep their energy levels up. Some gentlemen noted their men could consume up to six pounds of meat in a sitting, and the Canadiens saw food as a pleasure and a reward for their hard labours.

The express could not, however, carry endless supplies of provisions. On the west side of the Rockies the men packed biscuit, dried salmon, and potatoes, and the gentlemen purchased fresh meat or fish from First Nations on their way upriver. Sometimes they traded for edible roots, such as camas. They could not easily locate game in the heavily forested country west of the Rockies. Deer were small and hard to find, and moose had not yet moved into the territory.

Hunting for fresh food was an important aspect of the voyageur tradition, and of Indigenous culture too. The Canadiens were used to the taste of wild meat, and the First Nations and their Métis descendants had grown up on it, probably preferring it to the milder flavour of the domestic beef available at Fort Vancouver. Hunting was also considered a proof of their masculinity.

Fresh wild meat, and the excitement of the chase, were their reward for the hard work and short provisions they faced on their long journey to York Factory and return. The Canadiens were also excellent scroungers, collecting goose and duck eggs for their meals (they quaffed the ducklings whole), or eating raccoon, beaver, dog, and other non-traditional meats when they could find them. Fish were plentiful in these rivers, and they likely often fished for their suppers.

Provisions were not, however, a major worry on what was often a three-day jaunt from Jasper's House — unless, of course, Fort Assiniboine had little food on hand to spare. In 1827, that proved to be the case. David Douglas, who travelled as a passenger in Edward Ermatinger's express, noted that "as this place afforded us but little food, we pushed on without delay."[9] For the most part, though, the parties picked up provisions at the fort (Allan's party may be the only express party that delivered more provisions than they carried away).

The next part of their voyage took them 90 miles south, by horseback, via the Athabasca Portage to Edmonton House. Depending on the weather and the condition of the trail, it took them four or five days to make the portage. The trail had been carved out of the wilderness over the winter of 1824–25 by François Cardinal, on Governor

George Simpson's instructions. Unfortunately, Cardinal hacked out the rough road in the depths of an Edmonton winter, when the ground was frozen solid. In spring, the marshes along the route thawed, and the horses sank into the deep mud holes the trail ploughed through. In later years, the route was changed and many of the difficulties disappeared, and in the 1850s it was rebuilt on higher ground. But Aemilius Simpson crossed the portage travelling north from Edmonton House in 1826, when the trail was still new. On his arrival at Fort Assiniboine, he summed up his experience:

> We forded a branch of the Athabasca which forms an island of a few miles extent, & at 3 p.m. we arrived at the Main branch opposite Assiniboine Post, to which we Crossed in a Canoe. Thus completing our Journey from Edmonton, in a little less than six days, altho' only a distance by estimation of about 90 miles — and in a direct line, by my observations, only 62 miles N. 37° W True — which may seem to point out the difficulty of passing this Portage, which in any other part of the World, I really believe would be considered impassable. Yet so familiar is the Voyageur with difficulty, that he is better qualified to overcome them, than any other people I have met with.[10]

Edward Ermatinger led his men out over the portage in May 1827, one year after John McLeod had taken his express over the trail. We have no word on what McLeod said about the new portage, but Ermatinger did not have a good report of the now one-year-old trail. He was accompanied across the portage by John Stuart, of Lesser Slave Lake, whose men were coming up the Pembina River from the Athabasca in their canoes. Here is Ermatinger's 1827 journal:

> [May] Monday 14th. Fine weather. Take our departure from Assiniboine about 4 o'clock with 56 horses and men, part of the horses only being loaded. Proceed thro' the woods between 4 and 5 miles and encamp at a small creek. Many deep mires. Horses very poor and weak.
> Thursday [Tuesday] 15th. Weather rather overcast. Start at 7 a.m.

Breakfast at the Rivière Creuse [Cruche or Pitcher Creek]. Road to it very bad full of mires — ascend several hills. Several horses remain behind unable to come farther light. Men sent back to endeavour to bring them up — report one to be dead. Mr. McDougal with a man goes ahead to Edmonton to inform of the state of the horses &c. Proceed again having rested the horses 5 hours and encamp at Les Deux Rivières. Distance of today's journeys between 10 and 12 miles.

Wednesday, 16th. Morning fine — towards evening several claps of thunder. Shower of hail and successive showers of rain. Start between 7 and 8 a.m. Proceed thro' thick woods. Swamps — about 8 miles and take breakfast at first prairie. Afterwards continue for near 5 miles and encamp in the woods across the 2nd prairie. Our road the whole of this day has been thro' one continued mire — several horses too weak to come up with the rest, tho' light. Two men return to bring them up but are unable.[11]

As was usual, the horses had been left to forage for grass through deep snow over the winter, and had lost weight and condition as a result. No hay was cut to feed them, nor oats supplied. Working horses require good grass and fresh water, and this early in the year the new grass would not yet have grown. The Athabasca Portage was also hard on horses, which did not deal well with swamps. Sharp stones cut their unshod hooves, and safe fords over rivers were essential. Gradient was also important. As Fort Assiniboine was closer to sea level than Edmonton House was, the trail slowly climbed the dividing ridge that lay between the Athabasca River and the North Saskatchewan.

In addition to the above, all the horses used by the HBC were small, not much larger than ponies. At some posts the HBC men recognized this and loaded them accordingly:

Each bale weighing eighty pounds, two of which made a load for a horse and weighed 160 pounds, a load quite heavy enough for a common pony weighing from 700 to 1,000 pounds to pack over such roads and trails as are found in this mountainous country.[12]

Edward Ermatinger's journal continues:

Thursday, 17th. Fine morning. Start 6 a.m. Proceed 1 and a half mile
and arrive at the Paddle River — make a raft and get our baggage
across in about 3 hours — afterwards go on 3 miles and stop to breakfast. Detained here several hours by rain. Again continue 7 miles and
arrive at the Pembina River. The road from Paddle River lies along the
borders of small lakes, thro' swamps and woods — the track thro' the
latter being in some cases extremely bad — much fallen wood and
deep mires.

   Friday, 18th. Fine morning. Mr. [John] Stuart's craft not having
yet arrived, people set about making 3 rafts. Those being made cross
over all the property and load 20 horses therewith. Proceed to Lac la
Nane — distance 5 or 6 miles. Set a net. Two men also repair a weir
already made in the River. Find here Cardinal, a freeman, and family
with several tents of Indians. Mr. Stuart remains at Pembina with the
rest of the horses to wait his people.[13]

Lac la Nonne, and Berland Lake (Sandy Lake) to the south, were
the fishing lakes for Edmonton House, and knowing this, Ermatinger's
express-men set their nets. On Saturday, he reported that "Our net
last night yielded 60 carp and the weir 30 carp and pike." The carp
were Northern pikeminnow, a bone-filled but edible fish of the same
minnow family to which the common carp (*Cyprinus carpio*) belonged.
To further provision his men, Ermatinger sent men ahead to both
clear the road and to set another fish weir in the second lake. At last
word came that Stuart was on his way from the Pembina, and
Ermatinger took his departure with thirteen loaded horses:

Travel about 8 miles thro' woods occasionally very bad road and encamp. One of the horses is unable to bring up his load. The men
carry it.

   Monday, 21st. Fine weather. Start at 5 a.m. . . . . Near Berland's
Lake we meet 5 men with 22 horses from Edmonton — take 2 saddle
horses for Messrs. E. Harriott and Ermatinger. Send the rest forward
to meet Mr. Stuart. Take breakfast at Berland's Creek. Afterwards
proceed to the large scaffold and encamp. Our route to Berland's Lake

was for the greater part bad in the extreme — thro' thick woods full of deep mires — thence the road takes thro' the plains and is pretty good.

Tuesday, 22nd. Fine warm weather. Proceed at 4 a.m. reach the Sturgeon River about 10 o'clock with the strongest of the horses. Others do not arrive till 2 o'clock — occupy our time till 3 p.m. rafting our property across — afterwards resume our journey and arrive at Edmonton at 7 p.m. 5 men remain behind at the river their horses being too fatigued to proceed — roads thro' the plains often bad thro' swamps and mires — distance to Sturgeon River from our encampment about 16 miles thence to the Fort 9 miles.[14]

In 1828, Ermatinger's outgoing express experienced a different set of hardships. His party left Fort Assiniboine on May 10, five days earlier than the previous year:

Prepare our Baggage and cross our horses and commence our journey on the Athabasca Portage at 6 p.m., travel only 2 miles and encamp — 13 horses are employed transporting our Baggage &c. Messrs. [Michel] Klyne and [John Edward] Harriott accompany us with packs and horses.

11th. Messrs. McGillivray, McDonald [McDougall] and Ermatinger with 5 horses leave the party at 4 a.m. to go ahead to Edmonton having with them the accounts &c. Afternoon a tremendous storm of wind with rain overtakes us in the Burnt woods, bringing down trees in every direction — one fell upon one of the horses and killed him on the spot. Encamp a little beyond the Paddle River.

12th. Fine weather. Start at 3 a.m. Proceed near to Lac a Berland [Sandy Lake?] and encamp.

13th. Before we arrive at Sturgeon River, McGillivray's horse knocks up and is left. Arrive at Edmonton at 7 p.m.[15]

— • —

In April 1835, James Douglas described the country south of Fort Assiniboine. On the first night out, his express party set up camp at Eagle Lake:

The country through which we have passed is pretty generally covered with timber. There are certainly a few clear spots called Prairies but they are of small extent and scarcely merit any notice. There are no lakes of any extent save the one now near us, and the Paddle and [Pembina] are the only 2 rivers that deserve the name.[16]

Just before his party reached Sturgeon River, they camped "on the banks of a small river which runs thro' a narrow valley bordered with willows, and the banks thickly covered with grass, which is a most eligible situation for our encampment as we are completely shut out from observation, and run little risk of being discovered by any roving parties of horse thieves." The horse thieves were First Nations men such as the Assiniboine, who by tradition took great pleasure in "lifting" a few horses.

Douglas's journal continues:

From Eagle Lake to Berland's Lake the country is in general densely wooded with the white spruce, poplar & birch, but from that place to Sturgeon River it is totally different in its character. Instead of the gloomy interminable forest we have met with the extensive prairie variegated by pleasant groves of trees, and watered by numerous tiny lakes and small streams of water. The surface of these prairies is thickly covered with various grasses indicating a rich productive soil.[17]

He made no mention of the badness of the trail, so by 1835 it must have been much improved. No one now knows exactly where the trail ran, and its route changed over the years. Its general course, however, ran southeast from Fort Assiniboine through the historic town of Campsie, and passed a mile east of modern-day Barrhead. A later ferry site called McDonald's Crossing indicated where the then-trail crossed the Pembina, close to its junction with the Paddle River. Thirty-five miles south of Fort Assiniboine it touched on Lac La Nonne, the fort's fishery. Then it plunged through a swamp at Deadman Lake and followed a ridge through today's Alexander Indian Reserve, passing just south of present-day Rivière Que Barre. Crossing the ridge that separates the North Saskatchewan from the Athabasca River system, it ran through modern-day St. Albert to Edmonton House.[18]

— • —

The size of the express varied over the years. In May 1827, Edward Ermatinger started off with fifty-six horses, only some of which were loaded. In 1828, thirteen horses carried packs. In 1841, George Traill Allan's express departed Fort Assiniboine with thirty-three horses, fifteen of which carried loads. In 1847, Thomas Lowe started out with thirteen horses and nine packs of furs from Jasper's House, but George McDougall, now in charge of the Lesser Slave Lake post to the east, joined him with his forty-four packs of furs (on about twenty pack horses).

In 1848, Lowe travelled with fourteen loaded horses and eight saddle horses, leaving McDougall's Lesser Slave Lake party to straggle behind — and straggle they did. It snowed and sleeted for three days. When the sleet turned to rain, McDougall's party rode into Edmonton House, with many of their packs soaked by the rainfall. The work of opening the packs to dry the furs delayed the departure of the Saskatchewan Brigades.

In 1849, John Charles left Fort Assiniboine on May 20:

Beautiful clear day. Started this morning with 10 loaded horses and arrived at a small prairie about 5 o'clock, where we camped. Dark clouds gathering in the west.

Monday 21st. Commenced raining early this morning and continued all day — some snow fell towards night. We remained at our encampment in consequence.

Tuesday 22nd. The weather being so unfavourable for travelling with packs of furs without any covering to protect them from the rain we were obliged to remain at the encampment this day also.

Wednesday 23rd. Started this morning before sunrise. Camped on the opposite side of [Pembina] River which we crossed with a raft.

Thursday 24th May. Started about sunrise and camped at 5 p.m. Fine clear day. Blowing pretty strong.

Friday 25th. Before reaching Sturgeon River we were met by Edmonton Horse Guard who brought us word that Mr. [John] Rowand was anxiously waiting for us. We arrived at Edmonton about 5 o'clock.

Almost all the boats of the Saskatchewan Brigade have already left, and Mr. Rowand does not intend to leave his establishment until the arrival of Mr. [George] McDougall from Lesser Slave Lake with his returns and who is now momentarily expected.[19]

At Edmonton House, the express-men were absorbed into the Saskatchewan Brigades that carried their packs of furs to Hudson Bay. Their experiences would differ every year, but the one constant of the Saskatchewan Brigades was the boats in which they travelled. These were the HBC's York Boats, traditionally used by the Company men on the Saskatchewan River from the early years. York Boats had a major advantage over canoes — they carried a massive load and needed fewer men. These flat-bottomed boats were about 28 feet long and 6 feet wide, with a shallow draft that made them suitable for the low river levels they often encountered.

Although the boats might in some ways resemble the clinker-built boats used on the west side of the Rocky Mountains, they were quite

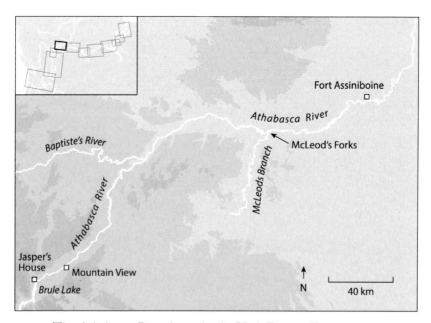

The Athabasca River brought the York Factory Express men from Jasper's House to Fort Assiniboine, 185 miles downriver.

different. York Boats were of carvel construction — the boards were fitted edge to edge and tightly pressed against each other. The HBC men believed that the smooth sides of the boats gave less resistance as they travelled through the water and allowed both faster speed and greater load-carrying. In fact, carvel boats sank deeper in the water and offered more resistance than clinker-built boats, although one HBC man said they only drew sixteen to twenty inches of water when fully laden.[20]

The same man described the stem and stern posts which were protected with strips of iron. The keels kept the boats rigid and made for better handling over portages; the false keel prevented damage to the true keel. Sharply raked ends helped the boat withstand the shock of the many collisions with rocks and sandbars, and the flaring sides made it more seaworthy. Three strong thwarts or cross-seats braced the hull without interfering with the storage of goods.

A platform in the rear of the boat allowed the steersman to push and pull on his enormous sweep oar without stumbling over the packs. The steersman's oar was set in a ring on the stern-post, and was used most of the time, particularly when descending rapids because of the strong hold it had on the water. The boats also had rudders, used only while under sail. The square sails were wrapped around masts and carried inside the gunwales of the boats. When not in use, the long, heavy oars were also stored inside the gunwales, on top of the loads the boats carried. One observer, a passenger who rode in these York Boats as a child, described the work of the men who rowed the boats:

The rowers sat on the opposite side of the boat to that on which their blade dipped into the water, and they were seated alternately on the left and right sides of the boat facing the stern, one man to each oar. They rose to their feet as they leaned on the huge sweep, pushing it forward and down to lift the blade out of the water, then sank to a sitting position on the thwart as it bit deeply into the water again. Then, as they pulled and strained mightily, the muscles of their arms, shoulders and backs stood out like bands of iron. Most of them wore around their foreheads and jet black hair a strip of crimson calico to keep the perspiration from rolling down into their eyes. The hand grip of the oars was bound with cloth or a strip of deer skin to prevent their hands from blistering. With their swarthy complexions, their flashing white teeth and bright, black eyes, they brought to mind vividly stories of pirates and galley slaves — except that these were laughing, kindly ones.[21]

Although the author is describing the Cree men who worked the HBC York Boats in later years, her description could, with a little imagination, be applied to any of the Canadien, Orkney, Iroquois, or Métis men who crossed the Rocky Mountains on their journey across the continent to York Factory and back every year.

At Edmonton House, the York Factory Express men are 1,258 miles from Fort Vancouver, and have 1,437 miles to travel before they reach York Factory. The next part of their journey would take these men and boats down the North Saskatchewan River to Fort Pitt and Carlton House. They wasted little time at these two provisioning posts before continuing their hurried journey downriver to Lake Winnipeg and beyond.

Although this image shows the colonists and soldiers who massacred
the bison by the thousands in the 1880s, the HBC gentlemen would
have looked much the same as they rode out after the buffalo.
(COURTESY: GLENBOW ARCHIVES, NA-1406-189)

The plains bison that roamed the natural grasslands of the prairies between
Fort Pitt and Carlton House provided both First Nations peoples and fur
traders with fresh bison steaks, dried meat for pemmican, and hides for robes
and leather. (COURTESY: SASKATCHEWAN ARCHIVES, S-B9275)

Fort George, the Hudson's Bay Company old headquarters at
the mouth of the Columbia River. (COURTESY: LAC, MIKAN 2897241)

Over the winter First Nations people brought their furs into the
Hudson's Bay Company posts to trade for goods (1879).
(COURTESY: GLENBOW ARCHIVES, NA-1406-45)

Trout Falls may not have been the longest portage on this Hayes River, but it was the most difficult, as well as the most dangerous (September 1819). (COURTESY: LAC, MIKAN 3949434)

On the outgoing journey to Hudson Bay, the men paddled the boats up to Boat Encampment and then walked over the Athabasca Pass, following the Wood River. On their return, they walked down the Wood River to be met at Boat Encampment by the boats that would take them home to Fort Vancouver. (COURTESY: BCA, A-05428)

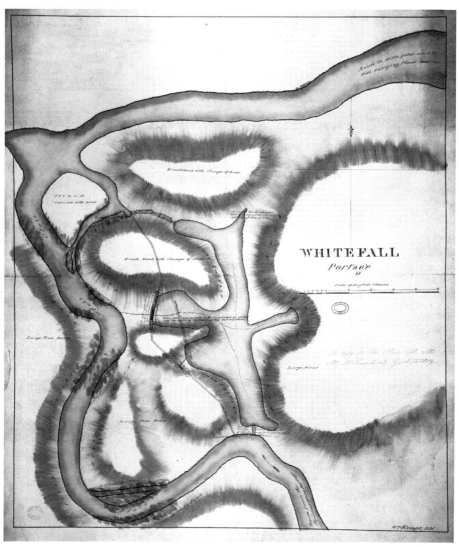

At the top of the hill above York Factory was the Whitefall Portage, now
Robinson's Portage. This long portage, seen as a thin line across a hill, avoided
a set of violent rapids created by the Hayes as it tumbled through a series of
twisting canyons on its way down the mountain.

(COURTESY: HBCA, 1985-44-34)

The HBC buildings at Norway House, Manitoba, 1955. The white-washed buildings and storehouses were surrounded by a palisade of boards twelve to fifteen feet tall. (COURTESY: GLENGOW ARCHIVES, NA-3040-11)

Launching a carvel-built York boat on the North Saskatchewan River at Prince Albert, Saskatchewan, by the HBC's competitors, Revillon Frères. Note the painted boards. (COURTESY: GLENGOW ARCHIVES, NA-1338-45)

The Grand Portage was at the mouth of the Saskatchewan River,
where it flowed into Lake Winnipeg through the rocks of the Canadian
Shield. One clerk, Augustus Peers, described the Métis men, who took
pleasure in showing off their strength in competition with one another, to
see who could carry the heaviest load across the Grand Rapids portage.
(COURTESY: GLENBOW ARCHIVES, NA-1406-48)

The express-men tracked their boats for days on end as they made their way up the Saskatchewan River on their return trip. The Guide shouted "Haul, Haul," and the gentlemen remained in the boats or walked up the river banks.
(COURTESY: GLENBOW ARCHIVES, NA-949-115)

By the 1840s the missionaries had set up at the place the HBC men and the early North West Company men, called the Pas, for the river Pasquia.
(COURTESY: GLENBOW ARCHIVES, NB-40-3)

Fort Pitt was constructed on a flat above the North Saskatchewan River,
in the territory of the Blackfoot, the Cree, and the Assiniboines.
The HBC men traded for bison meat, pemmican, and hides or robes.
(COURTESY: SASKATCHEWAN ARCHIVES, S-A97)

Massive herds of bison roamed the prairies around Fort Pitt.
(COURTESY: GLENBOW ARCHIVES, NA-1274-2)

CHAPTER 7

Edmonton House to
Carlton House

෯෯

EDMONTON HOUSE SERVED as the headquarters of the HBC's Saskatchewan District, and was the most important post on the North Saskatchewan River. In May 1827, when Edward Ermatinger reached the post, the fort stood on Edmonton's Rossland Flats, on the north side of the river close to its ford. But when the river ran high in spring, its waters occasionally flooded the flats, and in 1830 the HBC men rebuilt Edmonton House on the top of high bluffs that overlooked the curving river valley. In 1841, George Traill Allan described Edmonton House as he saw it, in its new location above the river:

> The fort . . . is built upon the Saskatchewan and is of great strength, having a balcony all round with a bastion at each angle in which we kept always charged a number of fire arms, there is also an observatory of considerable height which commands an extensive view of the adjacent country. All these presentations are by no means unnecessary as

Edmonton is frequented by bands of Blackfeet, Assiniboines and other lawless tribes who consider it almost a duty to plunder & even murder a white man when opportunity offers.[1]

On their way to Edmonton House, the men of the York Factory Express had travelled light and fast, carrying little more than papers and letters for the council meeting at Red River or Norway House. They had increased their load at Jasper's House and Fort Assiniboine, taking on a few packs of furs from those posts. At Edmonton House, the Columbia District men joined the Saskatchewan Brigades, to assist the Edmonton House men who were carrying out their winter catch of furs and casks of castoreum to Hudson Bay.[2]

The first leg of their long journey took the Saskatchewan Brigades down the North Saskatchewan River. This river, which begins as a rivulet trickling from the toe of the Saskatchewan Glacier in the Rocky Mountains, is, by the time it reaches what is now Edmonton, a powerful river that, in springtime, foams through a steep-banked valley that lies almost 200 feet below the level of the surrounding parklands.

It usually carried the HBC men downriver with ease, but the journey may have been a claustrophobic experience for some, as they ploughed down a coffee-with-milk-coloured river between looming banks of mud or clay of a similar shade. Even the grass was brown at this time of year.

Like the Athabasca River, the North Saskatchewan carried less water in some years than in others. In early May 1835, James Douglas described the hard work of travelling downriver when the river's uncommonly low water exposed its numerous sandbars:

The river is so very low that our progress is continually interrupted by the numerous banks of gravel and scattered rocks which are concealed from view by a small depth of untransparent fluid. The boats are incessantly taking ground on the one hand or striking heavily on the other, and the crews on these occasions have no other way of clearing these obstacles but by leaping out and dragging them [the boats] into deeper water, which is certainly not an agreeable pastime on a cold morning with ice forming all around them.[3]

Just before the boats reached White Mud Creek, on the northern-most bend of the river, the bluffs fell away and the riverbanks opened up to the fine parklands that surrounded this deep, brown valley. James Douglas wrote of his admiration of the countryside that sur-rounded his encampment two days east of Edmonton House:

Encamped a few miles below the crooked Fall or Rapides Croches. . . . We are surrounded on all sides by a fine country possessing all the natural beauties which can be well imagined in a wild uncultivated region. The banks of the river are lined with a narrow strip of trees, beyond which commences the extensive prairie embellished and di-versified with waving groves of trees, and refreshing streams of water. These prairies are the favourite resort of the Moose and Red deer [elk], and they are also visited by numerous herds of buffaloes, and there cannot be a more cheerful or pleasing sight than to see the whole country teeming with life, and forcibly reminding the spectator of the flocks & herds of more favoured lands where the mild virtues of reli-gion and civilization have refined and improved the human mind.[4]

In 1826, another gentleman, still new to the country, had expressed a similar view as his boats pushed upriver through the Eagle Hills, some miles downriver from Douglas's encampment. It was late sum-mer, and the grass was green. "The Banks have become very interest-ing," wrote Aemilius Simpson, "being finely ornamented, by Groves or plots of natural Wood, giving them the appearance of a gentle-man's Lawn, which is made more striking by the Vast Herds of Cattle, seen grazing along them."[5] At an even earlier date this same gentle-man had written:

The country now presents a face of rich Meadow Land, with occa-sional Groves of Wood interspersed on its surface, giving to the Scene a richness & beauty which even rivals the fine Lawns & rich pasture Lands of a civilized country. . . . Was this rich face of country made subservient to the use of civilized Man, how much would it enhance its beauty and value.[6]

The only persons who would have expressed their wish that the country be more civilized or settled were those gentlemen who came from England or Scotland to the wilderness of the fur trade. Few of the Canadien employees, many of whom chose not to return to Quebec when their contract was finished, would have wanted a settled country here. In the early years, many Canadiens were in the West because of their family's tradition of entering the trade: they had, in their way, grown up with the fur trade and understood it, although from a young man's point of view. To a lesser degree, this was also true of the Orkneymen who, generation after generation, joined the fur trade from their small communities in the islands.

But the mixed-blood children of these Canadiens and Orkneymen — the Métis — definitely did not wish for settlements and civilization. For the Métis, who were born in and lived in fur trade forts in the wilderness, York Factory was an enormously exciting community to visit, but they would not have chosen to make it their home. They had grown up with the stories of forts that rose and fell. They saw their routes change over the years, and sometimes they saw their methods of transportation change as well. But their lives did not change. Their work remained the same, as did their leisure time. This was their home, and they felt at home here. Here they were free, and their life excited them. They lived for the hunt, and for the hard work of the voyage, and they cared not a whit for the gentlemen's idea of civilization.

There was, however, one First Nations group that came from the settlements in Quebec, and many of these men rejected that civilized life to become freemen after years of service in the Company's fur trade. This group was the Iroquois-speaking Mohawks from the St. Lawrence settlements of Kahnawà:ke, Oka, and St. Regis. By the late 1600s, the Mohawks had moved north from their villages in modern-day New York State to settle near Jesuit Missions on the St. Lawrence River, becoming strong Catholics as a result. They had begun their fur trade careers by building magnificent birchbark canoes for the French. Then they joined the trade itself. By the time the Iroquois crossed the Rocky Mountains in the early 1800s, they were already known as tough negotiators, excellent trappers and hunters, and experienced canoe men. Although they were rarely mentioned in the York Factory Express journals, they were always here.

— • —

In May 1827, Edward Ermatinger and the gentlemen who accompanied him — chief factors John Stuart and John Rowand, chief traders Finan McDonald, John Edward Harriott, and George McDougall[7] — had a harrowing journey down the North Saskatchewan. Ermatinger began his journal at Edmonton House on May 26: "The boats leave Edmonton at 9 a.m. . . . . Proceed till 8 p.m. and encamp, distance 50 miles."[8] The next day he traded for beaver from a few Cree, and Finan McDonald shot an elk, which the men cooked on the river bank.

On that first night, the men lashed their boats together and paddled all night, with those not on duty sleeping. They breakfasted the next day at the ruins of old Fort George, a NWC post on the north bank of the river, five miles upriver from the mouth of Moose Creek. Later they put ashore at Vermilion Creek, where many years earlier the NWC's Fort Vermillion stood next to the HBC's Paint River post.[9] Here Ermatinger's men paused to hunt, and later they embarked to drift all night. This river was safe enough if the water was deep. There were no rapids here, as there were downriver.

On May 29, the men rowed against a headwind "from daylight till sunset, at intervals, and then put ashore to supper — after which go little below [sic] to sleep."[10] While continuing their journey after supper let them take advantage of remaining daylight hours, these men might also have slept on islands downriver from their supper place to avoid possible ambush by First Nations warriors.

On May 30, they set off at sunrise, later pausing to hunt for bison on both sides of the river. Fetching home the meat of the animals killed occupied the crew until nightfall. In these early years, before the provisioning post of Fort Pitt was constructed 217 miles downriver from Edmonton House, the men were forced to hunt to ensure they had enough to eat. Obviously this put them in danger of being attacked by the many wild animals that roamed these prairies. On Saturday, June 2, Ermatinger reported that he accompanied McDonald and Harriot into the plains to find two bulls that Harriot had wounded earlier in the day:

> Mr. H pursued and overtook one, followed by Mr. McD — the former fired but did not bring the Bull down. Mr. McD's rifle snapped and while he was endeavouring to distinguish his object in the dark of the night to have another shot the animal rushed toward him with the utmost impetuosity. . . . The first blow the animal gave him he tossed him with great violence and gored the most fleshy part of his thigh nearly to the bone. Mr. McD . . . remembers having received 6 blows, one of which was so dreadful that his whole side is bruised black and blue and some of his ribs appear to be broken — the last furious butt made him call out, and what is very strange the Bull at the same instant fell down as if a ball had struck him. In this state they both remained for above an hour while Mr. H ran to the Boats at least 2 miles distant for assistance. . . . A large armed party being collected were devising means of extricating Mr. McD from his painful situation, when one of the men's guns went off in the air by accident. This caused the Bull to rise. He looked at the party attentively for a moment and then galloped off.[11]

McDonald was carried on a makeshift stretcher to the boats, and they immediately set off for Carlton House to find medical help.[12] On arrival they found the hoped-for doctor had departed, so Ermatinger dispatched the injured McDonald in a boat to Cumberland House. This was the next major post downriver, and the remaining boats would follow in the first boat's wake.

Animal encounters were common on this river in the days when the fur traders hunted for their supper. In 1828, members of Ermatinger's party encountered a grizzly, which did some damage:

Shortly after starting a large grizzly Bear was wounded by Mr. Rowand and notwithstanding a large ball passed thro' his body and knocked him down, he escaped for some distance. A party pursued and were tracking him by his blood, when a rustling in the branches pointed out the spot where he had couched — all the guns were cocked ready to pour a volley upon him, but before the party had time to look about them he sprang thro' the thicket with a dreadful crash, seized one of the men and with his teeth bit him in many parts of the body — he also bestowed a pat on the back of a second, tore his shirt and marked him besides making an attempt at a third. A dog which happened to pass at the time drew Bruin's attention toward him and prevented his doing more mischief to the people and gave also an opportunity of firing at him, which could not well be done while he had a man in his possession for fear of shooting the wrong object — the dog got only one of the thighs bitten and the Bear was killed after having received at least a half dozen Balls.[13]

That year, Ermatinger had left Edmonton House on May 20 (meeting the bear one day later), with the Saskatchewan Brigade of sixteen boats laden with about eighty pieces per boat. Six days later he reached Carlton House, 431 miles downriver from Edmonton House. Later parties no longer hunted for provisions, but stopped at the new post of Fort Pitt, which was placed (but not yet built) on top of a high bluff on the north side of the river, almost equidistant from Carlton and Edmonton Houses.

For the first winter its traders lived in tents. Work began on the buildings in 1830, and by 1831 the main part of the small but sturdy post was finished. Although it was closed temporarily for fear of Indian attacks, in later years Fort Pitt was fully capable of defending itself against the ever-battling Cree, Assiniboine, and Blackfoot warriors, whose territories merged near its location.

The First Nations peoples who inhabited these prairies were one of the many hazards the men of the Saskatchewan Brigades encountered as they descended the river on their way to Carlton House. Roving bands of Indigenous warriors battled each other constantly, and at times also threatened the safety of the HBC men. On his arrival at Fort Pitt in May 1835, James Douglas wrote down the story of the most recent battle that had taken place on the plains surrounding the post:

> Here are 40 tents of Cree Indians encamped around the fort appar-
> ently with the view of being protected against any sudden attack of
> their enemies. A month or two ago a War party consisting of 300
> strong wood [Woodland Cree] and Beaver Hill Crees made a hostile
> incursion into the Blackfoot country, and accidentally fell in with a
> straggling party of 20 Circus [Sarcee] warriors who on perceiving the
> enemy threw themselves into a thicket of trees, and after hastily con-
> structing a temporary barricade boldly opened a spirited fire on the
> Crees who not relishing the idea of a rapid advance on their deter-
> mined enemy contented themselves with maintaining a weak and
> desultory fire during the day.[14] In the night the Circus who were not
> very strictly guarded escaped from their fortification leaving 11 of
> their number on the field of battle; of Crees, 3 killed and 10 wounded.
> The Circus who escaped reached their main camp and a strong party
> of their friends gave pursuit to the Crees who took up a strong posi-
> tion in the woods, where they could not be attacked but at a manifest
> disadvantage; and the two parties finally separated without any fur-
> ther attempt on either side. The whole Cree tribe are now living in
> continual alarm and are just on the wing for a flight to the strong
> woods where they may live in perfect security.[15]

In June 1848, Thomas Lowe noted that his party met a "large War party of Blackfeet, amounting to about 500 men. We had to put ashore for them twice, and Mr. Harriott made them some presents of tobacco. This is said to be one of the largest parties who have been here for many years."[16] And a year later, John Charles's party was de-layed at Fort Pitt for a day because of reports of "Blackfeet prowling about the vicinity of this Fort and their intentions to molest us on our way down to Carlton."[17]

At Fort Pitt, the express-men took in provisions for their down-river voyage to Carlton House, 214 miles downriver. Generally, this took the form of pemmican, but in June 1848, Thomas Lowe's provisions were large quantities of fresh meat "as pemican [sic] this year is very scarce, there not being above half the quantity in the boats that has been requested from below."[18]

Pemmican is a mix of dried and pounded bison meat, with boiled bison fat and local berries, all stirred together and wrapped in skin casings with the hair still on. This fatty food was packed with calories and fuelled the fur trade east of the Rocky Mountains. The men devoured it in enormous quantities.

In 1823, John Work commented on the number of 90-pound bags of pemmican his eight hardworking canoe-men consumed on their month-long journey from York Factory to Ile-à-la-Crosse, on the upper Churchill River north of Cumberland House:

> The men's provisions were just finished. On leaving York the canoes had 2 bags of Pemican (one of them turned out to be a bag of grease given in mistake) and a bag of flour. At Oxford House a supply of two bags more was got. Then at Norway House a further supply of four bags of Pemican and at Cumberland five bags more. Two of the bags got at Cumberland was unfit for use and had to be cast away, which leaves eleven bags that have been used in thirty days from York Factory, besides a half bag from McDougald. The men certainly worked hard but they eat as well.[19]

East of Fort Pitt, the wide valley of the meandering North Saskatchewan opened to a panoramic view of the parklands, so that even George Traill Allan, not the kind of man who enjoyed the countryside, admired the scenery:

> The country on both sides of the river is low and plains of immense extent meet the eye in every direction with stripes of wood along the banks. The water of this River at this season is very thick and muddy. . . . At certain seasons of the year Buffalo are extremely numerous along the banks; at present we saw none, but abundance of Antelope [Pronghorn], Wolves, some Red Deer or elk and Black Bears. Buffalo were so numerous last year that the Hunter attached to Fort Edmonton alone killed four hundred head.[20]

In 1828, Edward Ermatinger camped at a place he called the "Grande Sucrerie" (Big Candy), a short distance upriver from Carlton House. In 1835, James Douglas might have described the same beautiful countryside, a few miles above the HBC's Ash Island and one day's upriver journey west of Carlton House:

> The country on both sides very beautiful and picturesque, rising from the river by a sloping and undulating ascent to the highest level visible from the river. On this level the [eye] of the spectator ranges through the vast expanse of prairie variegated and adorned by innumerable groves of trees, smooth green hills and streams of water forming altogether one of the finest prospects imaginable.[21]

Wind, weather, and the depth of the river were important considerations in their downriver journey: all of these could affect the length of time it took to reach Fort Pitt and Carlton House. From Edmon-

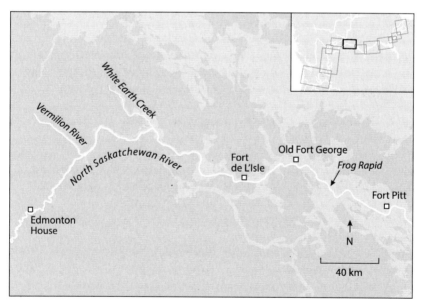

The provisioning post of Fort Pitt was built in 1830 on a bluff on the North Saskatchewan River, halfway between Edmonton House and Carlton House.

ton House it took George Allan's party two days to reach Fort Pitt in 1841, and two more to make Carlton House, with no mention of the weather. In 1847, Lowe's men rowed against a headwind for one day, and although the next day they had a fine sailing wind, it took them three days to reach Fort Pitt. Beyond Fort Pitt he found the river low, and they lost time running aground on the battures.

In 1848, high water and a good sailing wind for the first two days helped Lowe reach Fort Pitt in good time, but beyond that place his brigade was windbound for one full day, and delayed by snow another. It took Lowe eight days to reach Carlton from Fort Pitt. Even though the Saskatchewan River flowed eastward with them, the high flaring sides of the York Boats caught any wind from the east and slowed their headway.

On the prairies, weather hazards were always present in the form of rain, wind, and snow. In May 1835, Douglas noted the weather on his arrival at Fort Pitt: "We arrived here just in time to escape a heavy storm of hail and snow which continued to pour down upon us for nearly a full hour."[22]

Rain was a far more serious problem. In early June 1849, John Charles reported that it "rained very heavily last night and the greater part of this day so much so that we were obliged to put ashore and cover up the boats"[23] with oilskins to prevent the furs from being damaged by water.

When the party reached Carlton House, they pulled the packs from all the boats and examined any that had been damaged by water on their journey. This was no small job. The Saskatchewan Brigade that year consisted of twenty-five boats, each carrying loads of eighty to ninety-five packs of furs. Although they might not have opened every pack, the men would have unloaded some two thousand packs of furs, each weighing up to 90 pounds.

On his arrival at Carlton House in May 1841, George Traill Allan noted: "this fort is just a duplicate of Edmonton, upon a smaller scale."[24] The post stood at a shallow ford on the North Saskatchewan River, at a place where the rolling plains ended and the boreal forests began. It had been constructed at this spot in 1810 and, although once important as a fur trade post, its major role at this time for the HBC was as a provisioning post for the Saskatchewan Brigades.

In 1826, Lieutenant Aemilius Simpson described the fort:

> Carlton House is situated about a quarter of a mile within the South Bank of the Saskatchewan, a flat surface of Country extending for rather more than that distance to a Bank with rather a steep ascent, but moderate elevation, forming a rise of Hills running parallel to the course of the River. On gaining the summit of which immense plains present themselves extending to the utmost range of human vision; on the flat ground immediately in the neighbourhood of the Fort a considerable Track of Land is here cultivated, & produces very good returns of Wheat, Barley, Potatoes & vegetables in considerable perfection.... The evening was hot & sultry with vast numbers of mosquitos.[25]

In a matter of a day or two after arriving at Carlton House, the combined York Factory Express and Saskatchewan Brigades were once more on their way, heading down the North Saskatchewan River toward its junction with the South Saskatchewan. These two rivers made up the mighty and muddy Saskatchewan River, which would carry them east to historic Cumberland House, 275 miles away.

There were still hazards to contend with before they left the North Saskatchewan, however. Although travel down the river was fast and easy, the river itself remained shallow and strewn with islands and battures that changed its course and made travel difficult. Then, just before the North Saskatchewan flowed into the Saskatchewan River, the express-men faced the biggest hazard along the entire length of the river — Cole's Rapids.

CHAPTER 8

Carlton House to Norway House

§§

FROM CARLTON HOUSE, the Saskatchewan Brigades continued their journey down the North Saskatchewan River toward York Factory, now only 1,006 miles distant by river and lake. Their first stop would be at Cumberland House, a historic post that stood on an island in Cumberland Lake, close to the Saskatchewan River. In June 1827, Ermatinger's party left Carlton House and ran his boats down Cole's Rapids by moonlight. The men stopped for supper below the junction of the North and South Saskatchewan rivers. Now, in the safe, deep waters of the Saskatchewan River, the men of the brigade could "lash the boats together and drive — current very strong."[1]

The rapids that Ermatinger's party had just descended — today's La Colle Rapids but then known as Cole's Rapids — was a shallow, twelve-mile-long, boulder-strewn stretch of white-water that could be treacherous for the eastward-bound brigades. In that treachery they reflected the character of the person for whom they were named — John Cole.

Cole first appeared on the Saskatchewan River in 1772 as an employee of the North West Company. By 1779, he was interpreter at Fort Montaigne d'Aigle, an independent post run by American trader Peter Pangman, situated across the Saskatchewan River from the Eagle Hills. The unscrupulous traders there gave Cree hunters rum for furs, and dosed any troublesome hunter with laudanum.[2] One chief died after he was given a double dose.

The Cree mulled over this murder all winter, and in the spring they gathered on the hill behind the post to watch the traders pack their furs. After one First Nations man raised his gun and deliberately shot John Cole dead, a pitched battle began. Some of the traders retreated to their houses, but they had no chance of winning the fight. They surrendered rum and trade goods to the Cree hunters and escaped with nothing more than their lives. The incident served as a warning to future traders, who were much more careful in their treatment of the First Nations peoples.[3]

In 1827, Edward Ermatinger's men had little trouble with Cole's Rapids. In 1849, John Charles also enjoyed an easy downriver journey to Cumberland House. He left Carlton House on June 5, 1849:

Left Carlton House after breakfast with 26 boats, one having been added to the 25 brought down from Fort Pitt. We camped at a point where formerly stood a North West [Company] Fort.

Wednesday 6th. Blowing a pretty gale this morning. Towards night the wind abated. Put ashore at sunset and had supper, then embarked in the boats which being lashed together by threes we were able to drift all night. An Indian deserted from the Brigade this side of Bow [South Saskatchewan] River.

Thursday 7th. Men toiling all day against a strong head wind. At midnight when drifting down stream as usual one of the boats got a plank stove in by a tree lying in the River. We immediately put ashore and had the pieces taken out and spread in the other boats.

Friday 8th. Six of the boats arrived at Cumberland house late in the evening — the others will make their appearance tomorrow. Mr. [George] Deschambeault informs us that Cumberland Lake broke up on the 5th June and it is much feared that we will be detained by ice further down our route.[4]

For John Charles, Deschambeault's worries would prove prescient, as he would learn when he reached Lake Winnipeg. However, twenty years after Edward Ermatinger descended Cole's Rapids in 1827 (and a year or two before John Charles's men descended them), Thomas Lowe experienced serious difficulties with the troublesome string of rapids. His party set off from Carlton House on June 2, 1847,

at daylight, and were enabled to make a long days march, as the river has risen from the recent rains.

Thursday 3rd. Rainy. Came to Cole's Rapids before breakfast, but having broken two boats, put ashore to breakfast, and get them repaired. In course of the day 5 more boats were broken, one of them having gone to pieces, the crew saving themselves by springing into a boat which was passing. Most of the cargo was picked up and distributed amongst the Brigade, although the packs were very much injured with wet. Encamped half way down the Rapids.

Friday, 4th June 1847. Ran several of the Rapids before breakfast, but two more boats having been broken, the remainder were run down to the bottom of the Rapids by the experienced steersmen only, who had thus to make two trips, and it was 2 o'clock in the afternoon before we were able to start from the termination of Cole's Rapids, in which 8 boats were broken more or less severely, and 1 entirely lost.[5]

Taking risks, such as running rapids, was part of the voyageur culture, and a great part of the excitement of the journey. For the most part, the young and strong men were assigned the duty of taking out the York Boats, and guides and boutes were expected to keep their boundless energy under control. But even though they sometimes wrecked their boats in risky ventures, the men had talents enough to repair them. The boats' carvel construction allowed for easy removal of broken boards, and the gaps between the boards, which would later be filled with oakum (old rope) and tarred to make them water-proof, allowed for easy replacement of broken boards with new.

A good supply of new boards was always available. They could be scavenged from the boat that had been damaged beyond repair or taken from the supply of boards that each York Boat carried within. While few of these men could have built a York Boat from scratch, all knew how to repair them — and those who didn't know quickly learned under the guidance of the more experienced men.

Although the gentlemen tended to look upon their voyageurs as unskilled labourers, it was obvious there was no shortage of skills among this varied group of men. They were inventive and talented workers who carried out complicated tasks that demanded an ability to work together. Their willingness to share their skills with others was a great part of the strength of these co-operative men.

Many of the gentlemen in this business did not think twice about asking their voyageurs to do the impossible, but often did not give them credit for their ability to solve problems. One gentleman did: clerk A.C. Anderson remarked on his workers' abilities to overcome problems after they had completed the task of constructing the necessary driving gears for Fort Alexandria's new American-made wheat mill: "The mill itself was well made and efficient, but the driving gear, constructed at Alexandria, was a marvelous piece of workmanship. On those days of make-shifts, and appliances, to turn a Canadien voyageur into a mill-wright was nothing. Hence our mill, of which by the way we were very proud, rumbled round in a most eccentric manner."[6]

Lowe's men also proved to be good workers, and his journal indicates that they had repaired all eight boats that had been damaged in Cole's Rapids by the next morning. In spite of the hard rain that fell that day, the men made a long day's march:

> A short distance below these Rapids, the Southern Branch falls into the Saskatchewan, and as there happened to be a good flush of water in it, we made a good distance before camping. Raining at intervals during the day.

Saturday 5th. Raining hard. Made a long day's march.

Sunday 6th. Rainy, and a thunder storm in the afternoon. Pulled all day, and drifted at night.

Monday 7th. Fine warm weather. Arrived at Cumberland this morning at 8 o'clock.[7]

Shortly before the express-men reached Cumberland House, the Saskatchewan River flowed out of the prairie parklands and nudged the rocky Canadian Shield. High prairie riverbanks faded away, and the marshy bogs of the river's estuary took their place. The wide, sloping plain of the delta ran 120 miles from Thoburn Rapids (Tobin Lake) to Cedar Lake. There was more mud than rock in this part of the river, although the blue ridge of the Pasquia Hills loomed in the distance, as did the Canadian Shield. Going downriver the men hardly noticed the marshes. Coming upriver they would.

Cumberland House was the HBC's first inland trading post,

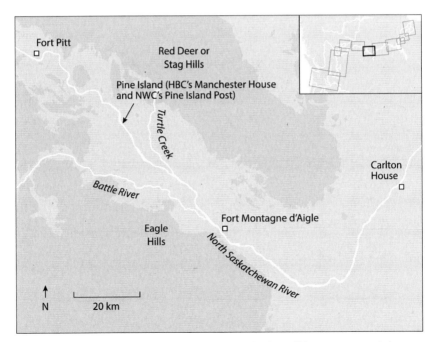

Coming downriver from Fort Pitt to Carlton House was a quick journey that took five to seven days in the high waters of the freshets.

constructed in 1774 on the only firm ground for miles around. The fort played an important role in the HBC's long history. Although Peter Pond is said to have invented pemmican, Cumberland House's Samuel Hearne further refined the greasy country food that became the familiar foodstuff for all prairie fur traders. William Tomison, who took over the post a few years later, built the first York Boats on the Saskatchewan. The French fur traders then on the river laughed at Tomison's clumsy boats but ate their words when those same boats transported massive loads of furs to York Factory.

Thomas Lowe's journal continues with his arrival at Cumberland House on June 7, 1847:

> Here two boats & the batteau were left, their ladings to be taken to Norway House by the Athabasca Brigade. Mr. Hector Aeneas Mc-Kenzie, who is in charge [of Cumberland House], takes a boat down with his Returns, and accompanies the Saskatchewan Brigade to York Factory. Started from Cumberland at 4 p.m. and pulled until sunset.
>
> Tuesday 8th. Very warm. Had a fine breeze all day, and reached the Pas in the evening, where we remained all night.[8]

Two days journey downriver from Cumberland House was the Pas, the narrowest part of the river, where a high ridge that served as lookouts loomed over the river. For more than one hundred years, First Nations men and French fur traders had used the Pas as a meeting place. Many early forts had been built at this historic meeting place, but in the 1840s only the free traders lived and farmed there. First Nations lived there too. "A sufficient number of Indians were engaged at this place to make up the boats crews to 3 men each, a few had 4, besides the steersman. About 10 pieces of Pemican were likewise taken out of each boat."[9] The pemmican would probably be stored at the mission station, now well-established at the Pas, with Reverend James Hunter acting as missionary to the local Cree:

> Wednesday 9th June 1847. Started from the Pas early this morning, and after a hard day's pulling, got as far as the commencement of the Muddy Lake [Lac Vaseux]. Very warm, and a few peals of thunder.[10]

Lac Vaseux was actually a widening of the Saskatchewan River that lived up to its name — Muddy Lake. After this, the express-men approached thirty-mile-long Cedar Lake, so named because it was surrounded by eastern white cedars that grew nowhere else on the river. In this part of the lower river, the channels constantly disappeared into mud flats and bogs that rarely rose above water level, and every storm or flood changed the course of the Saskatchewan River and confounded the express-men.

The last widening of the Saskatchewan east of Cedar Lake was Cross Lake or Lac Traverse, named because the lake ran north and south and the express-men generally rowed straight across rather than following its shoreline. From Cross Lake they re-entered the river and rowed toward two sets of rapids. The first was the Red Stone, a rapid that occasionally caused trouble for the Saskatchewan Brigades. East of the Red Stone was the Grand Rapids, a transportation bottleneck at the mouth of the river, where it flowed into Lake Winnipeg. These rapids flowed through a curving limestone gorge and descended seventy-one feet in five miles, almost sixty feet in one three-mile-long foaming section of river. Many a boat was damaged here, and some men lost their lives.

Thomas Lowe's journey continued east of Lac Vaseux, as his party rowed their boats down the Saskatchewan toward Cedar Lake and the Grand Rapids:

Thursday 10th. Beautiful warm day. Got into Cedar Lake by breakfast time, and sailed all forenoon, but the wind then headed us, and had to pull the remainder of the day. Encamped on an Island near the end of the Lake.

Friday 11th. Fine weather. Pulled through the remainder of Cedar Lake, and breakfasted at the other end of Cross Lake. In the forenoon 3 boats were broken in the Red Stone Rapid, and as a good deal of time was lost in repairing them, we only got as far as the head of the Grand Rapids, where we encamped. Rained very hard in course of the night.

Saturday 12th. Rained all morning, and could not start until after breakfast. In running the Grand Rapids, Laplante's Boat struck on the rocks, and blocked up the channel, when the Columbia boat, which was close behind, ran foul of it, and cut it down to the keel. The crew immediately jumped into the Columbia Boat, and left it in the middle of the Rapid. Before a boat could be unloaded and sent to haul it off, the cargo was completely soaked. Another one was likewise slightly broken, and we were obliged to encamp at the lower end of the Portage, having only come about a mile since starting this morning. Last night's rain rose the water a good deal.

Saturday 13th June 1847. Ran the remainder of the Grand Rapids today, the boats having taken out 30 pieces each, as the water was too low to run with full cargoes, and one half of them had therefore to make a second trip. Encamped at the bottom of the Rapids to mend the boats and dry the packs. In the afternoon the Portage la Loche Brigade passed us, in charge of L'Espérance the guide, consisting of six boats, with goods for McKenzie's River.[11]

According to Augustus Richard Peers, Alexis Bonami dit L'Espérance was "a Canadian of middle age, rather tall and of powerful frame."[12] He lived in the Red River settlement but worked as steersman and guide on the Portage La Loche Brigade. Every spring, he brought goods from Red River to Norway House. From Norway House he carried the Mackenzie River District's trade goods to Portage la Loche (Methye Portage), where he exchanged them for the furs, which he brought down to York Factory. Then he again loaded his boats with the goods for Red River Colony and returned home with them. He made this amazing journey every year for thirty years, and he often paused to exchange information with the express-men. It appears that during their brief conversation, Lowe learned that he had lost a day in his journal entries, and corrected the date in his next journal entry. Lowe writes:

[June] Monday 14th. Fine warm weather. Remained all day in the same encampment, drying the Furs.

Tuesday 15th. Beautiful day. Started in the afternoon and pulled down to the entrance of Lake Winnipeg. Encamped in the Horse Shoe.[13]

This was the sheltered horseshoe-shaped bay at the mouth of the Saskatchewan River, as it flowed into Lake Winnipeg. All the men were perfectly aware that the wide north basin of Lake Winnipeg could be a treacherous piece of water when winds from the south pushed the York Boats toward the overhanging limestone cliffs that lined its north shore. A wise man approached this fearsome lake with caution. Lowe's journal continues:

[June] Wednesday 16th. Started this morning under sail, and came about 10 miles, but as it began to blow a strong head wind, had to put ashore on an island in the Lake. A heavy thunder storm in the afternoon.

Thursday 17th. Remained on the same Island all day, and as it blew a strong gale, the boats were discharged, and hauled up on the beach.

Friday 18th. Raining and blowing strong. Remained in the same place all day, but as the wind lulled towards sunset, the boats were reloaded, and we pulled towards an Island about 5 miles distant, where we remained encamped until daylight.

Saturday 19th. Started early this morning, and had a fine side wind the whole day, which carried us through Lake Winnipeg, although we had much difficulty in rounding Mossy Point. [Mossy Point was the long point of land that separated Playgreen Lake from Lake Winnipeg itself.] Fine clear weather throughout the day, but a thunder storm at night. Mr. [John] Rowand who was the foremost of our Brigade, after passing Mossy Point, fell in with Sir George Simpson, who was in a boat on his way from Red River to Norway House. The governor was accompanied by C.F. [Chief Factor John Edward] Harriott & Mr. [Robert] Clouston. Mr. Rowand's boat and the governor's pushed on ahead, in order to reach Norway House tonight, but we remained behind with the Brigade, and encamped on an Island at the commencement of Play Green [sic] Lake.

Sunday 20th. Fine warm day. Arrived at Norway House at 3 o'clock in the afternoon. Sir George Simpson, Mr. Rowand &c arrived here about 10 o'clock last night.[14]

Norway House was a younger post than Cumberland House. It stood at various places (when it stood at all) on the shores of

Playgreen Lake, a weed-filled and shallow sheet of water that attached itself to Lake Winnipeg's northeast shoreline. The older Norway House had once stood on the southern tip of Mossy Point and overlooked Lake Winnipeg. But this post was consumed by fire in November 1824 and rebuilt nearby. A few years later the express-men pulled into the newer Norway House on Little Playgreen Lake, where the fisheries were. Wherever it stood over the years, Norway House was at the crossroads of the northern transportation system to Hudson Bay, and almost every HBC man passed through it. A young clerk, who saw Norway House in 1843, described the post he saw:

> Norway House stands on the bank of Jack River at its junction with Play Green Lake. The Fort which is built of wood is enclosed with high stockades. The houses are all of one story high and being whitewashed present a very neat and pleasing appearance. In front is the enclosure, intersected by platforms, the main one leading down to the river through the principal store.
>
> It boasts of an extensive kitchen garden in which are grown vegetables of various kinds A large farm is also attached and great quantities of excellent potatoes, barley, etc., are grown. It may therefore be seen that the inmates of this favored spot are well to do and enjoy a fair share of the good things of this life.[15]

— • —

In 1828, Edward Ermatinger's boats had drawn too much water to enter shallow Cumberland Lake, and the men camped across from the fort. His party left on June 2, retracing their way up the little river to the Saskatchewan. They drifted all night and arrived at the Pas the next morning. That night they camped at Lac Vaseux, and on Wednesday sailed and rowed across Lac Traverse. On Thursday, the men rowed against a head wind all day and reached Grand Rapids in the late afternoon:

> Water being very low find it necessary to take out half cargoes. People begin to carry. Rain.
>
> 6th. Rain all last night and continues till afternoon. Men run down

7 Boats and return with them light for the remaining cargoes — then run down the other eight boats and afterwards employed carrying the remainder of the cargoes across the Portage.

7th. Fine weather but cold. The 7 boats being found to be few to embark the half cargoes of 15 boats from this end of the Portage to the end of the Rapid, people fetch up another and afterwards the rest of the pieces are all got down safe. Sturgeon plentiful among the freemen here — trade nearly 100.

8th. Fine weather Leave the Grand Rapids early this morning and pull, the weather being perfectly calm, to the point opposite the Pine Island. Breakfast, then hoist sail across to the Islands, thence to the little Stoney Island and encamp.[16]

9th. Remain wind bound till afternoon and then pull to and along the mainland till 9 p.m. Encamp on a gravelly beach.

10th. Reload our boats (we were obliged to unload last night there being an appearance of wind from sea) and start at 5 a.m., pull for sometime and then hoist sail with a light breeze which forwards us to the head of the little Jack River, where we encamp.

11th. Start before 3 a.m. and reach the Fort about 6 o'clock.[17]

In 1849, young John Charles brought out the York Factory Express and the Saskatchewan Brigades. It must have been a long, late winter, because he had struggled against the ice in the Athabasca River. At Cumberland House he was again warned of the possibility of ice downriver. And at the Grand Rapids at the mouth of the Saskatchewan River, he was faced with the possibility of a frozen Lake Winnipeg.

[June] Tuesday [Thursday] 14th. By 10 a.m. all the boats were safely taken down to the end of Grand Rapids, here we found an Indian with his canoe, which with two men Mr. Rowand despatches to Lake Winnipeg to see if the passage was clear. The canoe returned after an hour's absence with the unfortunate news that the Lake appeared "like winter." Fearing that we might be detained here some time 4 nets were set in the River, which before night provided us with 12 sturgeon and upwards of 30 jackfish. One of the Indians succeeded in killing a moose deer.

Friday 15th. Peter Calder the guide with a crew of men in one boat visited the Lake, which he reports to be so full of compact ice as to preclude the possibility of our leaving the Grand Rapids for some time. A good many fish were taken out of the nets, this evening.[18]

On Saturday, it rained, and on Sunday the men awoke to a heavy fog and overcast that remained all day. Three days later they made their attempt to cross Lake Winnipeg:

Left Grand Rapids about 1 a.m. but were obliged to put ashore about 7 o'clock in consequence of the ice being in such large masses in the Lake and it not only being useless but dangerous for us to proceed. L'Espérance with 7 boats in his charge arrived at our encampment being on his way to Portage la Loche. He had been five days coming from Norway House.

Thursday 21st. Started this morning at 2 o'clock a.m. with a light breeze in our favour. The first boats arrived at the old Fort about midnight, the others arrived an hour or two afterwards. We had sail wind all day, and at one time a real gale, which lasted for some time.[19]

The "old fort" was the site of the abandoned Norway House at today's Warren Landing. On June 22, the boats crossed Playgreen Lake and arrived at the current Norway House, "where we found the governor and other gentlemen from the interior."[20]

At Norway House, Governor Simpson and many of the chief factors were holding their annual council meeting to discuss the concerns and difficulties that the gentlemen of the HBC had experienced that year, and to ensure that all HBC departments received Governor Simpson's new set of instructions.

Every year the chief factors in charge of Fort Vancouver and New Caledonia wrote their annual reports to the governor and committee. Each year their reports were carried out by the York Factory Express to Norway House or Red River. At these annual meetings, the governor and the gentlemen who made up his committee pored over the reports and created their own multi-page reports that must be copied out many times over and distributed to all the gentlemen in charge of territories spread far across the continent.

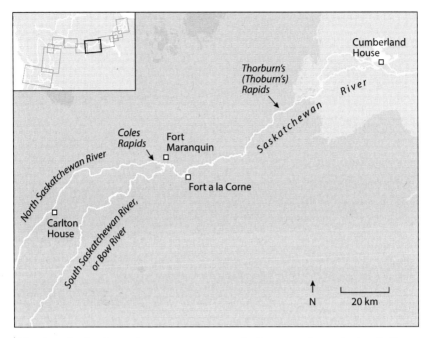

During the freshets, the express-men took shortcuts through the shallow muddy channels of the flooded river west of Cumberland House.

For the sake of efficiency, Governor Simpson used the leaders of the York Factory Express as his clerks: every year these clerks were delayed at Norway House, writing duplicate reports for the gentlemen of their district, while their men made their way to Hudson Bay unsupervised. In 1847, Lowe noted that he was "employed writing the Minutes of Council."[21]

On June 24, Governor Simpson "gave a Ball in the Council Room, at which we all mustered, and kept it up until midnight."[22] The next year, Lowe indicated he was "busy writing all day. Council sitting most of the day."[23] In his 1849 journal, John Charles reported the same: on Wednesday his day was "occupied in making copies of the Minutes of Council as well as other documents of a public nature."[24] He left Norway House on June 28, shortly after Governor Simpson's annual party.

Fortunately for these gentlemen who were delayed at Norway

House, the downriver journey to Hudson Bay was quick because it was made in lighter canoes and boats, and no delays occurred while their employees carted goods and packs of furs over the many portages along the route. Quite often the HBC gentlemen passed their employees' boats and reached Hudson Bay days before their various brigades arrived. The clerks may have ridden as passengers across the continent to Norway House or Red River, but at York Factory their Hudson Bay headquarters, it was the voyageurs' time to carouse, and the clerks' time to prepare their boats for the return journey across the continent.

CHAPTER 9

Norway House to
York Factory

§§

THE RIVER ROUTE FROM Norway House to York Factory was packed with historical landmarks and points of interest, but most HBC gentlemen did not bother to keep a record of the relatively relaxed downriver journey they made with their peers, especially as they had no responsibilities other than ensuring that they had a quick and easy trip to Hudson Bay. If the annual meeting was held at Red River, at the south end of Lake Winnipeg, the gentlemen left the York Boats at Carlton House and rode south across the prairies to Fort Garry. In 1835, James Douglas made this cross-country journey, and in 1841, George Traill Allan followed in Douglas's footsteps. When the meeting closed, they made their way up treacherous Lake Winnipeg to Norway House and thence to York Factory, travelling in birchbark canoes instead of York Boats.

In later years, however, the voyageurs delivered the gentlemen directly to Norway House, where the annual meeting was generally held. The voyageurs continued their journey to York Factory, following Playgreen Lake's intricate channels to Carpenter Lake. East of Carpenter Lake, the boisterous Nelson River carried the combined waters of the Assiniboine, Saskatchewan, Red, and Winnipeg rivers in a tumbling slide down the steep slope of the Canadian Shield to Hudson Bay. "The descent for a certain distance from Lake Winnipeg towards the sea, by a series of lakes terminating in Split Lake, is necessarily very gradual," one gentleman reported, "thence consequently to its mouth the Nelson rushes with great impetuosity."[1]

For the gentlemen who left the annual meeting for York Factory, their journey down the Nelson and Hayes rivers to Hudson Bay was faster and easier than for their voyageurs. They travelled in canoes from Norway House, taking the same river route their express-men had already taken, and passed the Saskatchewan boats at some point in their downriver journey.

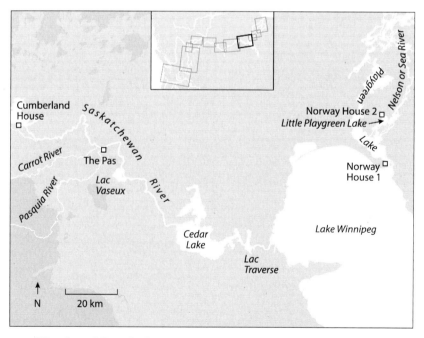

The Grand Rapids dam, constructed in the early 1960s, drowned much of the historic Saskatchewan River east of the Pas.

The first river, the Nelson, was far too dangerous for boat or canoe travel, and after a 25-mile paddle the voyageurs turned their canoes into a tiny stream so blocked by beaver dams that it was little more than a series of still ponds. This stream, the Blackwater, led them to the Echimamish River. At the point where the Echimamish flowed into the Hayes River near Painted Stone Portage, they were only 300 miles from Hudson Bay.

In its journey down the edge of the Canadian Shield, the Hayes River changed its name many times over. At the top of the hill it was called Hayes River, then Trout, Jack Tent, Hill, Steel, and finally Hayes once again. There were many obstacles along these various sections of river, and the falls at the top of the hill was the worst one. A quick paddle through Robinson Lake led the traders to Robinson's Falls (Whitefalls), a cascade that tumbled over five rockbound steps and forced the full fury of the Hayes between its massive granite walls. Here the men portaged their boats three-quarters of a mile to the base of the falls. Only the Grand Rapids on the Saskatchewan River presented a longer and more difficult portage.

After the chaos of Robinson's Falls, the canoes entered calm water for a short distance before stumbling into the scenic narrows they called the Hill's Gates, a ten-mile gorge with high granite walls that rose sixty to eighty feet above the foaming river. From the Upper Hill's Gate Portage, they crossed a second hauling place before entering the rapids-filled section of the river. The most dangerous part of this segment of the river was the Lower Hill's Gate. In his journals, Lowe called it The Lower Hell's Gates.

Beyond Lower Hill's Gate, Windy Lake led them through three or four sets of rapids, including Rapides Croches (Crooked Rapids), John More's Island, and the Lower Wipanapanis. At John More's Island, the river rushed with irresistible force through channels formed by two rocky islands. These landmarks were part of the narrow grassy Wipanapanis River, with its many channels that wound between islands large and small, separating and uniting time and again. This steep section of river was only the beginning of the Hayes' rapids-filled descent some 560 feet (170 metres) to the sea.

The gentlemen could, however, rest and socialize at Oxford House, which stood on the shores of Holey Lake (now Oxford Lake), named originally for the depth of its waters. Beyond Oxford House they paddled into rapids-filled Trout River and portaged over Upper and Lower Knife Handling Place and dangerous Trout Falls. At the east end of Knee Lake (which, like the Saskatchewan River's "Elbow," bent like the part of the body it was named for), they entered the Jack Tent River, whose island-filled river bed descended in giant steps toward the sea.

Four more portages in the Jack Tent River brought the men to Swampy Lake. Passing through, they paddled into another stretch of rapids-filled river, where thirty-seven portages over forty-five sets of rapids brought them into the relative safety of the lower river. But travelling downriver was fast and exciting. Not only did the boats run the rapids, but they shot the falls too, as a visitor to York Factory and the Hayes River wrote:

> As soon as the boat has safely descended, and is out of danger, all the crew lay down their oars, and give three cheers. This they do as each boat passes the fall unhurt; which is an expression of pleasure and congratulation, not considered necessary in simply coming down a rapid.[2]

At long-abandoned Rock Post, at the base of Rocky Portage, the HBC traders were 124 miles from York Factory. Eventually the Hayes delivered the gentlemen safely to York Factory, the HBC headquarters on the shores of Hudson Bay.

As a ten-year-old, John Charles had lived at Oxford House and at York Factory. In 1849, he made his first journey down the Hayes as an adult. His express boats had set off from Norway House on June 26, while he attended the annual meeting at Norway House. A few days later he travelled down the Hayes in a light canoe, making his way to York Factory with other gentlemen who had attended the same meeting. His journals indicate how busy this river was at the height of summer, when every post from Fort Frances on Rainy Lake to Edmonton House on the North Saskatchewan delivered its furs to York Factory and returned upriver with trade goods. Charles's journal begins at Norway House, on June 28, 1849:

> Thursday 28th. We overtook and passed Mr. [John Lee] Lewes & Co. about sunset. We camped at the Damn [man-made dam on the Echimamish River].
>
> Friday 29th. Came up with Messrs. [John] Rowand and [John Edward] Harriott at Robinsons Portage which is computed to be about three quarters of a mile in length. We left the portage at half past twelve and about an hour afterwards were across the Mountain Portage.[3]

Charles was born and brought up in the fur trade, and his journal is the only one to call Robinson's Portage by its correct name; all others called it Robertson's Portage:

> Saturday 30th. Overtook Peter Calder this morning, with his brigade at [blank] Portage. After breakfast we came up with the Lac La Pluie Brigade and before 4 p.m. overtook the Oxford House boat and arrived at the Above place about half an hour before them, where we put ashore and had dinner given us by Mr. Robertson.
>
> Sunday 1st July. Made two Portages before breakfast, the "Knife handled Place" and "Trout Fall." Had two hours sail in the evening. Put ashore for the night almost at the end of Knee Lake which Mr. Sinclair informs me is 60 miles in length.
>
> Monday 2nd. Entered Swampy Lake about 4 o'clock a.m. Made 4 Portages and 3 demi charges [running half-loaded canoes] today. Met the Red River Freighters towards evening. Put ashore at 5 o'clock and had supper when we embarked and drifted and paddled all night.
>
> Tuesday 3rd. Entered "Steel River" about 4 a.m. Sailed for about two hours, just before arriving at the Factory which was at 2 o'clock p.m.[4]

Like the other gentlemen who made this journey, John Charles had travelled downriver in a light canoe or boat. The goal was to get to York Factory as quickly as possible. The voyageurs would enjoy a well-deserved holiday at York Factory, but the gentlemen and clerks had work to do.

— • —

York Factory was an old place that had seen much history. The first British explorer to sail through Hudson Strait's fierce tide rips was Henry Hudson, who wintered in James Bay in 1610–1611. His crew mutinied and returned to London without him. Sir Thomas Button arrived in 1612 in Hudson's old ship, spending the winter at the mouth of the Nelson River, but fleeing the place when the mosquitoes woke up in the spring.

Luke Foxe and Thomas James were the next British explorers of note: they sailed through Hudson Strait in 1631. Foxe explored the top of Hudson Bay and returned home, but James overwintered on the bay later named for him. In spring, he sailed for London with stories of the wealth of fur-bearing animals he found on James Bay.

It was not until 1668 that two men who searched for furs rather than the Northwest Passage arrived on Hudson Bay — or at least one of the two arrived. Pierre-Esprit Radisson's ship was forced by a storm to return to England, but Médard Chouart des Groseilliers wintered in the same place that Henry Hudson had done fifty-nine years earlier. He returned home with a shipload of furs, and Charles II signed a comprehensive charter granting Radisson and Groseilliers' backers a fur-trading monopoly for all the lands draining into Hudson Bay.

Four weeks later, the ships of the Governor and Company of Adventurers of England Trading into Hudson's Bay, the Hudson's Bay Company, sailed west to establish a permanent post on their namesake bay, on a point of land that jutted into Hudson Bay a few miles north of Hayes River.

At this time, France and England were involved in a series of wars, and the English traders on both Hudson Bay and James Bay, lost York Factory and other posts to French invaders on at least four occasions. In 1713, the Hudson's Bay Company regained the fort once more, when Louis XIV of France signed the Treaty of Utrecht, surrendering significant portions of his empire, including the HBC posts, to Britain.

The French left and the British returned to Hudson Bay, building a new post at the mouth of the Hayes River in 1715. It was burned to the ground in 1782 by French naval officer Jean-François de Galaup, comte de Lapérouse. Because of bad weather, however, Lapérouse immediately departed Hudson Bay, and the HBC men stubbornly rebuilt. Five years later, a flood encouraged them to rebuild again, this time on higher ground.

By the 1820s, York Factory resembled a crowded village, but its appearance changed rapidly over the next decade as the HBC men constructed their enormous two-storey warehouse. By the 1840s, York Factory sprawled over the barren landscape, its fifty or more buildings dominated by the massive whitewashed warehouse. In 1842, a new arrival, Apprentice Clerk Augustus Richard Peers, described York Factory as he first saw it:

Like most other forts in the country it is built on three sides of a square, the whole surrounded by high pickets except in front where low ornamental palisades are substituted. The buildings are all of wood, the damp nature of the ground rendering it necessary to raise them on logs as a means of keeping them out of the wet and most of them are covered with tin on the roof to prevent accidents from fire. In the centre of the square stands the principal, or as it is called the General Store, wherein are deposited the goods for the Indian trade throughout the north. On its right and left are the summer mess room and a range of low buildings which are appropriated as summer residences for visitors. The private dwelling house of the gentlemen in charge of the depot, the clerk's dwelling house and those of the numerous artizens [sic] and labourers, with the sale shop, fur store, and Indian trading shop etc., form the plan of the fort.[5]

Some visitors remained unimpressed by York Factory. Robert Ballantyne called it "a monstrous blot on a swampy spot, with a partial view of a frozen sea."[6] The fort was surrounded by scrub willow and sawgrass, and its docks lay at the far end of three miles of boardwalks that stretched across flooding bogs. The ships that arrived every summer anchored in Five Fathom Hole, seven miles from York Factory and the only deep water nearby. Goods and passengers were transported to headquarters by smaller schooners, which at high tide could sometimes sail over the shallow mudflats that lined the bay's shores. Augustus Peers described his arrival on the London ship:

> About the tenth of August the sight of land once more greeted our longing eyes and we entertained agreeable expectations of a speedy termination to our voyage. Soon after we arrived in Ten Fathom Hole, and as the water grew rapidly shallow and the weather looking lowering, giving palpable indications of a coming storm, the Captain deemed it advisable to cast anchor. . . . The morning was fine and the sun shone bright and when the tide was at its full height, the ship was once more put under weigh. We soon passed over the bar, touching the bottom here and there, and brought up in the anchorage in Five Fathom Hole under a salute announcing our safe entry to the folk at the Factory.
>
> Dr. N[evins] and I gathered up our traps and betook ourselves on board one of the small craft which sheered out and set sail for shore but ere we got far, the tide having turned, we speedily stuck in the mud. As we were doomed to remain a fixture till the evening tide, we made the best of our lot by leaning over the side, like horses in a pound and surveyed the scene before us — a scene, by the way, which partook but in a very slight degree of the picturesque.
>
> Before us lay the land in bleak sterility, terminating below the Factory in a long low point whose limits were marked by a wooden beacon. Behind us lay the bay bounded by the distant horizon. . . .[7]

In contrast to its barren surroundings and primitive harbour, York Factory was a very modern place. The clerks who brought out the expresses came with shopping lists from all the forts along the Saskatchewan River, who had placed their orders for the trade goods they would require for the next winter's trading. The quality of the trade goods shipped upriver was important, as First Nations peoples would not trade furs for goods they neither wanted nor thought were not of good quality. It was the clerk's job to fulfil the orders for the interior forts as best he could, and a great deal of work was accomplished while they were at York Factory.

Trade goods for the Saskatchewan — items such as tobacco, flintlock guns, balls and powder, flints, powder horns, knives (large and small), awls, files, cloth, and blankets — were selected and packed in large pactons (packs with carrying straps), for shipment to the interior posts. The employees of the post included craftsmen such as blacksmiths, tinsmiths, coopers, and sailmakers who manufactured goods such as kettles, teapots, camp plates, axes, ice chisels, traps, and other goods necessary to the fur trade.

Many thousands of trade items were shipped west to Edmonton and other posts along the Saskatchewan and North Saskatchewan rivers. In 1847, Thomas Lowe reported that each of the 11 boats that left York Factory carried 60 pieces, each weighing 85 pounds, which was fewer packs per boat than usual, but the Saskatchewan River had little water that year. On visiting each upriver post the crew unloaded the outfit (the year's supplies) for that post. At Fort Pitt, the smallest post along the North Saskatchewan, Lowe (who had ridden ahead) reported:

> Shortly after breakfast the boats arrived. They were windbound the whole of yesterday. Had the Outfit taken out (more than 100 pieces). As the water is very low the whole of the 8 boats are going up (although it is usual to leave one here). They start from here tomorrow with 65 pieces per boat.[8]

All of the goods that were delivered to the various posts along the Saskatchewan and North Saskatchewan River were packed up by the clerks of the York Factory Express, although major posts such as Edmonton and Cumberland Houses sent their own clerks to Hudson Bay. Innumerable lists were written and rewritten, as the clerks itemized the products wrapped in the various packs for delivery to the interior posts.

Each pack was numbered and labelled with the initials of the post it was intended for — FP for Fort Pitt, for example. Duplicate lists were also written and left behind with the clerk at York Factory for purposes of inventory. Because the York Factory clerk would copy these lists into his own ledgers, there were duplicate and triplicate copies of all the lists that the express clerks made out. In July 1849, John Charles wrote of his time at the post:

> [July] Monday 4th/15th. This period was spent at the Factory in equipping the Saskatchewan and other Brigades, also in packing and making up Outfits. With the assistance of Mr. [Robert] Clouston the accountant I was enabled to get everything necessary for the Columbia in the way of documents &c. The weather during this interval was very changeable.[9]

The clerks also had to take care of the furs that were being shipped to London to be sold. Thousands of furs had travelled downriver in the boats to York Factory, and all must be unpacked, shaken out, and repacked in barrels for shipment to London. If the furs were damp, they must be dried to prevent mould and rot. In addition to that, as the furs were unpacked, they were credited to the post from which they came, which created more bookwork for the clerks who were in charge of this chore.

Everyone was in a rush and working to a very tight schedule. The London ships could remain at York Factory only a short time — a maximum of six weeks — before they were threatened with the possibility of being stalled by the ice in Hudson Strait at the north end of the bay. Nor could the boats of the outgoing York Factory Express be delayed, and all the goods they carried home must be sorted, labelled, and packed in time to prevent delays to their return journey.

At times, the clerks came with shopping lists for others left behind in the interior. In 1848, Thomas Lowe carried instructions to purchase a vinegar and oil cruet for the man in charge at Fort Colvile, and fiddle strings for one of its employees. They would also shop for themselves. The officers' stores sold goods that came straight from London on the London ships every summer. There were sextants, flannel and gingham shirts, trousers and shawls, tobacco and clay pipes by the dozen, and enamel basins stacked next to fur hats and candies. Items such as these would also be packed and delivered to the interior posts, to be sold in their own stores to employees or to visitors.

The normal work of the York Factory employees went on, although the work load was dramatically increased by the constant arrivals and departures of brigades from posts as far away as Rainy Lake, Severn, Swan River, and English River. After his arrival in August 1842, Augustus Peers described his first day at York Factory:

> Next morning — not at the fashionable hour of eight, but at the healthy hour of five — the inmates of Bachelor's Hall were astir and this being a particularly busy season, they betook themselves to the office there to scribble till eight at night or even later. At eight o'clock the bell tolled for breakfast and a precipitate rush was made from all quarters — from office, from shop, and fur store — the centre of attraction being the mess room. This room, which was about forty feet long by about twenty-five wide, containing four long deal tables, and numerous benches and warmed by two capacious stoves served the inhabitants the three fold purpose of summer mens room, church and ball room, for all which purposes it was well adapted.[10]

(The summer men's room Peers mentions would be familiar to all voyageurs in the Saskatchewan Brigades and the York Factory Express, as this was where they slept each night.)

An important job at this post was the maintenance of the York Boats that arrived every summer, and this work was done by the boat-builders who worked at York Factory. Any broken or rotting boards in the hull or elsewhere were replaced, and the boat's repair box filled with new supplies of wood, oakum (made by shredding old rope to pieces), and tools. The top two boards of these boats were lapped, and tradition had it that those boards were painted inside and out with a bright red paint. It is possible that at York Factory the carpenters made a point of applying a fresh coat of paint to the top boards of all the boats that arrived there.

The visiting gentlemen had some time for personal things. Those who had injuries or medical problems visited the doctor who, as a rule, was little more than a barber-surgeon. Many must have done so, as the doctors were kept busy during the times the brigades were at York Factory, although they had few patients the rest of the year. The gentlemen read the current English newspapers and scoured the library for books to read. They could also enjoy a more refined social life than was available at the isolated trading posts.

In the early 1840s, the new wife of Chief Trader James Hargrave arrived at the post from Scotland. Although her first reaction had been to cry in despair, she came to enjoy her privileged position. In 1841, George Traill Allan enjoyed a cup of tea with her, remarking that "when seated at table [he] could not help thinking myself once more across the Atlantic, enjoying that beverage with some of my own dear friends."[11]

Six years after Allan enjoyed his civilized cup of tea with Mrs. Hargrave, Thomas Lowe said this of his time at York Factory:

Thursday 1st July. Very warm. Working in the Office at the Columbia Accounts. [James] Cromarty a Postmaster, arrived with the Returns from Severn.

Friday 2nd. Rain in the morning, but fine & fair throughout the day. The Norway House Brigade arrived, and brought the Columbia letters [that Thomas Lowe had handed them at Norway House].

Saturday 3rd. Beautiful weather. [Charles] Roussain a Postmaster started with the Lac La Pluie [Rainy Lake] Brigade of 4 boats, with the Outfit of that District.

Sunday 4th July. Fine warm day. All quiet at the Factory.

Monday 5th. Rainy. In the evening 4 boats of the Saskatchewan Brigade arrived.

Tuesday 6th. Very close and oppressive. In the afternoon Messrs. [Augustus] Pelly & Burke arrived with one boat, the rest will be here tomorrow.

Wednesday 7th. Still unusually warm. Thermometer at 90° in the shade. The remainder of the Saskatchewan Brigade arrived today.

Thursday 8th. Sultry. Mr. Pelly began today to work at the Furs for England.

Friday 9th. Rain & thunder. Most of the boat crews drunk and fighting.

Saturday 10th. Very squally weather. In the afternoon all the men were called up and told where they were to go. We have got 20 pretty good hands for the Columbia.[12]

— • —

While the gentlemen enjoyed a cup of tea with Mrs. Hargrave or spent hours sorting and packing the furs for London or the trade goods for their return journey, the voyageurs celebrated.

The voyageurs arrived at York Factory as much as a week after the gentlemen. Before rounding the last bend in the river, they would pause to wash their faces and don fresh shirts. They decorated themselves with their traditional feathers and ribbons, and, picking up their oars, raised their voices in song, rowing quickly over the last stretch of water to the fort.

An exaggerated manliness was very much part of the voyageur culture. This was an all-male group, separated for months at a time from the women they had left on the far side of the continent. They had laboured hard for three months or more. Now, at York Factory, they received their regale of rum and celebrated their Canadien culture with games and contests. They wrestled to prove they were stronger than all around them. They challenged each other to boat races — York Boats vs canoes.

They claimed they could out-paddle a Swampy Cree man — and probably proved they could. They purchased duffle, cotton cloth, and blankets for their families in the West, and beaded shirts and woollen capots (coats) with long fringed belts for themselves. And they ate. These men were prodigious eaters at the best of times, but many had lost pounds of weight in their long journey across the continent. They ate to make up for their loss. They feasted on stews and soups and roasts, and berry pies that were two feet long.

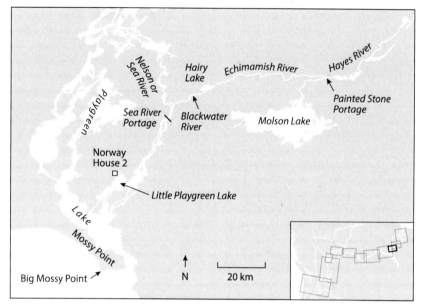

The HBC boats travelled from Norway House to the Blackwater River, which would take them over a shallow height of land to the Hayes River.

Most attended the church services that were offered at this place. Some had liaisons with First Nations women who visited the post, or who lived outside its palisades. They celebrated their time here with men from other posts with whom they had worked in the past, and who had not come from so far away.

The gentlemen at the post were used to the cavorting of the summer-men, as they were called at York Factory. "The men of the brigade got their Rum this morning, and there has been a good deal of fighting,"[13] Thomas Lowe reported in 1848. Fighting was a part of their time at York Factory, as the best boxers in each brigade challenged other boxers to a match to discover who would be declared "bully" of York Factory.

As the brigades arrived at headquarters, York Factory's champion boxer arranged matches that almost everyone in the fort attended. Each brigade had its own bully, and each winning bully went on to fight the bully from the next brigade, until the championship was decided. In the years between 1830 and 1855, the Saskatchewan Brigades' guide, Paulet Paul, was most often the last man standing.[14]

Music was also a part of their culture, as was dance. A young clerk who served at York Factory over a summer when everyone laboured hard to keep up with the work that had to be done described the antics of the Métis men who most often made up the bulk of the brigades in the early 1840s. To these men, who were born at isolated posts in the interior, a visit to York Factory was an entirely new and exciting experience. A young clerk described them this way:

> As the crews of these boats were formed principally of half-castes who scarcely know fatigue and who being naturally of a buoyant disposition, an incessant din was kept up; for let a half-breed be ever so tired if he but hear a discordant jingling of an ill-tuned fiddle he must be up and capering with ever and anon an inspiriting "Hi! Hi! Hi!" inviting the others to join in the dance.[15]

— • —

The clerks and apprentices who joined the Hudson's Bay Company in the 1800s arrived at York Factory on the London ships, which had departed from the Thames three months earlier, in spring. The ships stopped for provisions in the Shetland and Orkney Islands, at the same time picking up new employees for the HBC fur trade. In the early years, York Factory and Red River had claimed the best of the new employees, and the worst were shipped across the mountains into the Columbia District. By 1847, that bad habit appears to have been overcome. As noted above, Thomas Lowe expressed his pleasure at the quality of the men who were to cross the Rocky Mountains with him ("We have got 20 pretty good hands for the Columbia").

In the early years, many of the voyageurs who joined the York Factory Express would have come from the Shetlands or Orkneys with the ships, or they might have come from Quebec. There was a difference between these two kinds of men. As one clerk put it, "the chief characteristics of the highland Scotch and Orkney servants are

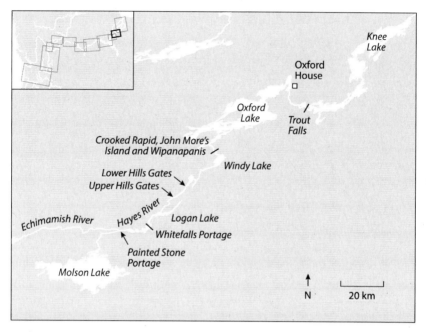

At Whitefalls Portage, the Express men began their journey down the
steep eastern edge of the Canadian Shield to York Factory.

honesty and prudence. They make excellent fort and farm labourers,
but indifferent voyageurs. The Canadiens are generally noted for hard
swearing and are excellent voyageurs."[16] Orkneymen tended to return
home when their contracts were finished, but the Canadiens often
stayed in the HBC's employ for some time.

By the 1840s, however, many of the new men were the Métis descendants of the earlier Canadiens, who had grown up in the HBC's
fur trade at Red River or on the Saskatchewan, and were now ready
to take their traditional place in the Company. In 1878, retired Chief
Trader A.C. Anderson wrote of a generation of Métis men who "had
sprung up, embodying in a marked degree the paternal characteristics
of their origin; and these native voyageurs became at an early period
a very useful class."[17]

From early days the Métis culture differed from that of their Canadien or Orkney fathers. The clerk who described the Orkneymen

and Canadiens, above, noted that the Métis men were "proverbial for light heartedness, recklessness, and the love of voyaging both winter and summer."[18] Voyaging was an important part of the HBC's fur trade, and the voyageurs' skills would be needed for some time into the future.

CHAPTER 10

York Factory to Norway House

෨෩

WITH THE YORK BOATS repaired and the clerical work done, most of the gentlemen who had come to York Factory with the outgoing express from Fort Vancouver prepared for their return home. Some did not. Edward Ermatinger brought out the express twice, in 1827 and 1828. He did not return to Fort Vancouver on his second voyage, but retired to Montreal.

In 1841, George Traill Allan brought out the express but went on furlough and did not return to the Columbia District that year. However, a transcript of the journal he wrote when he first came into the Columbia in 1831 still exists, and excerpts from that, beginning at Norway House, will describe elements of the return journey.

James Douglas returned to the Columbia District in 1835, and his journal will be continued in the next chapters, as will the account of Thomas Lowe, who went out to York Factory twice, returning home to the Columbia District in both 1847 and 1848. In 1849, he retired from the HBC, and John Charles took his place, leading the express back toward the Columbia District, although his story is cut short sometime after he passed through Edmonton House.

In the second half of this book, we will also hear from Aemilius Simpson, who was not the leader of the York Factory Express but a passenger in it. His cousin and childhood friend, George Simpson, governor of the Company, had strongly encouraged the London Committee of the HBC to employ this man as a combined surveyor, hydrographer, and ship captain in the Columbia District.

Aemilius Simpson's assigned duty on reaching Fort Vancouver was to manage the HBC ships that travelled up and down the West Coast of North America and crossed the Pacific to the Sandwich Islands (Hawaii). He would trade for furs in some places and do business with the Russians at Sitka and the Spaniards in what is now San Francisco Bay.

In addition to all this travelling to relatively distant lands, he played an important role in establishing some of the new trading posts along the Pacific coast — Fort Victoria on Vancouver's Island, Fort Langley on the lower Fraser River, and the first Fort Simpson on the Nass River of the Northwest Coast.

Aemilius Simpson's first duty, however, was to produce a detailed survey of the entire route from York Factory to the Columbia District, complete with compass directions and map co-ordinates, and to describe the difficulties of travelling on what was, in 1826, a newly established route.[1] His journal, titled "Journal of a Voyage Across the Continent of North America in 1826," is in the Hudson's Bay Company Archives. For many years it was ignored by historians, but in August 2014 it was published in *The Journal of the Hakluyt Society* under the title "Lt. Aemilius Simpson's Survey from York Factory to Fort Vancouver, 1826," edited by William Barr and Larry Green.

These six gentlemen — Ermatinger, Allan, Douglas, Simpson, Lowe, and Charles — are now the men who will be telling the story of the York Factory Express on its homeward journey. In the HBC correspondence, the York Factory Express was now referred to as the Columbia Express, as its final destination was the Columbia District (whether the lower Columbia River or northern New Caledonia via the Rocky Mountain Portage). However, it still travelled with the Saskatchewan Brigades. Unlike the Columbia Express, which brought in no trade goods from York Factory, the Saskatchewan Brigades carried in their trade goods the necessities for the next year's business.

The Columbia Express men were there to help push their boats the 1,437 miles upriver to Edmonton House and carry their loads over the portages. They were also there to bolster the Saskatchewan Brigades' numbers as they travelled through territory inhabited by people of the Blackfoot Confederacy, who might be tempted to attack a smaller brigade.

The upriver trip to Edmonton House was perhaps the most difficult leg of the journey home. From there, the men of the Columbia Express would continue their journey over the 90-mile Athabasca Portage. By the time they reached Jasper's House, they would have travelled an additional 185 miles up the Athabasca River. From there, another 983 miles separated them from Fort Vancouver, although once they reached Boat Encampment that distance was measured in downriver miles.

The departure from York Factory was not always easy, although the men were eager to leave. At times the Columbia men were exposed to viruses imported from England, which some had no ability to fight. However, in 1834–35, the mysterious disorder the HBC men called "the York Factory Complaint" was affecting many of the men who worked at that establishment.

The complaint, which went on for three years, was lead poisoning, caused by consuming food from cans made with lead, and it killed three people outright and sickened others.

In 1835, James Douglas reported that the contagion "rendered the sufferer unfit for duty, and in many instances, particularly with the Natives, terminated by inflammatory diseases of the lungs, generally proving fatal."[2] On his arrival at York Factory that year, Douglas could clearly see the effect of the complaint on the gentlemen and employees of the post, but the second part of his comment referred to the tuberculosis so common among the Indigenous employees of the HBC.

There were other reasons the men might not feel up to par. In July 1848, Thomas Lowe reported: "As the men had made too free with their regale before leaving we made poor progress, and encamped at 6 Mile Island."[3]

The factor that likely slowed travel most was that they were travelling west with many new and inexperienced men, who had not yet become accustomed, physically or mentally, to the hard labour of rowing these boats upriver.

As mentioned above, an interesting young man travelled with the departing 1826 Columbia Express. Retired Royal Navy lieutenant Aemilius Simpson was a total stranger to the continent and to the fur trade, and his journal bursts with the newness of his experience. As the brigade set off from York Factory, Simpson recorded a tradition that remained unmentioned in every other journal. "On Embarking we were accompanied to the Wharf by all the gentlemen and Servants assembled at York Factory, which at this time was very numerous."[4] In mid-July 1826, Simpson described how the sixty men of the brigades, including eight gentlemen on their way to Edmonton House and beyond, "commenced our journey across the Continent of North America. . . . We embarked in five Boats which were fully laden with the Supplies for the Interior. Our Crews were in high spirits and commenced their laborious journey with as much apparent indifference as if a few days was to bring it to a conclusion. . . ."[5]:

> On Embarking at 3 p.m. we had a favourable breeze which assisted us in our ascent of Hays' [Hayes] River, but on its dying away, our Crews were obliged to commence Tracking by line, which was a very laborious duty, the path in many places being along the face of steep cliffs of adhesive clay, yet such is the spirit of emulation among these Voyageurs, that they are regardless of every obstacle & perform their sworn Duty with a cheerfulness & perseverance that cannot be exceeded.

We continued our ascent of Hayes' River until a short Distance below Eighteen Mile Creek, where we encamp for the night, at 9:20 p.m. The weather throughout the day was fine, but we were very much persecuted by Moskitos.

Saturday 15th. The morning commenced Hazy, but cleared up on the Sun's rising when the Weather became fine & pleasant. We Embarked at 2:50 a.m. and continue our ascent of Hayes' River, which we complete at 5 p.m., when we arrived at the confluence of the Shamattawa [Gods River], making the estimated Distance from York Factory 56 Miles. . . . As we continue our ascent the current gains additional force, which adds very much to the labour of Tracking, but we were occasionally favoured with a breeze which gave us assistance, & the Tracking path was in many places very good, having a beach covered with rounded stones, as compactly [laid] as if done by human labour, & forming a good causey.[6] We continued to ascend Steels' River until 9:30 p.m. when we were 12 Miles above the junction of the Shamattawa, & having made a distance in the course of the day of 50 Miles by my estimation in a very Winding Course. . . .[7]

This was the section of the Hayes River called the Steel. Where the Fox River flowed into the Steel, the Hayes became the Hill River. Simpson's journal continues:

July 1826, Sunday 16th. The morning commenced Hazy, with a cold Dew followed by a warm day. At 2:30 a.m. Embarked & continued our ascent of the Steel River until noon, when we arrived at the confluence of the Fox and Steel rivers, making the latter by my estimation a distance of 29 Miles, we now commenced our ascent of Hills River, which we continue until 8:30 p.m. having ascended it 12 miles & making a distance in the course of the day of 29 Miles in a Winding course to the SW when we Encampt. Our men having had a hard day Tracking, over a very indifferent path, it being in many places along the face of perpendicular clay cliffs, affording frequently a very unsafe footing. These cliffs often attain a height of a hundred feet, with their Summits perfectly level & bearing a stint'd growth of Pines.

Monday 17th. The morning Hazy but fine Weather during the day. We Embarked at usual hour & continue our ascent of the Hill

River by Tracking, the path generally better than yesterday, as those steep clay Cliffs no longer occur, but its' being flooded in some places still renders it a very laborious duty, we do not travel therefore at a rate exceeding two Miles per Hour, at 4:45 p.m. we arrived at the Rocky [Rock] Portage, which I estimate is 34 Miles above the Mouth of the Hill River.[8]

It took the men two hours to complete this portage. This was the beginning of the steep climb to the height of land between Hudson Bay and Lake Winnipeg; the riverbed rose sharply and was full of treacherous rocks and islands. Simpson's journal continues:

We proceeded for 2 miles & got to Borrowicks' [Berwick] Falls, & having hauled above them at 8:15 we continued our ascent for a Mile when we encamp for the night, at 9 p.m.

On getting above the Rock Portage we discontinue Tracking, and proceed by Poling, an operation at which our Canadian Voyageurs are very expert. . . . The Scenery about the Rock Portage is very picturesque & romantic.

Tuesday 18. Commenced a heavy Fog which cleared up at 5 a.m. . . . At 3 a.m. we continued our ascent of the Hill River, which now presents a constant chain of rapids, obliging us to make frequent discharges and Portages, viz the White Mud Portage, Rocky Point Discharge, 1st & 2nd Brassa [Brassey] Portages, & minor Rapids, & at 7 p.m. we arrived at the lower burnt Wood Portage where we Encamp for the night, having after a day of great labour & fatigue, come a distance of only 13 Miles.

Wednesday 19th. . . . Some of our Boats having fallen on the rear, we were detained in our Encampment until 6 a.m., when we pursued our Journey, opposed by a constant succession of strong rapids requiring the utmost exertions, alternately at the Poles, hauling line & oars, & making frequent Portages, viz. South Handing [plain], Morgans Rocks, Portage des Isle, Upper burnt Wood, Smooth Stone Portages, above which we Encamp for the night, having only come a distance of five Miles from our Morning's Encampment. The fatigue from the great labour attending this Mode of travelling is very great, and notwithstanding the fine scenery presented by many of these falls &

rapids, which are well calculated to please either the Eye or imagination of the Traveler, yet their frequent repetition & the serious obstacles accompanying them, Divests them in a great measure of that interest which under different circumstances they must create, the attention of the travelers is principally directed to his progress, & you hear a constant repetition of the query: how far Distant is the next Portage?[9]

Of all the gentlemen who travelled in these expresses, Aemilius Simpson is the only one who noted, specifically, how hard the voyageurs laboured to get the clumsy York Boats upriver and down. As a group, these hard-working labourers performed near-impossible tasks, transporting goods and boats over the challenging portages that faced them in this steep, rocky part of the route. The Canadiens in particular, and the Métis men they had fathered, took pride in spectacular displays of strength and endurance. And when the brigades reached the Dramstone Portage at the top of the hill, tradition demanded that the gentleman-in-charge reward his voyageurs with a regale of rum, although Aemilius Simpson does not mention this in his journal:

Thursday 20th [July]. Fine clear Weather, some of our boats being still in the rear we did not proceed on our Journey until 4:30 a.m. We were occupied until 8:40 in getting above the rapids of the Mossy Portage, at Noon we were making the 2nd Portage, the Day extremely Warm. Notwithstanding our increasing exertions our advance today has been very trifling in Point of Distance being only 4 and a half Miles but taking Portages and rapids as an equivalent we have certainly made a fair days March, having made four Portages two of them launching places for Boats, besides hauling by line thru' several strong shoots [chûtes] & rapids, some of them Dangerous & the best tedious & fatiguing, the Crews being frequently obliged to leap overboard in the Rapids to Launch the Boats over Rocks. The heat of the day was followed by Showers in the evening. Two of our Boats having fallen in the rear, we Encampt at 8 p.m. above the Rapid of Ground Water Creek.[10]

All of these places bore names given for good reason. At Morgan's Rocks the river widened, and the low flat rocks along the shoreline allowed the men to enjoy the view of the cone-shaped hills that surrounded them. At Mossy Portage, the men carried their boats through a deep bog for a quarter of a mile. Above Mossy Portage, the river spread out again, and the men rowed between wooded islands, taking pleasure in the long beautiful vistas.

On Friday 21, Simpson's party continued the ascent of the Hill River, which he described as a continued chain of rapids and spouts that took the express four days to ascend. Sometimes the men tracked the boats upriver and at other times they rowed them. At the crest of the hill, the men tracked their boat through the Dramstone, the last and worst rapid on Hill River:[11]

> We now Entered Swampy Lake & being favoured with a sailing Wind, we landed on the Sail Island, a short distance from the Dramstone, & furnishing ourselves with Masts we made sail up this Lake, an agreeable change in our mode of travelling. . . . Entered Jack Tent River at 5 p.m. & having Carried across the first Portgage, which is about 1 mile up the River, we proceeded on to the Long Portage when we Encampt for the night. . . .[12]

On July 22 they completed their ascent of the Jack Tent River which, although only nine miles long, was a constant chain of rapids with four Portages in a distance of two miles. At 3 p.m. they rowed into Knee Lake and continued to ascend it with a fine breeze until evening, when they set up camp on a small island in the lake. By the time the express-men reached Knee Lake, they had traversed more than forty portages on this river.

Simpson's journal continues:

> Sunday 23rd. Commenced fine clear Weather, wind NE. We remained in our Encampment until the arrival of our sternmost Boats at 7:30 a.m., when we continued our ascent of Knee Lake, at 9:20 we arrived at the Magnetic Island, mentioned by [Sir John] Franklin. . . . On a close approach to this Small Island, which was hardly above the

surface of the Lake, I found the compass became greatly agitated, veering about with great rapidity, until at last it became stationary, the North Point being fixed in the direction of the Island, and altho' I applied a Key it had not the effect of withdrawing it from that Direction, but as we left the Island, it gradually resumed its true direction.[13]

The islands in Knee Lake contained deposits of magnetite or lodestone, common iron oxides with magnetic properties. As John Franklin passed these islands in 1819, he also noted that the magnetic properties of the rocks overpowered his compasses.[14]

Simpson's journal continues:

We now commenced our Ascent of the Trout River, which having done for 1 and half miles, we arrived at the Trout Falls, one of the most dangerous Rapids or falls on the line of Communication.[15]

At Trout Falls, the river tumbled over a sixteen-foot precipice between two high rocks, and the men hauled boats and loads up the precipitous rocky bank on the south side of the river. All along this section of the river, sharp fragments of broken slate rock cut through the men's moccasins and lacerated their feet:

We Encampt at the Head of these falls, two of our Boats having fallen again in the rear. These falls with the surrounding scenery afforded a fine subject for the Pencil of poor [Robert] Hood, but the heightening of the Landscape, by the Silver tints of the Moon's rays shooting above a projecting point of wood on the opposite shore, & playing upon the agitated surface of these fierce falls, made me regret that they were not similarly presented to him, as they were to me this Evening, which added much of their natural grandeur.[16]

Above the Trout Falls a five-mile long chain of rapids and falls made progress difficult, and at the Knife Handling Place the men once again cut their feet on the sharp slate rocks. They would rest at Oxford Lake, but west of that lake were the two Hill's Gates Portages, and "Robertson's":

Monday 24th. Commenced fine clear Weather, we remained in our Encampment until 5:30 a.m. Waiting the arrival of our sternmost Boats, when we continued our ascent of the Trout River, a very rapid stream, five miles of it being a constant chain of Rapids & falls. At 9:35 we got above the Knife Portage & having hauled by line above a number of Rapids at a quarter past Noon we arrived at comparatively still Water, enabling us to proceed with greater expedition. At 3 p.m. we arrived at Oxford House, a small Trading Post on Holey Lake.[17]

The old post of Oxford House was built before 1800 and for many years had contributed significantly to the HBC fur trade. More recently the post had declined in importance, as the land around it had been trapped out, and its Cree hunters had moved west to the Saskatchewan River. But the fort remained. As has been mentioned on the voyage out, it stood, as always, on the shores of a lake, then called Holey (Holé) for the deep pool of water near its outlet that could not be sounded. Holey Lake is now Oxford Lake. In 1819, Robert Hood described the post as being

> built like all the rest, of wood and inclosed [sic] by stockades. These lonely buildings are more widely scattered than the cities of Siberia. There is no difference in them; they were raised for the primitive object of shelter; and variety is only to be found in decoration and arrangement, here neither attempted nor desired.[18]

In 1843, a young clerk who reached Oxford House for the first time, described it this way:

> The fort is built of wood and according to the prevailing plan consists of the officer's dwelling house with a store and mens' house, the whole surrounded by a wooden stockade. It is airily situated on an eminence overlooking the lake and surrounding country. The land on the right margin of the lake [where the fort stands] is high and somewhat imposing so that when viewed under a more favourable aspect, there are, no doubt, many more unpicturesque localities than Oxford House.[19]

At Oxford House, the Saskatchewan Brigades were halfway to Norway House, and the men had spent an average of twelve days pushing upriver against the Hayes' strong current. Although the most difficult part of the journey was finished, there were more rapids and falls to come.

In 1849, John Charles's westbound brigades arrived in Oxford House on August 1, and the men breakfasted on whitefish. They left "under full sail. Made one portage and camped a little below a strong rapid called 'Rapides Croches,'"[20] or Crooked Rapids:

[August] Thursday 2nd. We came up today to the Head of Lower Hills Gate, where the Columbia boat on being hauled up full cargo, sustained some injury, but which was before night, repaired.

Friday 3rd. Arrived at Robinson Portage about 11 a.m. Before night all the boats together with part of the cargoes were taken over to the other end. Warm weather.

Saturday 4th. About 10 a.m. we left "Robinsons" having taken breakfast before starting. Were about three hours on a rock, drying, washing and resting, Camped a few miles from the "Height of Land."

Sunday 5th. Made the "height of land" portage before breakfast. Arrived at the Dams about two or three hours before sunset, and camped on a rock, half an hour's pull above the last launching place.[21]

Robinson's (Robertson's or Whitefalls) Portage was the longest portage on the Hayes River. In 1826, Simpson described it as "being across a Hill of Considerable Elevation and a distance of three quarters of a Mile & performed entirely by Main Strength, our Crews despising the Aid of art, they are not even furnished with a Tackle, which would if judiciously applied render great assistance, a chain of falls on our right as we ascend forms this serious obstruction on this part of our route."[22] Once in Robinson's Lake, the Saskatchewan Brigades crossed the low height of land between the Hayes and the Nelson via the Echimamish River, which flowed both east and west from a pond called Swampy Lake, or Hairy Lake. The dams Charles refers to had been built by the HBC men on the Echimamish River,

replacing the beaver dams that had once kept water levels high enough
to allow easy boat and canoe travel:

> Monday 6th. Pulled through Swampy Lake, where we had the good
> fortune to trade some fish from two canoes of Indians. Put ashore for
> the night a little way below the last Portage or Rapide. Raining almost
> all day.
>
> Tuesday 7th August. Took breakfast on an island immediately
> above the "Derniere Rapide on Monton."[23] The wind being favour-
> able we hoisted our sails and arrived at Norway House about 10 min-
> utes before dinner. After dinner I got all the letters and small bundles
> for the Columbia packed up in the express box. Fine weather.[24]

John Charles's express was already running a week later than
Lowe's had done the year before. Clerk Charles John Griffin, who
travelled west with Charles, had spent time at York Factory, where he
had come to know Governor Simpson. On his arrival on the west side
of the mountains, he wrote the governor a letter describing what he
referred to as his hazardous journey to the West, "rendered much more
so by the infeebled [sic] state of the miserable creatures who accompanied me, the long journey from Canada to here being more
than they were capable of undergoing, however, by encouragement &
perseverance we managed to surmount all our difficulties."[25]

The miserable creatures described by Griffin were the Canadien
and Métis boys new to the express, and the Orkneymen who had just
come in to York Factory on the London ships. All were now adjusting
to the hard work of hauling the York Boats up the Hayes River.

There are many possible reasons that Charles's express might have
been delayed. John Charles was young and had less experience than
most who led the express, although as son of an HBC chief factor he
would have had more authority with his men than many. A number
of his men were brand new to the HBC and to the heavy work of
tracking and rowing these York Boats upstream. Others who had
come all the way from Fort Vancouver and were now returning might
not have had the experience of express-men in the past.

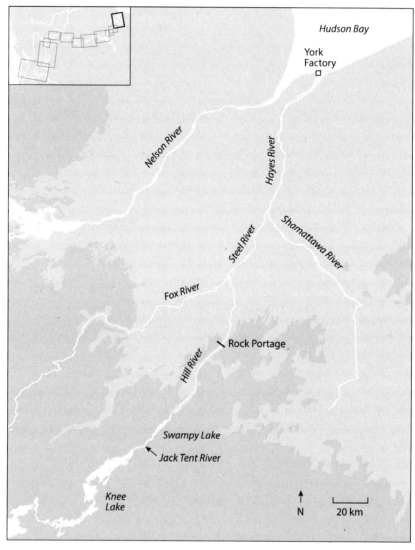

Between Knee Lake and York Factory, the HBC men traversed
more than forty portages, rapids and carrying places.

There were many reasons for this. The most obvious was that many
employees in the Columbia District had abandoned the fur trade for
the excitement and riches of the California gold rush, now in full
swing. As well, many Columbia River employees were killed by the

measles and dysentery that raced through the Columbia District over the winter of 1847–48. These diseases killed thousands of First Nations people and many HBC employees who had Indigenous or Hawaiian backgrounds also succumbed to complications of the disease. Measles destroys the immune system, and many died of the tuberculosis they already had, after being sickened by the measles.

Thomas Lowe's private journals give evidence of the exhaustion experienced by the HBC gentlemen over the winter of 1847–48 as employee after employee succumbed to the measles. The gentlemen doctored the sick and the clerks did the work the employees were unable to do, as well as their own. On December 8, 1847, he wrote that "almost all our working hands are laid up with the measles, and it is only the white who are able to work."[26] Six or eight Hawaiians had died in the first week of the contagion, and more deaths occurred over the following month.

In February, Lowe wrote: "Early this morning Joe Tayentas died of inflammation of the lungs, after an illness of only 4 days. He was guide to York Factory for 8 years running, and was one of the most efficient men in the Columbia. His loss will be much felt."[27] Not only had Thomas Lowe's 1848 express lost the services of their guide; so too had John Charles's 1849 express. Charles's guide was the less experienced Iroquois man named Michel Kaonassé, who was introduced in our prologue.

CHAPTER 11

Norway House to Cumberland House

෧෮

ON THEIR ARRIVAL at Norway House, the Columbia Express men knew that they had completed the most difficult part of their journey, the 400-mile climb up the east side of the Canadian Shield from sea level at York Factory. Oxford House, through which they had passed a week or so earlier, stood 632 feet above sea level, and Norway House at 720 feet. The actual climb, however, was not yet finished. Edmonton House stood 2,200 feet above sea level, and Jasper's House was at an altitude of 3,450 feet. Before the express-men reached Jasper's House (1,712 miles from York Factory), they would paddle or track their way upriver another 2,730 feet above the height of land at Norway House.

In the first leg of this part of their journey, the express-men made their way across the top of Lake Winnipeg. If they followed the northern shoreline of the lake, their journey would be 85 miles in length, as they knew from the trip out. In his 1835 journal, James Douglas described the shoreline past Mossy Point (at the end of the long point of land that separated Playgreen Lake from Lake Winnipeg):

Mossy Point which is about 6 miles distant [from new Norway House] rises abruptly from the water's edge, and during stormy weather the heavy swell breaks angrily against its steep ascent, and renders it at such times quite inaccessible. The coast for 27 miles beyond Mossy Point partakes of the same inaccessible character & forms but one continued unbroken line of abrupt ascent, undistinguished either by bays or rivers wherein a secure harbour might be found in case of boisterous weather, whence it becomes a matter of necessity never to attempt this part of the Lake particularly with loaded craft except when nearly in a calm and tranquil state.[1]

Impatient express-men and fur traders often took risks, rowing or sailing straight across the lake to the mouth of the Saskatchewan River. As Augustus Richard Peers notes: "From the shallowness of their build," however, these boats "are ill adapted for a side wind in a heavy sea."[2] In September 1832, after the Saskatchewan Brigades reached Edmonton House, the clerk recorded that "much risk was run in the crossing of Lake Winnipeg."[3]

In 1827, Edward Ermatinger's York Boats had experienced some difficulty in crossing the north basin of Lake Winnipeg:

[July] 31st, Tuesday. Weather being moderate started after sunrise and rowed to the Mossy Point — here finding that wind was likely to be too much for us we about ship to regain our last Encampment — however afterwards thinking that it had calmed we put about again when about half back — then the wind veered a little to the SW. We were enabled to hoist sail — but we soon perceived that a storm was coming on and had only time to run our boats ashore and get out the cargoes when it began to blow a gale with thunder and lightening [sic] and heavy showers of rain. The place where we were forced to put ashore is a very bad landing and never approached but in cases of danger — here we were fortunate enough to find Tom Firth with two Sask'n Boats who was forced ashore yesterday by bad weather. His people were useful in assisting us to land our cargoes which was done with little damage. One Boat however got two planks knocked out by the violence of the waves before she could be hauled up and 16 of her timbers broken.

August 1st. Fine weather. Wind westerly blowing hard — people employed drying some of our wet things and repairing the boat broken yesterday. Remained here for this night.

2nd. Wind being more moderate loaded the boats and got under weigh about 8 a.m. — rowed along the shores of the Lake till 6 p.m. and then hoisted sail and proceeded with a fresh breeze till night.[4]

They sailed all night, and reached the safety of the Saskatchewan River the next morning.

The Grand Rapids, where the Saskatchewan River "bursts through the ridge of limestone which forms the north-western boundary of Lake Winnipeg,"[5] was a major transportation bottleneck. This was the longest portage these men would make on their entire journey across the continent. Situated only three miles up the Saskatchewan, the Grand Rapids rumbled with extraordinary noise around a long point of land, between limestone cliffs and through gorges that dropped the riverbed seventy-one feet in five miles, with most of the drop concentrated in one three-mile-long section of the river. Beyond the gorges, the land continued to rise for ten more miles before levelling off. But the gentlemen, who did none of the heavy work, had time to notice its beauty. In 1843, clerk Augustus Peers described the scenery at the Grand Rapids:

> The opposite bank of the river curved inwards, forming a beautiful bay whose waters being out of the influence of the current were as tranquil as a mirror and on whose bosom several wild swans were sailing to and fro in all their stateliness, while on some rocks close by a group of pelicans sat with outstretched beaks watching their prey in the water beneath. The expiring sun threw its gold rays on the emerald foliage and added splendour to a scene that would have graced a more southerly clime.[6]

In early August 1827, Edward Ermatinger's party suffered a flurry of troublesome incidents, not all of them common in these brigades. Accidents occurred regularly on this river; it was, perhaps, more unusual that voyageurs attempted to desert the brigades in these years — long before the temptations of the California goldfields were an attraction:

> Had our boats and cargoes over the portage and were ready to start about 4 a.m. However [Bazil] Larance's Boat by mischance got loose just as they were going to load her and was precipitated down the Rapids — fortunately an eddy brought her up before she got far down and in a short time she was brought back safe. As we were about to embark one of our Columbia young hands (Desaire) was missing and as it was thought he had deserted, people were sent off in pursuit. In a short time he came running to the boats in great consternation — it seems he had laid himself down in some part of the Portage and fell asleep which held him longer than he intended. While we were sending for him another man (E. Pepin) actually did desert and we only succeeded in finding him late at night. This fellow added the crime of theft to desertion — for it appears during the time we were occupied on the Portage he had concealed a small bale containing the property of two of his companions and when found he was already rigged out in their clothing. As a punishment he was tied for the night.[7]

In 1847, Thomas Lowe began his journey from Norway House on Saturday August 7. "As the wind was ahead we could not enter Lake Winnipeg, and encamped on an island at the end of Play Green Lake."[8] Later, as his men crossed the lake they were "obliged to run ashore and unload the boats."[9] On August 12, his express boats finally entered the mouth of the Saskatchewan River, where he encountered his first low water of the season in the Rapid River (the Saskatchewan River east of the Grand Rapids):

> The water in the River is low, and the boats will have to make 3 trips over the shallows before reaching the portage at the foot of the Grand Rapid. Most of the boats made two of these trips this evening, and the remainder will be brought up tomorrow.

Friday 13th August 1847. Raining towards evening. This morning the remainder of the pieces were brought up & in course of the day all the cargoes were carried to the upper end of the Portage. Five of the boats were likewise brought up by water, although it is customary when the River is in its proper state to take them across the Portage.[10]

In his 1826 journal, Aemilius Simpson gave a good description of the crossing of the Grand Rapids Portage. Simpson walked to the head of the Rapids where he found a great number of the local Cree encamped at their sturgeon fisheries. The Saskatchewan gentlemen traded for sturgeon, as well as an "abundant suply of Wild fruits, the strawberry, Poyer [Poire] &c which forms a very agreeable repast."[11] Simpson's journal continues:

Our Crews have been Employed in Transporting the Cargos & Boats across the Portage. We had throughout the Day fine & pleasant Weather.

Wednesday 2nd. Very warm and clear Weather.... Our Crews from daylight were employed transporting the Boats &c across the Portage, which is a most laborious operation, having to drag them up a steep Bank of 20 feet & then to Launch them across the Portage, a distance of 1800 yards & whose extreme height was determined by my Mountain Barometer to be 67 feet.[12] At 3:30 p.m. this difficult service being completed we Embarked & continued our ascent of the Saskatchewan, by Tracking and poling against a very strong Current, & with our utmost Efforts, did not advance above a League. At 9:20 p.m., we Encampt for the night, just below the Red Rock.[13] Several Indians having accompanied our Brigade our Encampment this evening presented a grotesque group.[14]

Thomas Lowe's 1847 journal continues from the upper end of the Grand Rapids:

Saturday [August] 14th. The other 6 boats were brought up by water this morning, and we started from the Grand Rapids after breakfast, but as the wind was strong ahead, and we had to put ashore more than once on account of very heavy rains, we only got as far as the head of the Red Stone Rapid.[15]

The Red Rock or Red Stone Rapid was about three miles above the west end of the Grand Rapids. Although the river was wider, its channel was intricate and the water flowed dangerously fast over the broken ridges of rock that jutted into the stream. In 1848, Thomas Lowe came west from York Factory with twenty-six new hands in all, which meant there was a high percentage of inexperienced men on the brigade. Not surprisingly, there was an accident below the Red Rock rapid, on August 9th:

> The Saskatchewan is at present unusually high, and the current strong. An unfortunate accident happened this morning in hauling one of the boats round a strong point below the Rocher Rouge. The Boat sheered round, and the men having been hauled into the water, one of them (a young Canadian named Xavier Silveste [Sylvestre] was drowned. He came up from Canada this season, and was going to the Columbia. His body was not found, as the current swept him into the middle of the River. Breakfasted at the head of the Rocher Rouge, and got up to the entrance of Cross Lake afterward, but as there was a strong head wind blowing we were windbound here.[16]

Lowe said little more about the accident in his journal at the time, but certainly a ceremony of some sort took place at Red Rock — a ritual that would have included a prayer at the riverside. Some might have fired their guns in the air, or thrown tobacco on the water. One man would have made a wooden cross and planted it on the riverside. It is also likely that, as part of the ceremony, the gentleman would have handed out rum.

One more tradition may have been observed. As the men continued their way upriver, they may have created a song called a complainte. The voyageurs always sang as they worked, but after Xavier's death their singing would take a different form. A complainte was a song composed by the voyageurs themselves, a song that commemorated a sad death — a eulogy, in effect, for the man who had died. The complainte might be sung every year as the Saskatchewan Brigades passed this point, or it might be quickly forgotten. But almost certainly, in

1848, the voyageurs created Xavier Sylvestre's complainte and sang it
as they continued their upriver journey.

Thomas Lowe's 1847 journal continues as his party journeys west
from Red Rock Rapid:

> Sunday 15th [August]. Wind strong ahead, and having gone as far as
> the entrance of Cross Lake, remained windbound there the rest of the
> day. The English River Brigade of 3 boats in charge of Chief Factor
> [Hector Aeneas] McKenzie came up to us in the forenoon, and
> camped alongside. The wind fell about sunset, and we then pushed off
> and pulled across the Lake.
>
> Monday 16th. Made a portage at the Grand Descharge [the rapids
> at west side of Lac Traverse] before breakfast. When we reached
> Cedar Lake had a fine side wind, which carried us to Rabbit Point a
> couple of hours before sundown. Had to remain there until the wind
> lulled, and then pushed off about sundown with the oars. Carried on
> until midnight with the assistance of a slight breeze, and put ashore
> near the end of Cedar Lake.
>
> Tuesday 17th August 1847. Pulled through the remainder of Cedar
> Lake this morning, and likewise got through Muddy Lake [Lac
> Vaseux] in course of the day. Camped about 10 miles up the River.
> This has been an exceedingly warm day. The Portage La Loche Bri-
> gade of 6 boats in charge of [Alexis] L'Espérance drifted past us at
> night.[17]

Muddy Lake was well named. In June, Lowe's express boats had
floated over the muddy sandbars in this part of the river with ease. In
August, the water was much lower, and the York Boats made their
way upriver by rowing or poling up the narrow channels of water that
wound between the extensive mud-banks in the bed of the river:

> Thursday 19th. Exceedingly warm. Reached the Pas about 2 p.m.,
> and spent the rest of the day there settling with the Indians who have
> been working in the boats from Norway House.
>
> Friday 20th. Last night 3 Iroquois who were to have gone to the
> Columbia stole a canoe and deserted from the Brigade. It is supposed
> that they went down the River to Norway House. It had evidently

been a preconcerted business, as they decamped with all their clothes and a good stock of provisions. Spent all the morning on the lookout for them but in vain, and started from the Pas after breakfast, having taken in a supply of Pemican. Mr. O'Brien started ahead in a canoe for Cumberland to arrange matters before the Brigade arrives there. Made good progress today as the state of the River admitted of tracking in many places.[18]

Tracking was a major part of the express's upriver journey. Whenever the wind opposed them or the river flowed so heavily against the boats that use of the oars became ineffective, and the riverbanks had good footpaths clear of mud, the men tracked their boats. The "tracking grounds" are sometimes mentioned in these journals, and the location of these grounds might be places where the express-men almost always tracked their York Boats. But in 1847, Thomas Lowe's express-men were able to begin tracking east of Cumberland House because the water in the river was abnormally low.

John Work travelled up this section of the Saskatchewan River in 1823 on his way, via the old route, to Spokane House. His canoe brigade had some difficulty crossing Cedar Lake because of its heavy swell, but they continued their journey next morning. At Cedar Lake, the marshes that were a feature of the Saskatchewan River's estuary replaced the rocks of the Canadian Shield, and the muddy riverbanks plagued the Columbia Express men all the way to the Pas and beyond.[19] Work's journal gives an excellent description of this swampy, boggy section of the Saskatchewan River:

We proceeded part of day up the River through narrow channels formed by Islands where the water was very shallow and nearly choked up with mud. At the lower end of the River the shores and islands are very low composed of soft mud or clay and covered with reeds, & flags [rushes], & here and there some willows to the water's edge. A little further up the river the banks continued still low and are entirely thickly clothed with willows, poplars, &c, they are sometime [sic] so thick that it would appear difficult to get through them, some places there are a few poplar trees but not the appearance of a pine near the edge of the river. Considerable quantities of drift wood, some of it of a large size, in some places deposited along the shore. The banks on both sides of the river are very low and appear to have been over-flowed in the spring. Where we encamped it was so soft & wet that a dry spot could scarcely be found to pitch the tent on.[20]

Thomas Lowe's 1847 journal continues with his arrival at Cumberland House:

Saturday 21st August 1847. Very warm. This evening got as far as the mouth of the River leading to Cumberland Lake, where we encamped, waiting for the return of Mr. O'Brien from the Fort.

Sunday 22nd. Remained at the same place the whole day. In the afternoon Mr. O'Brien returned, and the Cumberland Outfit was taken from the Boats, and put into the Cumberland boat, which of course leaves us here.[21]

In the early years of the York Factory Express, the men took the boats up the two narrow rivers that led to Cumberland Lake, where Cumberland House stood. But the narrow channels eventually silted up, and if the water in the main river was low the entrances were not useful to the express-men.

In 1826, Aemilius Simpson's incoming express entered Cumberland Lake without difficulty, although they took a very complicated path that appears to be different from that used by later Saskatchewan brigades:

Tuesday 8th. . . We struck out of the Main stream into a small channel which led us into a Lake which we proceeded to cross in a Westerly direction for 5 Miles which brought us to a chain of Swampy Channels leading in to the Westward by which Track we cut off a great part of the Distance to Cumberland House. . . . At 8:30 p.m. we put up for the night under a Clump of Willows, having come an estimated Distance of 36 miles during the day. The night presented a rich display of the Aurora Borealis.

Wednesday 9th. At 3 a.m. we continue our Journey & having come about 5 Leagues we arrived at Cumberland House at 8:30.

This Post [Cumberland House] is in a very good order, a considerable extent of ground around it is in a high state of cultivation, yielding abundant Crops of Wheat, Barley & Potatoes, & a garden affording an excellent supply of Vegetables for the Table. The soil appears of an excellent quality being a black loam of considerable depth upon a subsoil of lime stone. The surrounding country is swampy. Pine Island, on which the Post is situated, is low, but bears a good growth of Pines. I saw few Indians at this Post, they were engaged at the different fishing situations, procuring a Winters supply.[22]

In 1835, James Douglas described the variable weather that he and his men had experienced on their way up the Saskatchewan River to Cumberland House.[23] Unsettled weather such as this would be a common experience for all the express-men who travelled these rivers. Even on the prairies, the hot, sun-filled days of summer were regularly interrupted by thunder storms and periods of heavy rain and wind.

In 1827, Edward Ermatinger arrived at Cumberland House from the west but reported that four boats had taken the wrong channel. In 1828, he found the entrance to Cumberland Lake too shallow to enter. In 1847, Lowe's outgoing express boats made their way into Cumberland Lake, but on their return from York Factory the water in the Saskatchewan River was so low they camped opposite the entrance to one of the streams.

One year later Lowe's boat arrived at Cumberland Portage from the west, and Lowe walked across to the fort. On his return journey, however, he attempted to enter Cumberland Lake:

15 Tuesday [August]. Beautiful weather. After breakfast entered a small channel which leads (through a lake) to Cumberland, but as there was not water enough, after working hard and hauling the boats through the mud the whole day, we had to return to the main River by the same road as we came, and encamped at our breakfasting place, at the entrance of the channel, long after dark.[24]

Coming downriver in the high waters of the spring freshets, it generally took eight days to make the 320-mile journey from

Cumberland House to Norway House. But not always: in 1847 Lowe was delayed five days by rain, broken boats, and low water. In 1849, a frozen Lake Winnipeg stopped John Charles's express in its tracks.

Coming upriver the problems were different. The water level in the Saskatchewan was always lower in August than it had been in the spring. The freshets dislodged mud and trees which stuck in shallow parts of the river, changing the channels and confounding the guides who had studied the river on their way down. The silt made the muddy lakes and streams along their course shallower. In almost every year the York Boats took thirteen days to make the journey upriver to Cumberland House from Norway House, which meant they travelled only about 25 miles a day — a far cry from their exciting descent of the river with the freshets.

The next stage of their journey would take them to Carlton House, 275 miles away. But there were good things about travelling up this section of the river: they would be tracking through the most beautiful and historic part of the river, where most of the stories the men told were born. Even better, at the end of their journey the gentlemen, at least, could anticipate an exciting buffalo hunt on the high prairies.

CHAPTER 12

Cumberland House
to Carlton House

§§

FROM CUMBERLAND HOUSE, the Saskatchewan Brigades continued their push up the Saskatchewan River toward its junction with
the North Saskatchewan. Their next stop was Carlton House, 275
miles to the northwest, located on the North Saskatchewan at the
boundary between open prairies and aspen parkland. This was an
ideal location for a fur trade post — near the northern woodlands,
which gave the traders access to furs, but also near the prairies, which
provided pemmican and dried meat from the buffalo grounds. In
1826, Aemilius Simpson described the differences of landscape as
they approached the eastern edge of the open prairie. His party had
left Cumberland House on August 10:

> At 3 we had a severe Thunder storm which continued for some hours.
> As we ascend the Banks of the River become more elevated, but are
> still too Muddy to afford an Encampment. The Trees along the River

are becoming larger; in some instances the Poplar have attained a considerable growth. Having come 25 and a half Miles by estimation, in a very winding direction we put up for the night at 8 p.m. & slept in our Boats.

Friday 11th. Showers occasionally with a strong breeze from the SW which combined with the current against us, retards our progress very much, not averaging a greater rate than about 2 Miles per hour. . . . We pass thru channels formed by Islands, lying in the bed of the River, which appear to owe their origins to drift Wood covered with muddy Deposits.

Saturday 12th. Fine weather, a breeze from the SW. At 3:30 a.m. Embarked & continued our ascent of the Saskatchewan. . . . As the Banks attain height the Current appears to gain additional force. The greatest part of our Journey today has been made by the Track line, which did not average a greater distance than 2 and a half Miles per Hour.[1]

Two and a half to three miles an hour was reasonably good tracking time for these men as they hauled their boats upriver. Their speed depended on how strongly the river flowed against them, and whether the banks of the river were muddy or firm underfoot. Simpson soon learned that this heavy work went on for weeks at a time, with an average travelling distance of 25 miles a day.

In August 1827, Edward Ermatinger started his journey west from Cumberland House:

12th, Sunday. Overcast with rain. Some changes having been made in the Boats cargoes to embark the families of Messrs. McLeod and McDougal we took our departure from the place at 8 a.m. The last Boat arrived at the encampment at 10 p.m.[2]

The women were the wives of Alexander Roderick McLeod of Fort Vancouver and of James McDougall who was suffering from a stroke at Fort St. James, New Caledonia. George McDougall had crossed the Rocky Mountains in the spring to pick up Mrs. McDougall (as mentioned in Chapter 1). Although George McDougall reported that he had spent his summer at Carlton House hunting bison, he must have travelled to Cumberland House to meet the brigades.[3]

Despite Governor Simpson's orders, it was not uncommon for women and children to travel in the York Boats, although they are rarely if ever mentioned in the express journals. In 1835, John McIntosh travelled west as far as Jasper's House with his wife and five children in James Douglas's incoming express. When Finan McDonald retired from the trade in 1827 (as mentioned in Chapter 7), he was accompanied by his wife and children, although no mention is made of them in Ermatinger's outgoing journal.

Edward Ermatinger's journal continues:

13th. Overcast with rain. Embarked at 4 a.m. having made some further alterations to equalize the Boats cargoes. Encamped at half past 8 p.m.

14th. Showers of rain during the day. Started at half past 4 a.m. Passed the River Cebanac [Sipanok] about 10. Encamped at the head of Thoburn's Rapid at 8 p.m.

15th. Slight rain. Wind ahead. Started at 4 a.m. At dusk having arrived at a very shoal part of the River we had much difficulty in passing it and only reached our encampment at half past 10 o'clock. Mr. [John] Rowand's Boat having taken a different channel found it barred at the top and was obliged to remain there for the night.

16th. One shower of rain to-day — part of the crews of the 5 Boats went at daylight to assist in extricating Mr. R.'s boat from its confined situation, which being effected we resumed our journey at 5 a.m. Encamped at 8 p.m.

17th, Friday. Rain afternoon. The Dog Prince having strayed from the Boats yesterday, a man was dispatched in search of him this morning. Started at quarter past 4 a.m. Encamped at half past 8.[4]

It is unlikely that the dogs mentioned in these journals were pets that journeyed with their masters. Probably these animals were butchered when provisions fell short. As Aemilius Simpson noted at Norway House: "The scanty supply of Provisions has reduced our Crews to the alternative of Eating Dogs, which however is considered a choice article of food by some of the old Voyageurs."[5] Ermatinger's journal continues:

18th. Fine weather. Started at half past 4 a.m. At noon came to point La Corne and breakfasted. McKay and Guilbauche fought at the point above — 2 rounds — Guilbauche beaten. Encamped 2 points above Fort a Batosh. Man returned without the dog.

19th. Rained in the evening. Started at half past 4 a.m. Breakfasted at 11 opposite the South Branch. Encamped at 8 o'clock below the 7th of the Cole's Rapids. . . .

20th. Fine weather. Started at 5 a.m. A Point below Campement des Femmes — found a man from Carlton with the meat of 2 Buffaloes, off which we took breakfast. . . . Encamped at half past 7 o'clock above Rapides Croches.

21st. Fine warm weather. Started at 5 a.m. Encamped a point above Sturgeon River.

22nd. Fine weather. Started at half past 4 a.m. At 9 o'clock we were met by Gadana with meat from Carlton. Breakfasted and afterwards hoisted sail with a fresh breeze. . . . Encamped about 8 p.m. in sight of the Steep Banks.

23rd. Fine weather. Mosquitoes very thick. Started before 4 a.m. Sailed for a short distance; arrived at Carlton after 3 p.m. Yesterday it appears the last of a party of about 400 Slaves, Sourcis [Sarcee] and other Indians took their departure after having stolen 7 horses and committed other depredations about the Fort.[6]

— • —

The First Nations peoples were a constant presence on the prairies, and many HBC gentlemen mentioned them in their journals. In August 1826, Aemilius Simpson told the story of a friendly meeting with a party of Crees, who asked for assistance from the gentlemen of the York Factory Express:

Saturday 19th. Commenced heavy rain, with the wind NW, at 4:15 a.m. Embarked & continued our Journey. At 7 a.m. it cleared up and became fine. We discovered on an Eminence skirted with Woods on the right Bank of the River a few Indian Lodges and horses, we put on shore to breakfast that we might communicate with these Indians, whom we found to be a party of Crees, who had been attacked a few days before by a strong War Party of the Blackfeet & Blood Indians, who had succeeded in killing ten of their nation & destroying their property. They however asserted that they had retaliated amply, by killing more than an equal number of their Enemies but no reliance can be placed on Indian authority in such cases, & it is evident they had the worst of it as they were flying out of the reach of the Blackfeet, with the sacrifice of their propertys. They say they were taken by surprize & that the most of their Enemys was dispatch[ed], their apprehensions of another attack is so strong that they have requested that we will cross them & their familys to the opposite Bank, so as to ensure greater safety. This request was readily complied with. These Tribes have perpetual war, for a long time the Crees had the advantage, I am informed, but the Blackfeet & Blood being now as well supplied with Arms and Ammunition, the scale is rather turned against them, & instead of gaining ground they are gradually retiring to the Woody Countrys.[7]

In 1841, George Traill Allan told the story of a conflict with First Nations men that could have led to the murder of three Edmonton House employees. Fortunately, the man-in-charge was respected and the HBC men survived the ambush, although they must have been very frightened:

Mr. [John Edward] Harriott himself, who came to the Country when quite a boy and is much liked by the natives generally, being upon a voyage once, accompanied only by two men, fell in with a band of Assiniboines to whom he was well known and as it is almost a universal custom when we meet Indians to give them where-with to smoke, he drew up his horse and in order to get the Tobacco from his pocket laid his gun for a moment across his saddle, he had no sooner done so than an Indian snatched it up. Mr. Harriott was now defenceless and his two men were in the same predicament, their arms being taken from them by force. To endeavour to retake them was useless; they therefore returned to the Fort, too happy to escape with their lives; and had it been any one but Mr. Harriott ten to one had they never returned.[8]

In 1835, nine years after Aemilus Simpson travelled this route and six years before George Traill Allan told his story, James Douglas filled his journal with observations of every sort. His story begins at Cumberland House:

Monday 17, August. Early this morning left Cumberland House, the entire party of nine boats being in company. Proceeded through the narrow channel leading from Cumberland Lake to the main river which is still very high and is in consequence full from bank to bank.[9] The water is so thick and muddy as to be scarcely fit for use. As we ascend, the banks are more elevated than in the lower parts and are covered with the aspen, poplar, and willows. I observed a red currant bush today. The oar was in constant use the whole day.

Tuesday 18. Continued our journey early this morning and received during the day some trifling assistance from the sail. Country of the same description as yesterday. Encamped a few miles above Sturgeon River.[10] A gentle northerly breeze induced our crews to extend the boat sails, but it proved of short duration, and afforded little relief to the harassed men. At 10 o'clock the tracking lines were put in requisition and were not withdrawn excepting for a very short distance until we had ascended Thoburn's Rapid when the oars were once more set in motion until our encampment a few miles farther on.[11]

Douglas's Thoburn's Rapid was named (with incorrect spelling) for William Thorburn, a NWC fur trader who, in David Thompson's time, had been in charge of a series of posts around what is now Nipawin. Today these rapids are buried under Tobin Lake.

James Douglas's journal continues:

On the opposite side of the river some Crees are encamped who brought us a little venison which they bartered for rum. From Cumberland to the place where we commenced tracking today I did not observe a single stone, there however and along the rapid the beach is in most places covered with stones of different kinds. I notice one or two limestones, blue and grey granite, but the others are unknown to me. In a walk thro' the woods I found the common strong scented black currant, and another kind of black currant, with gooseberry leaf, wood covered with soft weak prickles; berry well flavoured & fursed [sic] colour jet black. Banks covered with the willow, aspen, birch, poplar, and occasionally a few spruce.

Thursday 20. Pretty severe frost during the night, ice formed on the oars. Fine clear weather with oppressive heat during the day. Proceeded today at times with the oar, at others with the tracking lines. The country improved in appearance as we ascend, the banks being of greater elevation and are covered with tall and graceful poplars intermixed with birch, and the dark green foliage of the pine. Passed a number of islands. Some of them rather extensive formed by diverging branches of the river. Reached Pemican Point in the afternoon. Encamped a few miles above Rowand's Portage.[12]

The voyageurs had long memories: "Rowand's Portage" probably referred to the place where, in 1827, John Rowand's men portaged his boats around the sand banks west of Thoburn's Rapids. This is an example of the river's moveable islands, when the freshets swept away the battures in the season of high water and created new islands of gravel and driftwood when the water slowed. James Douglas travelled up this river almost ten years after John Rowand was forced to portage across battures that had blocked the usual channel, and yet the name survived.

James Douglas's journal continues west of Rowand's Portage:

Friday 21 [August]. Rather cold this morning. Left our camp about our usual hour half past 3. At 5 o'clock reached the tracking ground, and travelled with the line out all day.[13]

The place they called the tracking ground was not the only spot on the river where they tracked their boats with lines, but it appears that they always tracked them here. In 1843, a clerk described the hard work done by the men who hauled these boats up a ferocious rapid on the lower river. One end of the tracking line was tied to the boat, the leather straps (the same straps they had previously used to portage their loads) were attached to the other end of the line, one strap for each man. The men leaned into the loop of the strap they wrapped around their shoulders, and hauled the boat up the river:

> Such was the strength of the current, the trackers were often obliged to bend themselves till their hands touched the ground, giving them the appearance of walking on their hands and feet, as in fact they were, for the former served them at times as much as the latter. . . . The bowsman with a long iron-shod pole watched every movement, changing his pole from side to side as occasion required while the steersman plied his long sweep-oar in concert and every now and then cried out at the top of his voice to those on shore to "Haul! Haul! Haul!" when, in fact, they were hauling to their utmost and straining on the line which was brought to an alarming state of tension as the boat creaked and quivered between the contending force of the water and the trackers.[14]

For the most part, on this section of the Saskatchewan River, the work of tracking the boats would not be as hard as this, but it was still wearying work, carried on for hours at a time. At the end of the "pipe" — the traditional measure of distance and time in the fur trade — the men would rest and smoke, or hand off their lines to others who were already rested.

James Douglas's journal continues:

> Saturday 22. Slight rain during the night, and showers with intervals of sunshine during the day. In the evening very heavy rain. Broke one of our boats at Fort du Tremble and were detained one hour & a half in repairing it. Encamped 8 miles below Fort La Corne.
>
> Sunday 23. Constant rain the whole night and during the early part of the day. It ceased in the afternoon & before sunset the sky was clear & unclouded. Passed Fort La Corne at 8 o'clock and 2 hours after Batoche's Fort, and encamped for the night 3 miles below Fort Maranquin.[15]

There were numerous old forts in this part of the river. Fort Aux Trembles was constructed by independent traders and was in business between 1773 and 1777. Fort à la Corne (also called Fort St. Louis) was built in 1753 by Chevalier Louis-François de la Corne and stood just south of the confluence of the North and South Saskatchewan rivers. West of Fort à la Corne was Batoche's Fort or Point. This might be the location of the NWC's old Fort Batoche, which operated for a single season. Finally, Fort Maranquin once stood just east of the deep dramatic valley where the North and South Saskatchewan (Bow) rivers joined to form the Saskatchewan River. Douglas's journal continues:

> Monday 24. Passed the Bow [S. Saskatchewan] River Forks early this morning where a small party of Carlton Crees who have fled the storm of war are resident. It appears from their information that a war party of Blackfeet or Slave Indians have lately visited Carlton with the view of retaliating their spring disasters on the hostile Crees. Having encountered none of their actual or natural enemies to allay their savage rage and to quench their eager thirst of vengeance they directed a portion of their ill will against the Traders, and by way of compensation for other disappointments carried off Mr. Pruden's saddle horses after possessing themselves of the clothes and property of their guardians. No other violence seems to have been committed. Met with an hour's detention in consequence of an accident happening to one of the boats in Cole's Rapids. Encamped at a place called the Women's Camp.[16]

This was Campement des Femmes, a place where First Nations men may have left their families in safety while they went hunting. As this was Cree territory, it was likely the Cree who made this their safe place, out of the way of the Blackfoot and other southern bands that might attack the undefended women. Douglas's journal continues:

> Tuesday 25. Departed at the dawn of day from our encampment, and after a few hours travelling ascended the Crooked Rapid [Rapid Croche] without accident. The sky rather overcast and threatening

but no rain fell. Proceeded with the oar almost all day. Country on both sides of the River of some elevation, wooded with intervals of prairie land.

Wednesday 26. Rained during the night and nearly the whole of the day. Found a camp of Crees at Sturgeon River from whom a quantity of provisions was traded.[17] Encamped nearly 10 miles below the willow banks.

Thursday 27. Rained during the great part of the night. At dawn of day we continued our journey, tho' the weather is by no means favourable for the preservation of the property as the rain still continues.[18]

A clerk who travelled in the York Boats described how uncomfortable it was when it rained. "Rain is a disagreeable thing at any time but particularly in an open boat," he wrote. "True, you may manage to keep yourself dry by submitting to be smothered under the oil cloth, but you soon find this even worse than the rain, and so it was with me. As there was no alternative I chose the lesser evil of the two and submitted to the pelting of the pitiless storm."[19] Douglas's journal continues:

After a few hours rowing a gentle breeze from the North East aided the exertions of the crew very considerably in propelling the boats against the powerful current, and as it gradually increased the oar was entirely laid aside our advance being too rapid to admit of them being used to advantage. Arrived at Carlton at 3 p.m.

Saturday 29. The rest of the boats which we had left behind arrived late this evening. A party of Crees also arrived from a war excursion which they had entered into in conjunction with their allies the Stone Indians. They have been but too successful in executing their barbarous projects, having surprised and by their accounts nearly destroyed a camp of nearly 200 Fall Indians. The leader of the party is the man who holds the knife.[20]

The Fall Indians so often mentioned by the fur traders were the Gros Ventres (Atsina). In his 1835 journal, James Douglas recorded a list of Indigenous tribes who inhabited this country, including additional information on them:

The Blackfeet, 300 Tents
The Piegan, 500 Tents
The Blood, 400 Tents
Gros Ventres or Fall, 250 Tents
Circus, 100 Tents[21]
Crees

The three first named tribes speak the same language and may be regarded as different families, having one common origin. The latter are distinct from the first, and from each other both in language, in appearance, and in the general features of character. The Piegans, Blackfeet and Fall Indians are friendly and well disposed, but the Blood Indians are a fierce and violent people detested by all their neighbours.[22]

It is not always easy to identify the First Nations peoples that the HBC men wrote of in their journals. The Cree were originally Woodland Cree who had followed the fur trade from northern Manitoba and western Ontario, but when they obtained firearms, they expanded into present-day Saskatchewan and Alberta until their numbers were checked by two massive smallpox contagions — the first epidemic in 1781–82, and the most recent in 1837–38.

Although they were entirely separate tribes, the Blackfoot, Peigan, and Blood formed a powerful confederacy to limit the intrusion of the Cree into their territory. The confederacy caused some trouble over the years for the HBC traders.

The Gros Ventres (which translates as Big Bellies) retreated southward into American territory under pressure from the Cree and Assiniboine, and disappeared from the Canadian prairies toward the end of the 1800s.

The Assiniboines, or Stoneys, had also travelled west to the southern prairies from the eastern woodlands and resided mainly in the area of the Assiniboine River.

The Plains Crees had come west with their cousins, the Woodland Crees. One of the modern-day Plains Cree bands is the Checachas, who could be Circus Indians. However, it is more likely Douglas's

Circus Indians were the Sarcee, who inhabited an area next to the Rocky Mountains and spoke an Athapascan dialect used by no one else.

— • —

Every man who was keeping these journals was beginning to show his exhaustion with the long upriver haul from York Factory. Those who came from Fort Vancouver had been away from their home since late March, and it was now mid-to-late August. No one other than Aemilius Simpson is excited, especially as this part of the journey is little more than a long slog against the heavy current of the Saskatchewan and North Saskatchewan rivers. Thomas Lowe's 1848 journal entries for this section of the journey are brief and not descriptive, and John Charles literally mashes his days together:

22nd, 23rd, and 24th August [1849]. The weather during these three days was variable. Met with several Indian canoes, which were laden with furs &c and bound for Cumberland House. On the evening of the 24th we arrived at the tracking ground.

August 25th, 26th, 27th. Tracking from morning until night. About 4 p.m. of the 27th, we had a very heavy shower of rain. Passed a few Indian lodges on the same evening. Saw two horses grazing on the beach.

Tuesday 28th. Pass the Forks of the Riviere Pend D'Oreille [South Saskatchewan River] at 3 p.m. — at half past three came to the foot of "Coal's Falls" where all the hands saving the Boutes per each boat were obliged to track.

Wednesday 29th. At 2 p.m. we reached "Rapides Croches" and at half past four the men put away the tracking lines and took to their oars. Camped at half past seven. Some parts the channel, very shallow indeed. On the beach some of the men in the guides boat found a slip of Birch Bark on which was written the accounts of Mrs. Rowand's decease.

Thursday 30th August. At 1 p.m. we arrived opposite the Sturgeon River where we traded a few sturgeon, some berries, &c from Indians encamped there. Warm weather.

Friday 31st. Pulling and tracking all day. Wind pretty strong towards evening. Encamped below a high bank, a quarter after eight.[23]

On September 1, John Charles's express arrived at Carlton House. John Rowand, who had been travelling with the Saskatchewan Brigade, made haste to return to Edmonton House on horseback to deal with the death of his long-time wife, Louise Humphraville. She was the probable daughter of an earlier HBC and NWC trader named Edward Umpherville who, in 1788, left his Indigenous wife behind when Louise was only three years old. This was not uncommon in the fur trade, and the abandoned wives of Company men had a status among First Nations people that allowed them to secure good second marriages. Daughters, too, were adopted by the wife's new husband and were generally well treated.

Most daughters of gentlemen raised in the Indigenous villages that surrounded the posts were aware they had a Company father, and that, too, gave them status. In 1810, Louise appeared to be a very determined young woman who wanted to acquire the best husband she could find. Whether or not she fixed on John Rowand, she did rescue him when he had a serious fall from a horse out on the prairie where he had been hunting bison. Marriage *à la façon du pays* (in the custom of the country) soon followed, and she brought into the relationship a valuable herd of horses. By 1849, John Rowand and Louise had been together forty years, and Rowand called her his old friend. If Louise was born in 1785, she was sixty-four years old when she died.

Carlton House was on the edge of bison country, and generally had supplies of meat with which to feed the men. Allan, who appeared to be a sportsman who was greatly interested in hunting and in country food, reported that on his arrival at Carlton House in August 1831, his brigade was "regaled by Mr. [John Peter] Pruden, the gentleman in charge with an excellent breakfast on Buffalo stakes."[24] But in 1849, John Charles reported that "No buffalo meat to be had at this Fort in consequence of those animals being at such a distance. The brigade feeding on domestic beef."[25] No other gentleman made mention how they were "regaled" on their arrival at Carlton House, but this feast of steaks, vegetables, and fresh baked bread, would have been a meal to which all the gentlemen and voyageurs looked forward.

CHAPTER 13

Carlton House
to Fort Pitt

֍

BEFORE FORT PITT was built in 1830, the Saskatchewan Brigades travelled straight through to Edmonton House from Carlton, which meant the men were delayed by having to hunt for the food for those who worked on the boats. Hunting and preserving their food were activities that we have seen delayed their arrival at York Factory on the downriver journey and it also slowed their trip home. Aemilius Simpson comments on this in his August 22, 1826, journal entry:

> As this Post cannot furnish a supply of Provisions to our Brigade, it will be necessary to send our Hunter on before us to endeavour to kill Buffaloe which are said to be in great abundance upon the Banks of the River a short distance above here. Our business being brought to a close we embarked at 6:45 p.m. & proceeded to an Encampment at Irroquoise Point.

Wednesday 23rd. Commenced fine clear Weather. We had a heavy dew during the night. At 4:45 a.m. we Continued our ascent of the Saskatchewan, alternately Tracking & Rowing, at 9 we landed to breakfast, our Horse Party joining us, but after breakfast they proceeded to the Hunting ground, Messrs. Rowand & MacMillan accompanying the Hunters. As we ascend Deer are occasionally seen grazing along the bounding Plains, Mr. Barnston succeeded in killing one this afternoon, which afforded us a Venison Supper. These Deer are a small kind resembling the fallow Deer and are called Chevreuil by the Canadians.[1]

The place where the party breakfasted, to be joined by the post's horse party, was called the Montée, and was located close to a ford where the Carlton House men crossed their horses. As was usual, the Carlton hunters accompanied the Saskatchewan Brigades upriver, keeping the men who rowed the boats well fed with fresh meat from their hunts.

After the boats rounded the North Saskatchewan River's bend (the Elbow) and approached Eagle Hill Creek, Simpson writes:

Being anxious to Witness the Hunting of the Buffaloe, I accompanied the Hunting Party, and Mounting our Horses we struck into the Plains in pursuit of that object. . . . Our Hunter Mounted one of the fleetest Horses & went in pursuit of a band of Animals, & was soon out of sight, except occasionally on his showing along the rising ridges in the distant horizon, we could discover him in close pursuit of a band of Cows, out of which he succeeded in killing 2. . . . We took up our abode for the night under the shelter of a few Willows, which to a stranger appears rather an uncomfortable night's residence.[2]

A high wind discouraged their hunting the next day, and Simpson returned to the boats. A few gentlemen "went upon a Pedestrian excursion on the south Bank of the River, and succeeded in killing a few Animals, but not being furnished with Horses to transport the Meat, they were obliged to leave it behind to be devoured by the ravenous Animals of the Plains. Our Hunters were very successful today, having killed nine Cows & to afford them an opportunity of joining us with the Meat we Encampt at 6 p.m. in a very pleasant situation."[3]

The next day Simpson hunted on his own:

In passing between two Clumps of Wood I came in contact with a few Bulls & almost succeeding in killing one, my Ball having pierced his body. On first receiving the shot he made a great leap & then seemed as if going to fall, but to my astonishment he again took to his heels — in fact it is far more difficult to kill one of these Animals than a person would suppose — for unless you pierce him in the heart or brain you seldom bring down the Animal.[4]

That evening, the hunter brought five more buffalo to the camp, and Simpson described the express-men's ability to eat large portions of the roasted buffalo meat:

It is pleasing & amusing to see our Encampment, on first view you might suppose from the immense quantity of Meat set roasting at the different fires that some special feast called for these preparations, as you would suppose it impossible that our men could devour so much at a meal, but on seeing a single man very deliberately attacking six pounds of Meat for his supper, you are soon conscious of the real cause.[5]

By the next evening, the hunters had killed an additional seven buffalo, and Simpson reported that

the quantity of Meat already on hand with the addition of this supply suggested the necessity of preserving a quantity of it according to the Indian Mode, viz Smoking it over fires. We therefore Encampt at 2 p.m. for that purpose. Was salt & other necessarys on the spot, the Animals are so abundant, that any quantity of Meat might be cured, and that of an excellent quality, for the beef of these Animals appears to me as good as our English beef.[6]

By August 30, the hunters had supplied the boat party with more meat than was likely to keep. They had killed and cured the meat of some thirty-seven bison, and left behind the carcasses of three more. Had an entire bison carcass been preserved, at 400 pounds of meat per cow (which were preferred to the bulls), these three dozen animals would have provided something in the neighbourhood of 15,000 pounds of meat. However, in spite of the effort put into drying and preserving the meat, Simpson reported that "Nothwithstanding our late abundance our Provisions was falling short. The Most of the Meat that had been cured, having been spoilt, caused perhaps by the heat of the Weather, but I suspect it was not well cured."[7]

— • —

On August 20, 1831, George Traill Allan's Saskatchewan Brigades pushed away from Carlton House. "The face of the country is now entirely changed," he wrote. "Large plains instead of woods now surround us:

> Monday 22nd. Mr. [John] Rowand having brought six horses from Carlton Mr. Douglas and I went on shore today to take a ride, accompanied by an Indian and Canadian as guides, we rode from 2 p.m. to half past eight when we joined the other gentlemen at the encampment. The horses in this part of the country are small but swift and hardy. During our ride across the plains we fell in with a large company of Cree Indians. The Crees when on horseback and with all their warlike accoutrements have a formidable and fine appearance, most of the present company were mounted and accompanied by an immense number of dogs. Some of them, the dogs, I mean, dragging sleighs, others loaded with parcels of furs etc. We remained nearly an hour talking to them by means of our guide, and then set out to overtake the boats. We now lived in style having taken as much fresh meat from Carlton as the boats could carry.[8]

Within a day or two, the boats were close enough to the new provisioning post that Allan "went on shore today and walked to Fort Pitt, a small establishment under the charge of Mr. [Patrick] Small who received us kindly. We found at the Fort about two hundred tents of Cree Indians. They are in general a quiet people, except when they get liquor, when they become very troublesome. I reached Fort Pitt about an hour before the boats, where I waited their arrival."[9]

— • —

At Carlton House four years later, September 1, 1835, James Douglas concluded his "various arrangements" and "recommenced [his] journey at 6 o'clock [in the] morning. The sky was overcast and threatening rain, but these vapours were quickly dispersed by a brisk northerly breeze which was of great assistance to us during the whole day. Encamped about 6 miles above Ash Island."[10]

On the next day, the express-men were provided with fresh buffalo meat by the Assiniboine Indians, and they camped twelve miles below Lower Eagle Creek. On Thursday, they passed that stream, and Douglas noted the weather was fine, but cold for the season. On Friday, he recorded:

Rather severe frost last night. Many of the people who slept with wet garments or bed clothes found them this morning stiff as boards. The oar is now principally in use the water being too high to admit of any advantage being derived from the line. Sky overcast and frequent showers of rain. Several bands of buffalo were seen by the hunters but none slaughtered.

Sat. 5. A very dense fog occasioned considerable difficulty to the boats, being in continual danger of becoming entangled amidst the numerous flats which obstruct and render the ascent very tedious and circuitous. Beautiful clear day and very warm. Mr. McLeod a gentleman who accompanies us to the Columbia, joined us today at 10 o'clock nearly opposite Battle River. It was near this spot that Mr. [John] Cole after whom the rapids in the lower part of the river are named was shot by a Cree Indian in a transport of jealous rage on account of the seduction of his wife.[11]

Cole's story was told in Chapter 8, and it involved traders from Peter Pangman's Fort Montaigne d'Aigle murdering a chief with laudanum and the Cree men retaliating. Douglas's above comment suggests there was an additional reason for the targeted shooting of John

Cole by the First Nations man, not mentioned in the original reports.

Many stories circulate along this part of the North Saskatchewan River. Some of them are recorded in the post journals that survived; others were told many times until a gentleman recorded them. We don't know if all the stories of this river are true. We only know that they are told.

The Canadien and Métis voyageurs knew the stories of this river, which their ancestors had opened to the fur trade long before a Hudson's Bay man had set foot on the riverbank. The Canadiens and Métis had been told the stories by earlier voyageurs, who had heard the stories from others who had been working for earlier companies. These stories were passed down by word of mouth — or perhaps in song — and were remembered by men who travelled this river every year, paddling past the familiar locations of old posts.

The Canadiens and Métis also remembered the old French names given many years earlier, and they applied new names all along the river as new stories unfolded. (For example, in 1848, Thomas Lowe and his men breakfasted at the Bas-fond de Giboche — a shallow place in the river that might have been named for the man (Giboche) who escaped from Fort Montaigne d'Aigle after John Cole's murder.[12]) With these names, they introduced their French presence up and down this river, and in doing so they claimed the Saskatchewan and North Saskatchewan rivers for themselves forever. These were the voyageurs' rivers, and no HBC Gentleman could take that away.

James Douglas's 1835 journal continues with a new story, along with a reference to an old story that had been passed down for decades:

[September 6] Clear warm weather. Encamped 7 miles Basfond Desnoyer. Early today a poor Red deer [Elk] which was hotly pursued by a pack of fierce wolves was observed rushing at full speed down the hills on the opposite side directly towards the river. This circumstance having engaged our attention the foremost boats stopped to await the issue of the pursuit. On gaining the water the red deer dashed into the stream with reckless haste having distanced all its pursuers. The boats lying close ashore were not perceived by the poor animal until within 50 yards when a badly aimed shot gave intimation of its danger. Gun after gun were discharged without effect. The deer crossed the river and was seen coursing through the prairie apparently uninjured having escaped with equal good fortune both from wolves and hunters.

Monday 7. Fine clear weather, and strong westerly breeze which considerably retarded our progress. Landed on the upper or South Western extremity of Basfond Desnoyer at half past 9 and were detained there waiting the arrival of a boat which had fallen far behind until midday. Passed Manchester House or Fort Brulé so called from the manner in which it was destroyed by the Fall Indians, at 5 o'clock, and we encamped near 9 miles above it.[13]

Douglas only needed to mention Manchester House and its nickname, as everyone in the fur trade would know the details. This fort had been one of five posts that once stood on the North Saskatchewan River's Pine Island, 400 miles west of Cumberland House. It was built by the HBC in 1786, and stood close to the NWC's Pine Island Post.[14] In 1793, the Gros Ventres attacked the post and took it, stripping the employees of trade goods and personal possessions. The HBC abandoned Manchester House, and it was burned (brûlé) to the ground a year later.

— • —

In 1849, John Charles remained with the boats, continuing to update his journal. His entries ceased on his arrival at Edmonton House. Charles's boats left Carlton House on the afternoon of September 2, and "a party with 14 horses started the same time by the opposite side of the river in order to hunt buffalo to feed the hardworking men of the Saskatchewan Brigade."[15] They had enjoyed little success, but were soon to have better luck:

[September 4] About 1 p.m. we waited for the boats to cross our horses to this side of the river, where we thought of having better success. Two Buffalo bulls were killed today — one by [Jean-Baptiste] Carlton & the other by a man out of the boats.

Wednesday 5th. This morning about 11 o'clock, Mr. Harriott dispatched 5 of the best hunters in the brigade on horseback, the boats to wait for their return. One of them returned late at night with an animal. . . .

Thursday 6th. At 6 a.m. the hunters arrived with 4 other animals which were equally divided between the 10 boats.[16]

The men brought some seven animals to the boats for provisions. On Saturday evening, they "Camped above Battle River about half past 5 p.m. where we met a boat full of dried and fresh meat sent down from Fort Pitt for the brigade."[17]

The brevity of John Charles's journal entries shows the wear and tear of the long trek to Hudson Bay and return. By now, the men had been away from their homes at Fort Vancouver for five months, and had travelled more than 3,700 miles. They had 100 miles to go to reach Fort Pitt, and 300 miles to reach Edmonton House. By late August, they still faced two months and another 485 miles of upriver travel before they crossed the mountains and felt they were in reach of home.

Weariness might be a reason for not making journal entries. A shortage of writing implements for writing might also be a cause. In those days, pens and ink were not easily transported — pens were goose quills, and ink came in cakes or bottles. A shortage of paper is not a reason, at least not in 1849, as there remain a number of blank pages in Charles's original journal.

Another possibility is suggested by Thomas Lowe's 1848 journal, which was written on sheets of paper, covered with ink on both sides, kept folded in Lowe's pocket and transcribed into his small leather-bound journal when he had time. The wording changes in places as he does so. It is possible that some men kept their entire journal on sheets of paper without ever transferring the information into an actual journal. Perhaps there are many unrecognized segments of York Factory Express journals written on loose sheets of paper, stored away and lost.

For whatever reason, the men were exhausted and bored; the

gentlemen's journals were brief and to the point. Only Aemilius Simpson and James Douglas appeared to take enough pleasure in their journey to record their thoughts. But even they must have looked forward to the civilization of the HBC headquarters at Edmonton House, at this point still 217 miles to the west.

This photograph shows both the location of the old fort on today's Rossland Flats (see the man lying on Rossland Flats), and the second location of the post where it stood high on the hill above the North Saskatchewan River. (COURTESY: LAC, MIKAN 3303099)

Thick woods, fallen trees, and massive bogs made the pack-horse journey across the Athabasca Portage difficult at all seasons, but especially in wet weather. (COURTESY: GLENBOW ARCHIVES, NA-3934-16)

View of the Athabasca River at Prairie Creek. When the express-men got their first sight of the Rocky Mountains at the "Mountain View," they celebrated the fact that they were approaching their home territory and the end of their long upriver journey to the west.
(COURTESY: GLENBOW ARCHIVES, ND-18-11)

The second Jasper's House, looking toward the Northwest at the mountains behind. Photographer Charles Horetzky (1872).
(COURTESY: GLENBOW ARCHIVES, NA-382-5)

The Committee's Punch Bowl at the summit of Athabasca Pass. There are many traditions connected to this historic lake, which every man, woman, or child passed, as they travelled across the Rocky Mountains by Athabasca Pass. (COURTESY: GLENBOW ARCHIVES, NA-3490-26)

The Rocky Mountains from Boat Encampment on the Columbia River, May 2, 1846. Henry James Warre. Every man who reached Boat Encampment from Jasper's House looked back in awe at the impressive range of mountains they had just crossed. (COURTESY: LAC, MIKAN 2834211)

This image, drawn in the 1840s, describes the same sort of First Nations scene that Aemelius Simpson had seen in 1826, as he came into the Columbia district with the first incoming express. (COURTESY: ROM, B-10483)

The Columbia River above Sioux Island Rapid, Washington. Henry James Warre. No one now knows where the Sioux Island Rapid was, but it was probably in the Nespelem Canyon east of Fort Okanogan. (COURTESY: LAC, MIKAN 2834204)

In 1811 Fort Okanogan was established on the Okanagan River, on a
flat of land half a mile from the Columbia. By 1826 it appears to have
moved south to the junction of the Okanogan with the Columbia River.
(COURTESY: GLENBOW ARCHIVES, NA-1274-17)

As the incoming Columbia men approached The Dalles, the last major
barrier on the Columbia River, they enjoyed a clear view of Mount Hood
ahead of them. (COURTESY: LAC, MIKAN 2834205)

The North Saskatchewan River snaked its way between
high river banks until it reached Edmonton House.
(COURTESY: GLENGOW ARCHIVES, NA-1328-175)

The North Saskatchewan River at Batoche, Saskatchewan, 1950s.
The open grasslands of the unsettled prairies was a beautiful sight to the
HBC gentlemen, but the gravel battures caused a great deal of trouble
for the express-men. (COURTESY: GLENGOW ARCHIVES, NA-3632-60)

Portrait of Governor George Simpson of the HBC.
His fur trade employees called him "the Little Emperor".
(COURTESY: BCA, PDP02186)

The incoming Columbia Express men and their pack-horses travelled
from Jasper's House all the way down the Mountains to Boat Encampment,
at the junction of the Columbia River with Wood River.
(COURTESY: GLENGOW ARCHIVES, S-233-68)

Fort Vancouver, at the mouth of Columbia River, Washington Territory,
1853. In 1846 the HBC's Fort Vancouver was surrounded by gardens and
farmland. After 1849 the property was shared with the U.S. Army.
(COURTESY: GLENGOW ARCHIVES, NA-1274-19)

CHAPTER 14

Fort Pitt to Edmonton House

§⸙

THE NORTH SASKATCHEWAN was a complicated river that changed its character many times over. In the spring, the Saskatchewan Brigades had descended the river so quickly that the men barely noticed its transitions. But in late summer, they pushed their boats up a very different river, travelling considerably more slowly and with more effort, and the gentlemen who wrote the journals had time to notice the varying landscapes that surrounded them. They also noticed the river's heavy flow, which at Fort Pitt seemed to gather strength and push against them more strongly than it had done before. In late August to mid-September, when they were making the homeward journey, the river was shallower than it had been in the spring. This created a different set of problems for the men, whose boats grounded on the gravel bars that were now barely covered by the river's water.

"The River is becoming Narrower," Aemilius Simpson reported

when he passed the North Saskatchewan's junction with Vermilion, "not Averaging a greater breadth than 150 yards, which is not above the half it had some distance below here. Its course is occasionally obstructed by rapids, formed by projecting points of rounded stones, obliging our Crews to use the track line principally today."[1]

This was one of two rivers named Vermilion during the fur trade era. One, now called the Redwater River, is in Alberta, north of Edmonton and Fort Saskatchewan. The other, which Simpson mentions, tumbled into the North Saskatchewan from the southwest, at a place where the Saskatchewan flowed through "a well-defined valley with deep cuts in the landscape," according to Simpson. "For about 2 Leagues below Vermilion Creek the River has a bend South & SW, when it gradually turns again from the West & NW. My observation placed the latitude of the junction of the Vermilion Creek, at 53° 39' North. Opposite its Mouth there were two Trading Posts, situated on a Low point upon the South Bank (& the opposite one to the Vermilion Creek) before the Coalition."[2]

The two posts that had once existed opposite the mouth of Vermilion Creek were the NWC's Fort Vermillion, and the HBC's Paint River House. Both had disappeared ten years before the "coalition" Simpson refers to, which was the merging of the NWC and HBC in 1821.

"The face of the country continues the same as that passed yesterday," Simpson noted. "For some days the Moskitos had disappeared, but the great heat & rain today, brought them back in great numbers to our great annoyance."[3]

In 1835, when James Douglas's party left camp just south of Vermilion Creek, he observed "a luminous circle or halo around the moon, and sky wearing a rather threatening aspect." He concluded "that a change of weather was not distant, and truly enough for about 7 this morning after ascending Frog Rapid [at Frog Creek] the rain commenced falling rather heavily and continued throughout the day."[4]

Aemilius Simpson gave an excellent description of this stretch of river:

The course of the river has been very Winding, with numerous rapids on rounding the projecting points, rendering the Tracking a very difficult duty, our men are frequently obliged to Wade out to their Middle, in the River, where the projecting Points of rounded stones, or Battures, makes it necessary to keep the Boats a distance offshore.[5]

The next landmark these men passed as they travelled north and west from Vermilion Creek was the mouth of Moose Creek, a river that would take them northeast to a lake of the same name if they had wanted to go there. "At 9:15 we passed Moose Creek," Simpson wrote, "a small stream falling in on the left [right] or North Bank. I am told it communicates with a lake of the same name [Moose Lake], & then by making a few Portages to a chain of small Lakes we get to Beaver River, which communicates to the Athabascaw [Athabasca]."[6] For many years this was one of two or more routes into the Athabasca District.

The NWC's Fort George had once stood close to the mouth of Moose Creek. Constructed in 1791, Fort George gave the company's men access to the rich furs of the Athabasca via Moose Lake and Lac la Biche (Doe Elk Lake).[7] The HBC followed, building Buckingham House less than a mile upstream from the NWC post. By 1800, these two posts had trapped out the furs and moved farther west, to Fort de L'Isle. Although by 1826 the old site of Fort George had been long abandoned, the men in Aemilius Simpson's brigade still acknowledged its history. "At 4 p.m. we passed the ruins of Fort George, an old Establishment situated on the right [left] or North Bank."[8] Simpson described the country that surrounded the abandoned post:

The Country along the right or South Banks of the River, is now covered with extensive Forests, consisting principally of the Poplars, on the left, the Country is a mixture of Forests & plains, with swamps in some places.[9]

It may confuse the reader that Simpson described the south bank of the river as the "right," when it is clear that, as they ascended the North Saskatchewan River, the right side of the river was to the north, and the left to the south. His usage reflects a fur trade convention that holds true everywhere in the exploration journals of the time, even on the west side of the Rocky Mountains. Riverbanks are described as "right" or "left" based on their location as men descended the rivers. These men were going upriver — hence, the left bank was the bank on the left as they went downstream, the north bank, although it was actually on the right-hand side as the boats ascended the river.

In 1827, Ermatinger's men took breakfast at "the Old Fort below the Dog Rump Creek,"[10] probably a reference to Fort George, although there was at one time a post just south of Dog Rump Creek. Eight years later, James Douglas writes: "Passed Lovers Rapid at 2 p.m. and encamped 2 miles below the old fort of Dog Rump Creek,"[11] also likely a reference to Fort George. The fort is not mentioned in later journals. Perhaps it slipped from the men's memories because it was no longer visible from the river, and by 1835 many of the logs that belonged to the old fort had been floated downriver to build Fort Pitt.

Dog Rump Creek was ten miles or so northwest of old Fort George and had been named for a nearby ridge of hills that resembled, to some imaginative Canadien, the rump of a dog. James Douglas noted, "The banks of the river are on both sides covered with wood but we still have at times a distant view of the lofty smooth hills peering out from beyond the intervening thickets."[12] Aemilius Simpson noted the Dog Rump Creek post was "situated on a low Point of Meadow Land, on the Left Banks of the River. About here the river is very rapid & Winding."[13]

As his men departed Dog Rump Creek post, Ermatinger noted that the "Wind still continues to favour us and assists us in ascending many strong rapids. Continued sailing till 6 o'clock in the evening when it calmed and we proceeded tracking till half before 8 and encamped at 4 or 5 miles above the Island House."[14] Island House, or Fort de L'Isle, is where the XY Company's post of the same name was constructed in 1799. It did not last long. James Douglas hints at the tragedy that occurred there. "At half past 2 reached Fort de L'Isle where the deceased King shot by Lamothe lies interred."[15]

Fort de L'Isle had been constructed on an island in the river (near present-day Myrnam, Alberta) by the short-lived XY Company. The post competed with both the HBC's Buckingham House and the NWC's Fort George. Within a year, both those posts had moved up-river to compete more directly with the XY Company's post. The NWC "bully," James King, worked out of the new Fort George, and young Joseph-Maurice Lamothe was employed at Fort de L'Isle.

"Bully," as has been seen, was an actual position in the fur trade of the time, and as the title "bully" implies, King was a large, strong man who was willing to intimidate. Yet these two men from competing companies appeared to be friendly. Both King and Lamothe had been warned by their superior officers not to travel together to the First Nations villages to trade, and both ignored the advice.

At a tent in a village some distance from the post, James King claimed some of the furs that the much younger Lamothe had collected in trade. Lamothe refused, and the men struggled for possession. In the fight, Lamothe shot and killed King.

He was charged, in Canada, with murder, but since the crime scene lay outside the borders of Upper and Lower Canada, it was not clear if the courts there had jurisdiction. This led to the creation of the Canada Jurisdiction Act, passed in 1803 by the Parliament of England, which ensured Canadian courts had jurisdiction over crimes committed in the fur trade country.

North and west of Fort de L'Isle, James Douglas wrote of the Rapid of Bas-fond du Lac des Œufs (Egg Lake):

> While at this place, a gentle easterly wind which had been gradually increasing in strength since morning induced the men to elevate the mast, and after concluding our meal the sail was spread to the breeze which carried us forward so rapidly as to render the exertions of the crew unnecessary, a respite from labour which is very acceptable to the poor fellows who are dreadfully fatigued by the long continuance of the toils.[16]

Ten years earlier, Aemilius Simpson had also reported that his boats were "favoured with a fair Wind for some hours which gave our Crews considerable relief from the labour of Tracking."[17] Once the mast was erected and the sail drawing the York Boat upriver, the men stopped their heavy work. The clerks lay back on the packs, and the tired voyageurs slept, or brought out their playing cards.

There were many traditions developed over the years of sailing up and down this river when the men could erect their simple square sail and let the wind do the work for them. One man must always watch the sail, ready to react quickly when the wind grew too strong. But the others relaxed and almost certainly gambled.

In later years, the Cree men who worked the York Boats played poker. But in the 1840s, these men would have played a simpler version of the game, such as Vingt-et-un (Blackjack), or an earlier version called Trente-Un. Faro is a possibility, as are early poker variations called Poque and Bouilotte.[18] Some men may have brought out their fiddles, playing some of their traditional tunes to entertain the others: one man might play his fiddle with a bow, while another corded his fiddle, fingering and strumming the fiddle strings as if it were a guitar.

These men called the wind *La Vieille* or the Old Woman. Even in the midst of their card games, the voyageurs paid attention to the speed of the boat, yelling at the Old Woman if the boat appeared to be slowing. "Let the wind do the work" was the attitude here, and these men often sailed along a particularly straight stretch of the river where the wind seemed to serve them well. Eventually it would die, and the hard work of rowing or tracking up the North Saskatchewan River continued as before.

The Crooked Rapid was the next landmark along this river, some twenty miles west of Fort de L'Isle. Aemilius Simpson noted that "the course of the River is if anything becoming more Serpentine, & the rapids more frequent, making the labour of Tracking very severe. In the Evening we passed a very strong chain of Rapids, The Crooked Rapids, formed by a very sudden bend of the river."[19] In his journal,

James Douglas remarked that his party "Encamped four miles [from] the Crooked Rapid. Heard the calls, consisting of a loud whistle, of a great number of Red deer on the hills bordering the river. The buck red deer is at this season in full flesh and his branching antlers are now grown to their full size, and as he stands looking proudly from the lofty smooth hills amongst which at this season he delights to ramble appears the most superb animal of the deer kind."[20]

In contrast, Edward Ermatinger noted, "several lines broken at this rapid."[21] A broken tracking line meant that the men hauling the boat fell forward onto the beach. This was one of the occasions that the patient, hard-working Canadiens, who were known for their colourful curses, fell into fits of full-scale swearing.

By this time, every man in the York Boats must have felt the excitement of approaching home. The Edmonton House men were almost home; and although the York Factory Express men from Fort Vancouver still had more than a thousand miles to travel, they could anticipate the end of their journey. Although they were close to Edmonton House, they must still follow the great northern sweep of the river around its massive bend. Simpson noted that, from the Crooked Rapids, "the Journey has been made to Edmonton, I am informed, in one day by Dogs & Sledge."[22] It was approximately 155 miles as the crow flies to Edmonton House from Fort Pitt, but some 217 miles by water.

Douglas's crew continued to sail upriver until they passed Terre Blanche, or White Mud Creek. "The easterly wind still continues and we are not dilatory in availing ourselves of its assistance,"[23] he wrote. Simpson reported that White Mud Creek was about twelve miles upriver from Crooked Rapids. "We passed a small stream coming from the NW called the White Mud River, on account of a fine White mud found on its Banks, which the Indians use for Whitening their leather robes."[24] In their frequent perambulations up and down the North Saskatchewan River, both the HBC's Edmonton House and the Nor'Westers' Fort Augustus had stood for a while on the banks of the White Mud Creek.[25]

The express had now passed the northernmost bend of the river and followed its snaking course to the west, once again entering the steep-banked section east of Edmonton House. Here, according to Simpson, "The Banks of the River now rise into steep Cliffs of Considerable Elevation, the interval between these being Hilly ridges, those on the South Bank densely Wooded. The face of the Cliffs present Coal strata with very fine quarries of free stone, having a yellow hue & apparently of an excellent quality."[26]

In this stretch of the river, James Douglas's crews passed over a rapid they called Lac de Vivres, and encamped at half past 7. Some five hours after they set off the next morning, they passed the Rivière des quartre Poteaux, or Four Post River, that flowed in from the northeast. One hour's travel west of the Four Post River, past three or four sets of rapids on a bending river, they reached the Carp (Namepi) River.

A short distance above the Carp, where an island extended along the bed of the river, the North Saskatchewan bent southward, and the men now headed straight for Edmonton House. There were no more major diversions in this winding river. The Edmonton House men were, at last, reaching for home. For the Fort Vancouver men, Edmonton House was a major milestone on their way home.

However, they still had some distance to travel. Simpson reported:

> The course of the River has been very Winding some bends turning to the SE. We passed several tributary streams. Rapids occurred. I am informed the Interior Country from here, is no longer plains, but is very Woody & intersected by Swamps. Our Tracking path has been very bad today, being in many places a soft adhesive Clay, & the Men were frequently obliged to Wade nearly up to their necks in crossing the Mouths of the several small streams falling into the River.[27]

Douglas's party camped one mile above the Three Islands, where the ochre-coloured Vermilion (Redwater) River fell into the North Saskatchewan. Simpson described the Redwater as "a considerable Rivulet coming in from the North. From here to Fort Edmonton is only a short day's Journey on foot, tho' owing to the Serpentine course of the River & strength of the Current, it occupies the Boats generally two."[28] His party camped that night above a chain of rapids at the base of an elevated clay cliff. The next morning Simpson wrote:

> From our mornings Encampment the course of the River is particularly Winding, and bounded by very high cliffs, whose surfaces present a double Strata of Coals. Petrifications are very abundant on the Banks of the River. A little Distance within the Summits of the High cliffs, on the right Bank of the River, the country opens out into plains, on the left, or within a bounding rise or Bank taking its rise some distance from the bed of the river & running parallel with its course nearly & leaving a Margin of low Meadow Land between it & the River, from the Summit of this Bank the country presents a broken surface of Woods & Swamps intersecting it, tho' it is generally level — the distant ridges of Hills having little elevation.[29]

Aemilius Simpson's brigade arrived at Edmonton House, at that time in its Rossdale Flats location, on September 9, 1826. Edward Ermatinger's 1827 brigades pulled in on September 10, having taken eight days from the approximate location of the future Fort Pitt.

Unlike the journal-writers who came before him, George Traill Allan wrote nothing of his upriver journey to Edmonton House, where he arrived on September 4, 1831. By this time, the Saskatchewan headquarters had moved from its Rossdale Flats location and was "a very complete and handsome Fort." He described the fort as follows:

> It is built upon a very high bank of the River Saskatchewan and is surrounded by plains and woods. As the Indians who frequent it are dangerous some pains have been taken in making it efficient. A high well-contrived balcony is built all the way round, from when in times of danger an enemy's approach can be seen from a great distance. . . . Nor did the inside of Fort Edmonton belie its outward appearance as we found ourselves very comfortably lodged and entertained by Mr. Rowand with the greatest hospitality, fed upon excellent moose deer

and buffalo meat we might well have challenged all the tables in London to produce us something better. I had here an opportunity of seeing a couple of Blackfoot Indians. They are a fierce looking race and such treacherous villains that they have been know[n] whilst smoking the pipe of peace in one end of a camp of other Indians, to have committed murder in the other, nor do they pay any respect to the Whites but on the contrary, cut them off whenever they find themselves the strongest.[30]

In 1835, James Douglas's single boat, "pretty strongly manned and with less loading than the others in order to proceed on ahead of the brigade,"[31] reached Edmonton House on September 16, having left Fort Pitt on September 10.

In later years, the gentlemen took a different route to headquarters, leaving the men to work the boats upriver alone. In 1847, Thomas Lowe wrote that from Fort Pitt, "We started on horseback this morning [September 16] after an early breakfast, accompanied by one of the men of the fort as a guide. Took dinner at Frog Creek, and went on afterwards until we reached a lake on this side of Dog Rump Creek, where we camped."[32] The horse party set up camp the following night at a small stream not far beyond Egg Lake. They followed the north bank of the river around its big bend and camped close to Redwater River that evening, arriving at Edmonton House two days later, on September 20. In 1848, Lowe crossed the North Saskatchewan River south of Vermilion Creek and rode west by a chain of lakes, past Bute Noir and Eagle's Nest Creek.

The travelling conditions for the boats coming upriver from Fort Pitt varied. In 1847, Lowe's boats were delayed by bad weather and wind, and pulled into Edmonton House on September 23, three days after Lowe had reached the place. The next year at Fort Pitt, he "had the [Fort Pitt] Outfit taken out (more than 100 pieces). As the water is very low the whole of the 8 boats are to go up (although it is usual to leave one here). They start from here with 65 pieces per boat."[33] The "Outfit" is the years' supply of trade goods, and each "piece" weighed up to eighty-five pounds. They had unloaded 10,000 pounds of trade goods on their arrival at Fort Pitt, and carried almost 6,000 pounds away. Still, it took his boats only seven days to cover the distance from Fort Pitt to Edmonton House.

On September 13, 1849, John Charles departed Fort Pitt in one of nine boats, but recorded that "Messrs. Harriott, [Alexander] Young, [John Charles] Griffin and Frederick Lewes are to proceed on horseback across land to Edmonton House.

"Friday 14th. After breakfast all the boats hoisted sail and the wind being light aft we were enabled to come a great distance today."[34] On Saturday, they tracked the boats upriver in fine clear weather, and the same work continued for the next five days. "Men tracking from morning until night. Passed two camps of Freemen who were camped near the river sides. No animals of any sort to be seen."[35] "Freemen were ex-employees of the Company, who remained in the country, trapping and trading for themselves." Freemen were on the Athabasca River and at the Pas, but it would appear this is the first place they are mentioned on the North Saskatchewan River. Charles's journal ends here.

— • —

Aemilius Simpson gave an excellent description of Edmonton House on Rossdale Flats, and of the celebrations that occurred after the arrival of the Saskatchewan boats:

> Fort Edmonton is the most important Trading Post on the Saskatchewan. It is situated on the North Bank of the River & is in a good state of defence against Indian attack, a very necessary precaution, as the Indian Tribes visiting it are formidable, viz. The Blackfeet, Blood & Crees.
>
> There is a considerable extent of farm adjoining the Fort, which is now under an abundant Crop of Wheat, Barley, Oats & Potatoes — and a garden producing excellent vegetables. There is an extensive range of Pasture Land, also along the Bank of the River, affording an abundant Provision for Horses. Deer are very numerous in this Track of country — of the red deer Tribes principally. Bears both of the Black & grizzle kind are also numerous.[36]

Simpson spent several days at the Saskatchewan District headquarters while the men prepared to cross the newly constructed Athabasca Portage to Fort Assiniboine. It had rained heavily, so no one knew exactly what to expect on this first crossing from Edmonton House. On the evening of September 12, however, Simpson and his men were given a grand send-off:

> Mr. Rowan[d] favoured us with a Ball, in the Evening, which appeared to diffuse a great deal of delight, & pleasure amongst the numerous partakers of the Amusement. All appeared anxious to decorate themselves in their best attire, and altho' among so many there were some grotesque figures, yet the general appearance of the group was very pleasing, and I was not a little amazed to see Scotch reels, and even Country Dances, danced with a spirit & grace that would not disgrace a far more refined society. Among the half breeds and Canadians particularly, I observed some excellent dancers, & the half breed girls, tho' evidently not so proficient in that Art, made a very good appearance & seemed much pleased with the Entertainment. We have all reason to feel obliged to Mr. Rowan[d] for his great Kindness & hospitality since our arrival at his Establishment.[37]

CHAPTER 15

Edmonton House to Jasper's House

§∂

AFTER A FEW DAYS' rest at Edmonton House, the voyageurs of the Columbia Express resumed their homeward journey, taking the 90-mile "Assiniboine" (Athabasca) Portage to the new post of Fort Assiniboine on the north bank of the Athabasca River. The goods were carried over the portage by pack horses, and in the late 1820s this could be a difficult journey, as the trail had only been created in the winter of 1825–26.

Aemilius Simpson continued to record his experiences, describing how he stumbled through dangers other HBC traders did not mention because they were so familiar. On September 13, 1826, he wrote, "As the loaded horses cannot travel very expeditiously, I with several of the gentlemen continued at the Fort for the night, with the intention of following in the morning."[1] His journal continues:

September, Thursday 14th. Commenced cold but fine weather. After breakfast Messrs. Jon Stewart [John Stuart], [Joseph] McGillivray, [George] Barnston & myself mounted our horses & commenced our Journey across the Portage. At Noon we arrived at the Sturgeon River, which we crossed in a small thin Canoe. . . . On arriving at a small Creek Mr. Barnston followed a different Track, to what I conceive our Brigade had followed. I pursued what I thought the right one — until I arrived at a Deep Swamp & stream, when I began to suspect I had followed the wrong road. I therefore began to retrace my steps, but found Mr. McGillivray coming by the same Track. I returned again with him, & Crossing the Swamp & stream (which obliged the Horse to swim almost) we came up with the Brigade a short distance beyond it. Encampt. While retracing my steps in the dusk I had a rather un-wished for meeting with a Bear, but on taking a short survey of me, he turned into the Woods.

Friday 15th. A very coarse night, rain, sleet, with Thunder & Lightning. . . . We continued our Journey at 10 a.m. & pursued our route, by a road almost impassable to Man or Beast — the Horses & their loads frequently falling into swamps & ruts, in which they almost disappeared, & it required extraordinary efforts at times to extricate the poor Animals from their very uncomfortable situation, and calling down upon them the Most Awful imprecations from their Canadian guides.[2]

The curses were both colourful and descriptive: rough verbal ex-changes were part of the coarse and familiar language of the Cana-dien voyageur. Their swear words were creative, and generally based on their religious experiences. "Sacré," "mon Dieu," and "baptême" were used freely. They cursed the difficulty of their situation, they cursed the horses and the mud. Their curses were rarely if ever obscene, and in this instance eased a tense situation. Cursing made the work easier, and it amused their companions:

In the Tracks leading through the Woods, the loads, which were slung over the sides of the Horses projected so far, that they were constantly coming in contact with Trees & Branches, to the great injury of the loads, & to add to the comforts of our Journey it rained throughout the day. We traveled until 5 p.m. when we Encampt for the night, having come 14 miles by estimation, in a Winding course to the NW, over a broken & almost inaccessible face of country intersected by Swamps & Woods which afforded hardly a Track Sufficient for the Horses to get through.

Saturday 16th. Constant rain During the night, but cleared up at 6 a.m. At 8 a.m. proceeded on our Journey, over a continuance of extremely bad roads, leading thro' Woods, Quagmire & Marshes. At 2 p.m. We Crossed the Pembina River, a considerable stream, which the Horses forded, but not without having Wet'd some of their loads. We found a Canoe on the right or South Bank of the River, which was launched for the purpose of transporting a few of the Casets [cassettes], particularly my Instruments & Book Cases.[3]

As was explained earlier, these cassettes were travelling boxes with compartments to hold personal belongings.

Simpson's express party continued their journey over the portage, and he estimated that day that they had travelled "eighteen miles tending to NW, over the worst road I certainly ever saw travelled."[4] The next day they awoke to a sharp frost that formed a thin coat of ice on the lakes. They continued their journey through meadowland bounded by woods, and stopped for two hours to rest the horses. That night they encamped "in the skirt of a Wood, which formed a very comfortable Encampment. We travelled 15 Miles between North & West."[5] The next day:

Monday 18th. A hoar frost during the night with clear Weather. At 5:30 a.m. We commenced our March, & traveled through a Point of Woods until 8:30, Many parts of the Track being very bad, the Horses sinking under their loads up to their necks nearly. We breakfasted on the North side of the River Cruz [Cruche],[6] a small but deep stream. At 11 We resumed our Journey, passing several Creeks, Swamps & Points of Wood, where the Track is frequently almost impassable from the immense quantity of fallen burnt Trees strewed on the path, & which forms one of the worst obstacles on the line of route, as every gale blows down a new covering of these burnt stumps, however often you clear the path, & to Work your way thro' this confused Mass is irksome & tedious.[7]

Aemilius Simpson crossed the portage in the first incoming express that had ever used the trail. It took his party six days to cover what he estimated to be only 90 miles, or 62 miles as the crow flies, and on his arrival at Fort Assiniboine he commented on "the difficulty of passing this Portage, which in any other part of the World, I really believe would be considered impassable. Yet so familiar is the Voyageur with difficulty, that he is better qualified to overcome them, than any other people I have met with."[8]

Simpson also described Fort Assiniboine:

Assiniboine is a small Post situated on the North bank of the Athabasca, enclosed by a Woody country but has intervals of Meadow Land, which furnishes good pasture for Horses. It is much used for that purpose, a number being always kept here belonging to the Edmonton Establishment & to supply the Brigades Crossing the mountains & as it is safe from the depredations of the Blackfeet & other Indians, who do not cross this Woody country. A considerable quantity of dried meat is procured at this Post, which is made into Pemmican, to supply the passing Brigade to & from the Columbia &c. It gives fair returns of skins, I am informed.[9]

The next day, Simpson wrote of the "Coarse Weather, with rain & sleet, bearing all the appearance of Winter, I trust it is merely the equinoctial Storm as a continuance of this Weather would make our Journey across the Mountains a very difficult & disagreeable one."[10] The cold, wet weather delayed their departure as the men were unable to gum the canoes. On September 21, Simpson noted the "thin covering of snow on the ground & hoar frost in the morning, with constant rain during the day."[11] On Friday, the weather cleared but they still anxiously awaited the arrival of the Lesser Slave Lake party under John Stuart.

James Birnie and Sinclair rowed upriver "with a loaded Boat, and strong Crew, so as to enable her to get in advance, as much as possible, before we start in our Birch Canoes. Mr. Stewart [Stuart] with a few of his party arrived in the Evening Having had a most difficult Task to transport his goods across the Portage owing to the continual bad Weather rendering the road worse than we had them."[12] But the weather finally cleared and the work of preparing the birchbark canoes for their upriver journey proceeded.

In 1831, George Traill Allan crossed the Athabasca Portage from Edmonton House, and commented on precautions taken that no other person made note of. It appears from his journal that the Canadien and Métis employees must have crossed the portage on foot, as they were not provided with horses to ride:

> We remained two days at Edmonton, and on Wednesday the 7th (September), we started out for Fort Assiniboine with about 40 horses and as many men. Messrs. [Duncan] Finlayson, Douglas [George McDougall], [Pierre Chrysologue] Pambrun and I being mounted on excellent horses set out at full speed in order to overtake the men with loaded horses, who had already set out. Our kind host, Mr. [John] Rowand with two other gentlemen accompanied us a short distance and then bade us adieu. After a ride of about three hours over a rather barren country we arrived at the banks of a small river, called Sturgeon River where we rafted the goods and forced the horses to swim across. During the evening we established a watch at which I in conjunction with two other gentlemen took my turn of three hours in walking about to see that the men did their duty. We were apprehensive that the Assiniboine Indians might attempt to carry off our horses, but we were agreeably disappointed as we neither heard [nor] saw anything of them. During the first part of my journey over the Assiniboine Portage, as it is called, our route lay through extensive plains, but during the latter part we found considerable difficulty in passing through thick woods covered with fallen trees and in some spots morasses out of which our horses could scarcely extricate themselves.[13]

In 1835, James Douglas recorded that the combined Lesser Slave Lake Brigade and the Columbia Express departed Edmonton House on Tuesday, September 1, at 8 o'clock with our party for the Columbia consisting altogether of 24 servants, 6 gentlemen besides 2 families, with their attendants.[14] Our property is now conveyed by horses and will be thus forwarded as far as Assiniboine from whence we once more betake ourselves to the water. We have in all 51 horses, of which number 39 carry burthens, and 11 are for the passengers. Encamped opposite the Little Scaffold.[15]

On several occasions, Edward Ermatinger mentioned the Grande Echaffaud (Large Scaffold) north of Edmonton House.[16] These were meat scaffolds, where the hunters' game was cached to keep it safe from the depredations of wild animals until it could be delivered to Edmonton House.

James Douglas's 1835 journal is brief. On Tuesday, they stopped at Bridge River to rest the horses, and stayed at "Mr. Shaw's encampment." On Wednesday, they passed Eagle Lake and camped on the Pembina River. The next day, they reached Two Rivers, and on Friday passed the Grande Côté to reach Fort Assiniboine. Côté translates both as "side" and "coastline," so Douglas could have been referring either to the journey down the steep banks of the Athabasca valley or the crossing of the island mentioned by Aemilius Simpson in 1826. Douglas's journal continues:

On arrival here yesterday afternoon, we found the man who had preceded us from Edmonton busily occupied in repairing & strengthening the canoes, a work which was nearly completed this morning. Two of the canoes are old, and two of them were made at Slave Lake about the commencement of the present Summer. Though they were made at different times and by different persons they bear a close resemblance to each other in many respects, but chiefly in being Made of the most wretched materials, and the new ones of the very worst possible construction being very narrow, deep and consequently of a great draft of water. Three [Boats] built here last summer of 24 & 22 feet keel, and 8 & 9 1/2 middle thaft; being light and well proportioned offer strong inducements to abandon the canoes and adopt the boats as the safest mode of conveyance up the river. Advantages of canoes:

lightness of fabric, swiftness. Boats: strength, durability, insusceptibil-
ity of injury. Disadvantages of canoes: susceptibility of injury. Boats:
Weight, difficulty of propelling against a powerful current.

A trial was made this morning to ascertain the speed of the two
crafts which did not terminate so unfavourably to the Boat as I anticipated, and I am now of opinion that with the same cargo a boat will
reach the mountains nearly as expeditiously as a canoe. The one is
certainly more easily propelled than the other, but the canoe frequently
stands in need of repairs, and much time is invariably lost in that way,
wherever the boat moves on rather slowly it is true but without deten-
tion of any kind.[17]

The "thaft," mentioned above, was a strengthening brace or seat
installed between the gunwales of a boat or canoe; in today's termi-
nology, a thwart. Until this year, the only craft used on the Athabasca
River by the Columbia Express men had been birchbark canoes. As
Aemilius Simpson explained in 1826, the Canadiens favoured the
canoes:

> Our brigade being distributed into three Canoes, very deeply laden,
> each Canoe has seven Men, besides boys, but heavy laden as we are
> [we] make Comparatively quick progress to what we did in the Boats
> ascending the Saskatchewan, and the Canadian Crews appear very
> well pleased with the change, as they are much more used to and un-
> derstand the management of the Birch Canoes much better than the
> Boats. To the passengers however the change I think affords no ad-
> vantage, the heavy lading reducing our room to very small bounds.[18]

For two centuries, the birchbark canoe had been the craft that
opened the wilderness to the fur trade. It was the craft that still carried
the voyageurs west from Lachine, near Montreal, over the narrow,
portage-filled rivers east of Lake Winnipeg. But once the Canadiens
reached Norway House, where they began their journey west with the
Saskatchewan Brigades and the Columbia Express, they travelled in
York Boats. The only opportunity the express-men had to paddle
their beloved birchbark canoe was on the Athabasca River.

Now even that last preserve of their traditional craft in the west was threatened as James Douglas made the decision to replace the canoe with the Athabasca River boat. The voyageurs had lost many traditions over the years and were now losing another. They almost certainly mourned the loss of their treasured craft, but they had no say in the matter and so they adapted.

The Athabasca River boats differed from the York Boats the HBC used on the Saskatchewan River. York Boats had pointed ends; the Athabasca boats were sturgeon-nosed, meaning they had a flattened end at front and back. Sturgeon-nosed boats were quicker and easier to build, but may not have been as well-crafted as the old York Boats. Over the years, there were many complaints about these large, unwieldy boats, but by 1848 Governor Simpson advised the Board of Management at Fort Vancouver that, according to Thomas Lowe, the Athabasca River boats were "light handy craft of small draft of water, better adapted for the navigation, than any other we have in our power to institute."[19]

Douglas's 1835 journal continues with the journey upriver in the boats. On September 16, he wrote: "At 3 o'clock left Fort Assiniboine with 3 of the boats, 9 men in each and encamped at the lower end of the Grand Bas-fond. Experienced no unusual difficulty in ascending even the strongest points. Fine clear weather."[20]

The next day, the men worked their boats past Compass Point and camped five miles above the lower end of Big Island.[21] On Monday 28, however, Douglas reported that "Boats rather weighty in the strong points, a very harassing day's work for the men."[22] The reason for this was that the current in the river was "still getting stronger the farther we advance up the river,"[23] as John Work reported in 1823. In 1826, Aemilius Simpson mentioned similar conditions: "The Current is strong & the Rapids frequent. In hauling above one of these two of our Canoes got broke obliging us to Encamp at an early hour for the purpose of repairing them."[24] In 1831, four years before the Athabasca River boats were adopted by James Douglas, George Traill Allan described his experiences in making his way up the river:

We set off in the canoes. Two gentlemen and nine men in each, and during our voyage which continued thirteen days we encountered many hardships and delays. The river, so shallow and full of sand banks, or as the Canadians call them, Battures, as to break our frail bark canoes five or six times a day and force us ashore to kindle fires and repair them.[25]

In 1848, Thomas Lowe's party enjoyed a little excitement as they made their way up the Athabasca River toward Jasper's House. His journal begins on September 24, a day's journey west of Fort Assiniboine:

September 24th, Sunday. Fine warm day. In the forenoon while the men were walking ashore following the boats, a chocolate Bear which was running up from the water side found himself sandwiched in the midst of them, and was so taken by surprise that he jumped upon one of them, Norman Smith,[26] and before he could be frightened off by the others had inflicted a very severe wound on his forehead, with his teeth, besides two or three smaller ones below the eye, but nothing very dangerous. Made very good progress today, and marched about two thirds up La Crosse Isle.[27]

25, Monday. Fine weather. Breakfasted near the end of La Crosse Isle, and encamped at the further end of the Long Reach.

26, Tuesday. Exceeding warm, and the River has risen a little in consequence. . . . Encamped about a mile above McLeod's Forks.[28]

27, Wednesday. Strong head wind all day, but very warm. The two men who started ahead yesterday broke their canoe, and we embarked them again late in the afternoon. Encamped at Mr. McDonald's Cache.[29]

"Mr. McDonald's Cache" is where Finan McDonald abandoned a bark canoe in fall 1826, to be picked up by a later outcoming express. Although the canoe was long gone, the voyageurs' story remained. Thomas Lowe's journal continues:

28, Thursday. Rather cloudy most of the day, but no rain. Came on very well today, as there are even fewer Islands, and better tracking ground.

29, Friday. Fine day, Breakfasted at the Grand Pointe, opposite a small River which falls into the Athabasca on the right bank. About 2 p.m. we passed the Beaver River, and encamped on an Island a good piece beyond.

September 30, Saturday. Cloudy all day, but no rain until the afternoon when we had a thunder storm. Shortly after breakfast came to an encampment of 3 lodges of freemen, but they were all off, as we supposed, to bring home meat. Here we took a canoe which Mr. Colin Fraser had got made for himself, and put 5 men and 4 bags of Pemican in it. It will accompany us for the present.

October 1, Sunday. Raining nearly all day, but not cold. Encamped at Baptiste's River.[30]

Baptiste's River was named for Jean-Baptiste Berland, and now carries the name Berland River. It tumbles into the Athabasca from the north, 65 miles west of present-day Whitecourt, Alberta. Lowe's journal continues:

2, Monday. Snowing most of the day, and cold. A strong current all day, and made poor progress. Encamped on an Island where there was a beaver lodge.[31]

Interestingly, on large rivers such as the Athabasca and Saskatchewan, the North American beaver (*Castor canadensis*) built lodges but not dams.

Thomas Lowe's journal continues:

3. Tuesday. Clear cold weather. Made poor progress in the morning, but got on better afterwards. Encamped about a mile above a large open space on the right bank which has been burned long since, and now forms a sort of prairie. Encamped on left side.

4, Wednesday. Very cold in the morning, but warm during the day. Very strong current. In the forenoon had to put ashore to have Charlebois' boat repaired, as he damaged it yesterday in a Rapid. Stopped there about 3 hours. Encamped upon Canoe Island.

5, Thursday. Same weather as yesterday. Breakfasted at the bottom of Rapid Croche. Encamped about a mile below the Mountain View.[32]

Thomas Lowe's Rapid Croche is Rapids de Croix (Cross), where in 1814 two NWC voyageurs drowned. At the place Lowe called the "Mountain View," the men and boats were in the immediate vicinity of today's Hinton, Alberta, where the "first grand outline of the Rocky Mountains bursts upon the view."[33] Almost every passenger in the returning Columbia Express mentioned this spot and its stupendous views. Artist Paul Kane wrote that "the men gave a loud cheere on seeing them [the mountains]."[34]

John Work noticed that the banks of the river were high and covered chiefly with pine. George Traill Allan reported, "Today we came in sight of the Rocky Mountains and at sunset we had a splendid view of them, their summits towering to the skies and covered with snow. The view of these majestic mountains endowed the scene which had for some days back produced nothing for the eye to rest on but thick and almost impenetrable woods."[35] Aemilius Simpson questioned how they were to cross this impressive range of mountains:

> At 11 We came in sight of the Rocky Mountains, in the SW, their lofty summits towering up to the Vaulted Heavens, seemed to bid defiance to the efforts of Man to gain their eminences, it was not therefore easy for the traveller to divert himself from feeling anticipated hardships, on beholding this stupendous Mass of Mountains which he was about to Cross, & was it necessary to pursue our route across their Summits, I doubt much to practicability of gaining an access to the West side of this stupendous Barrier — but detached Mountains form Grand defiles, it is by these that the traveller is enabled to make his way across the Mountains.[36]

Thomas Lowe's 1848 journal continued west of Mountain View:

> 6, Friday. Fine clear weather. This morning Mr. Colin Fraser started ahead for Jasper's House in the canoe with 5 men light, and expects to get there in three days. Made good progress today as there were few Rapids & good tracking ground.
>
> October 7, Saturday. Fine weather, not cold. Came on very well today, and encamped at the foot of the Rapids below the Lake.[37]

This was Brule (once Brûlé) Lake, where the first Jasper's House had been built. At this point, the men of the Columbia Express were 3,232 feet above sea level. From the waters of Hudson Bay, they had rowed up the long, slow slope of the continent to this height of land. They had left York Factory in mid-July and reached Jasper's House in early October. Excepting the traverse of the Athabasca Portage by horseback, the men had rowed 1,712 miles from the HBC headquarters on Hudson Bay.

To accomplish this amazing feat in approximately sixty-six days (excluding ten days crossing of the Athabasca Portage), they had to cover an average of twenty-six miles a day, upriver, in all weather, in spite of accidents and despite the difficulties of the many portages and rapids they had to track their way through. But they also worked against gravity. On every day of their journey, they hauled their boats up an average height of 49 feet in order to reach the 3,232-foot altitude of Jasper's House.

From Brule Lake, Thomas Lowe took two more days to reach the current location of Jasper's House near where the town of Jasper now stands:

> 8, Sunday. Beautiful day. Breakfasted at the commencement of the Lake, and as we had a good deal of trouble afterwards in finding the channel spent the day in the Lake, and encamped about 2 miles up the River. It was fortunately calm weather, which is a very unusual thing in this quarter.
>
> 9, Monday. Fine weather. Arrived at Jasper's House about 3 p.m. and had the boats unloaded at once on the opposite side of the River. Mr. Fraser arrived here with the canoe yesterday. Had a dance tonight at the House, and there was no want of women as there are about a dozen lodges of Freemen here.[38]

Many Iroquois and mixed-blood freemen, who had worked for the NWC or HBC, spent the remainder of their lives in this valley.[39]

The dance at Jasper's House was a pleasant break for both the gentlemen and the hardworking voyageurs. Their work began again the next morning, as they proceeded up the valley toward the shining mountain range. Aemilius Simpson spoke for all the gentlemen and employees, when he described the scene as best he could:

> The view now in all directions presents a continued Mass of snow clad Hills towering their lofty summits in successive ranges, their outlines assuming a great variety of forms, giving to the whole scene a grandeur and novelty beyond my powers to describe — but it is truly sublime.[40]

CHAPTER 16

Jasper's House to Boat Encampment

ॐ

IN THE EARLY YEARS, the express-men began their journey across the Rocky Mountain Portage from the first Jasper's House post on the west side of Brule Lake. Later, HBC men started from the second house, constructed in 1831 on the west bank of the Snake Indian River at its junction with the Athabasca. As a result, the stories told in the journals differ. The names of the various encampments in this valley also changed a little over the years, and only a few express-men referenced the names of early fur trade locations, such as Henry's House or Larocque's Prairie.

The men endured many difficulties as they made their way up the Athabasca River west of Jasper's House, walking or riding toward the pass that would take them across the Rocky Mountains. The lakes were shallow and silted in with sand, and Miette's Rock sometimes proved to be a huge barrier to transportation.[1] Burnt woods and fallen trees caused problems farther up the valley. And, as always, there was the difficulty of travelling with fresh horses, as Thomas Lowe experienced in 1847:

> Had much difficulty in starting; the horses being wild and the men awkward, and got in consequence only as far as the head of the Lake, where we encamped.[2]

The next year, Lowe's party experienced less difficulty with the animals, but his journal brings to light another common experience for the men who, day after day, worked at rowing or hauling these heavy boats upriver:

> Started from Jasper's House late in the afternoon with a band of 34 horses, 27 of which were loaded. Encamped about 2 miles above the Lake. Sent off the guide with two men to arrange the boat at the Grand Traverse. . . . Four of our men who have sore feet and legs are on horseback.[3]

In 1823, three years before the York Factory Express came into existence, John Work's men would not have suffered from sore legs, because they worked their way up the Athabasca River in birchbark canoes. Work's party left old Jasper's House on horseback, and he described his passage up the Athabasca River:

> Having everything prepared, I was sent off with four men and the horses 22 in number and part of the provisions and baggage, to proceed by land to a place where the canoes are to be left. . . . As it was noon before we started we did not go far. The road was first along the shore of the Lake & river & then through the woods some parts of which were very thicketty & some places very swampy in the bottoms of the valleys. The mountains rising one behind another in succession still appearing higher the farther we advance.[4]

In 1826, Aemilius Simpson's account of his canoe journey west from the post on Brule Lake is filled with his excitement at the spectacular scenery that surrounded him:

We continued our ascent of the Athabasca, occasionally opposed by rapids alternating with sheets of comparatively still water — until 6 p.m. when we Encampt for the night at the Base of Millet's [Miette's] Rock upon a gravel flat or Batture, which extends to the base of the bounding Mountains that forms this grand defile, & through which the River holds its course. I certainly think our Encampment might vie in point of romantic appearance with many of far greater celebrity. On our left is the perpendicular face of this stupendous Rock rising to an elevation of upwards of three thousand feet, its shadow casting a gloom over the deep Defile, so opposite to the brilliant sky immediately over us, that the mind feels an impression as if this situation was somewhat supernatural.[5]

Aemilius Simpson's stupendous rock still stands on the banks of the Athabasca River, close to where the second Jasper's House was later constructed at the site of the present town of Jasper. In 1823, John Work described his passage to Miette's Rock, and his passing of it, once again on horseback:

Our road was through woods & along the banks of the river alternately. Over hills and cross valleys the horses often climbing up hills which a person would imagine sufficient for wild goats to ascend. We crossed the river to the West side & then recrossed it again, which saved the necessity of ascending a very steep rock [Miette's] which is dangerous. This cannot be done except when the river is very low as it is at present. Notwithstanding it was enough for the horses to ford it on account of its depth and the strength of the current which is very rapid. Except this place where we crossed our road lay along the East side of the river sometimes close on the shore and sometimes a little distance from it. The course of the [Athabasca] river is nearly from S to N winding through the valley and the mountains rising abruptly on both sides, not in one continued chain but here and there broken by a small valley or kind of fissure, out of each of which issues a small river or creek which contributes to increase the size of the main river.[6]

Four years later, in 1827, Edward Ermatinger's party camped close to the foot of Miette's Rock, and he wrote that it "is high and difficult to pass."[7] He was not referring to the pinnacle of the rock, which stood 7,600 feet above the ground, but to the large, slippery "nose" of rock that bulged out from the base of the pinnacle at a height of 1,300 feet above the Athabasca River. The rocky point of the nose, which forced the river to the west, was called Disaster Point because of the number of horses that slipped down its smooth surface and tumbled into the Athabasca. In his journals, a NWC gentleman, Ross Cox, described his arduous climb over Miette's Rock on his way north to old Jasper's House in 1817:

> About a mile beyond this river we arrived at the foot of a stupendous rock, called Le Rocher de Miétte [Miette], over which we had to pass. We commenced our task a little after eleven; and at half past two arrived at its base on the northern side, where we remained an hour to refresh the horses. The road over this rock is tolerably good, but extremely steep. The horses surmounted it with great labour; and the knees of the majority of our party were put to a severe test in the ascent. From the summit we had an extensive view of the country, the general features of which do not differ materially from the scenery through which we passed the preceding day.[8]

In spite of, or perhaps because of, its hazards, Miette's Rock, and the man it was supposedly named for, has its own enduring history. Aemilus Simpson reported:

> I employed myself in the forenoon, with the assistance of Mr. [George] Barnston, in measuring the height of Millett's Rock, the remarkable Mountain whose Northern termination falls perpendicularly & forms the Southern boundary of the grand defile thro' which our route lays — at its entry. This Mountain has its name from a Canadian who asserted that he had ascended to its summit, when he sat down on the edge of this enormous precipice nearly four thousand feet high & felt so little apprehension that he amused himself by raping [sic] his heels against the Rock. He must be very credulous that believes this story.[9]

The clamber over Miette's (or Millett's) Rock was a major hurdle in the early years when the NWC ruled this valley. In later years, however, the HBC express-men brought their boats up the Athabasca River to the new Jasper's House, located just west of the Snake Indian River which flows east and south into Athabasca directly across from Miette's Rock. This change made the traverse of the nose unnecessary, and Miette's Rock disappears from later journals.

Aemilius Simpson's 1826 journal continues as his canoe travels westward from the base of the Rock:

> Sunday 8th. Fine and clear weather, Embarked at 5 a.m. and continued our ascent of the Athabasca, on having done so for a few Miles, we Entered a small Lake which was so shallow, that we had considerable difficulty in finding a passage through it, & had to make a Portage over some sand banks, which detained us considerably. The proper channel lies along the Mountains on our right.[10]

At this point, Simpson's party is paddling their canoes through shallow Jasper Lake, having already passed the location where the new Jasper's House would be constructed in 1831:

> At 2 p.m. we met the men who were proceeding for [old] Jasper's House with an express from the West side of the Mountain Portage. As it was now unnecessary for them to proceed, their communication being directed to the gentleman in charge of our Brigade, they Embarked with us. At 6:15 p.m. we arrived at the Encampment from which we were to commence our Land Journey across the Mountains, and the point of separation from the Brigade for New Caledonia.[11]

This encampment, where the New Caledonia men separated from those travelling via Athabasca Pass to the Columbia River, was known as Larocque's Prairie. In 1822, HBC Chief Trader Joseph Félix Larocque had constructed a substantial post on the west bank of the Athabasca River, where Cottonwood Creek flowed into the Athabasca. In 1824, Governor George Simpson passed through the valley on his way to the Columbia District and ordered the post closed down. The name remained.

In 1826, when Aemilius Simpson reported on the separation of the

New Caledonia Express at Larocque's Prairie, it was an historic occasion. In the spring, Chief Factor James McDougall had left his New Caledonia post of Fort St. James via McLeod's Lake Post and Dunvegan. This return journey was the first time the New Caledonia men were choosing to come into their territory by way of the Rocky Mountain Portage (Yellowhead Pass) to the headwaters of Fraser's River at Tête Jaune Cache. At that lonely storehouse (an actual building), the incoming men would meet their Iroquois guide, who would bring them downriver in boats or canoes to Fort George, the first stop on their way to Fort St. James.

Simpson described the work done at Larocque's Prairie: "This day has been occupied in making arrangements for our Journey across the Portage, & the separation of the brigades for the Columbia & New Caledonia, the latter pursue a Route that has thitherto been passed by few. Report says it is a good one which soon leads them to the Head Waters of Fraser's River."[12]

In 1827, Edward Ermatinger wrote that he arrived at Larocque's Prairie on October 4, having spent the night before at "Campement de Cardinalle, a small creek."[13] The next day, "Having separated and Prepared the Baggage the Columbia people set off about 10 a.m. with 15 horses . . . Mr. [George] McDougal [of New Caledonia] has 40 horses to transport his packs."[14]

In 1835, James Douglas's journal differs from Simpson's and Ermatinger's journals in his description of travel between the new Jasper's House and the old location of Henry's House, across the Athabasca River from Larocque's Prairie. On October 10, his express "Left the fort and encamped at the Little Rocher, 6 miles from the fort."[15] Little Rocher is possibly what is later named Rocher du Bon Homme.[16] The next day Douglas's party camped at Henry's House: "Distance 20 miles; time 5 hours."[17]

According to Aemilus Simpson, Henry's Plain (or House) was on the east side of the Athabasca River, almost directly across from the place he called Larocque's Prairie. As Douglas had already transferred the incoming gentlemen and employees to the control of the New

Caledonia clerk who had been waiting for him at Jasper's House, this appears to indicate that the east side of the Athabasca River, through the old location of Henry's House, was the preferred route when travelling independently of the New Caledonia men.[18]

The next stop along the valley, south of both Henry's House and Larocque's Prairie, was known variously as Buffalo Encampment, Campement des Vaches, or Prairie de la Vache.[19] Aemilius Simpson described the relatively easy travel between Larocque's Prairie and Buffalo Encampment:

> We continue our Journey until 2 p.m. when we Encampt in a Small plain, extending from base to base of the bounding Mountains, with a small stream meandering through it. It is named the Buffaloe Encampment. Our route has been by a tolerably good Track. The path thro' the Wood being clear, with a good hard footing for our Horses, & no precipices of great importance.[20]

The precipices would come later. First these men had to make their way from the relatively open, narrow valley that surrounded Buffalo Encampment to the junction of the Whirlpool and Athabasca rivers:

> Wednesday 11th. Commenced with hail and rain Showers in the Valley, snow on the Mountains. At 6 a.m. we resumed our Journey. At 8 we arrived on the Banks of the Athabasca, where we waited the arrival of a Canoe that had been dispatched from Henery's [sic] House for the purpose of crossing our Luggage &c. That being completed at 11 we pursued our Journey, our route leading thro' a flat and woody face of country with a great quantity of burnt Wood strewed over the surface for about five Miles, when we arrived at another branch of the Athabasca, a narrow but deep and rapid stream, which we forded with some difficulty.[21]

The narrow, deep stream was the Whirlpool River, which would lead them almost all the way to Athabasca Pass. As has been mentioned earlier, in its early years the Whirlpool was called the Holé or

Holey River because of a section of deep water close to where it flowed into the Athabasca. John Work's 1823 journal informs us that his party

> proceeded on our journey along the East side of the S.W. branch of the river till noon when we crossed to the W. side at what is called the hole traverse. The course of this branch of the river is nearly from N to S through a deep valley between high mountains. Our road was almost all day through thick woods, some of which were formerly burnt and had fallen & rendered the road very difficult, there were also some steep and difficult hills to ascend.[22]

In 1827, Edward Ermatinger reported that this piece of road was "much encumbered with fallen wood."[23] Although it is difficult to ascertain exactly where George Traill Allan is on his 1831 journey west, he was probably describing the same piece of road when he wrote:

> Today we entered a point of wood and found the track so blocked up with fallen trees as to render it almost impassable to our horses. The mountains as seen today were really splendid, a thick fog having concealed the base, the summits appear, as it were, to tower above the skies.[24]

From the mouth of the Whirlpool River the express-men continued their journey southwest toward their next encampment, known as Campement d'Orignal, Moose Encampment, or Moose Deer Encampment. This campsite was situated on the banks of the river, deep in the narrow Whirlpool River valley. In 1826, Aemilius Simpson described his journey along the Whirlpool:.

> We occasionally ascend pretty steep Eminences & pass thru' Thick Wood, intersected by Swamps or Marshes into which the poor Horses sink with their loads, and costs a great deal of labour to extricate the poor Animals from their disagreeable situation. Having come about 18 miles we Encampt at the Moose Deer Encampment, situated on a flat or Batture through which the River has its course, bounded by

immense Mountains whose summit appear almost vertical to us. The evening was fine.[25]

In 1835, James Douglas had a difficult passage between the Hole of the Whirlpool River and the Grande Batture (Scott Gravel Flats), with a pause at Moose Encampment:

Tues. 13. Raining in the morning, and in the evening heavy snow which rendered this day particularly disagreeable; drenched to the skin by the rain in the early part of the day. We were by no means prepared for the transition which followed to heavy snow. The encampment and a good fire were highly relished by all. Stopped at Commencement of Moose encampment & encamped 2 miles below Grand[e] Batture. Distance 22 miles.[26]

In 1848, Thomas Lowe reached

the Grand Traverse about 10 a.m. and crossed without taking off the loads. Michel & the two others had arranged the Boat, but we did not require it. The Road beyond the Grand Traverse was very bad, and we had a great many trees to clear out of the way. Encamped at the Campement d'Orignal [Moose Encampment], but it was late when we got there.[27]

The next familiar encampment often used by these men was the Grande Batture, 24 miles south of Moose Encampment. From the Grande Batture (Scott Gravel Flats) it was another 14 miles to the summit of Athabasca Pass. South of the Grande Batture, but a few miles east of the summit, was the camp these men called Campement du Fusil, or Gun Encampment (now known as Kane Meadow, for artist Paul Kane). In 1826, Aemilius Simpson's party made its way from Campement d'Orignal to a place that might have been Campement du Fusil:

We commenced March at Daylight, and continue travelling until 3 p.m. having come a Distance of about 20 Miles in a Winding course to the SW, ascending & descending high cliffs alternately, over one of which a horse fell, and the poor animal was so much injured that it was deemed necessary to kill him, an expedient that was not atal [sic] disagreeable to our Voyageurs, his flesh being deemed, by them, a good and seasonable supply of food. The River has now dwindled away to a pretty stream, its course very much through flats or Battures confined by stupendous mountains, in some places again it forces its way thro' ravines and Cliffs of Rock. . . . We passed immense glaciers of Ice, that appear from the earliest time to have resisted the power of the Sun, and are now as compact as the Mountains that enclose them, they impart a frigidity to the surrounding atmosphere and cast a cheerless aspect over the Scene, that is by no means agreeable to the passing traveller, however much they may excite his curiosity.[28]

Edward Ermatinger, whose 1827 party camped a few miles west of Campement d'Orignal,

Started at 8 a.m. and encamped near the height of land, having passed thro' some very bad swamps and mires during the day. View of the mountains very grand. One [man] ahead all day clearing the road in different places — and as the track is much worse farther on, 4 [four men] will start early to-morrow morning for the same purpose.[29]

In 1831, George Traill Allan reported that on passing between the mountains,

I perceived at some distance large masses of ice suspended as it were in the air, to have a nearer view of which I took a gallop in that direction. Sometimes when the path lies near the base of the mountains that are so bedecked, travelling becomes dangerous by these immense masses suddenly giving way. We heard frequently at a great distance a noise similar to thunder and which we attributed to the ice falling from the mountains. It is not many years since a gentleman had a very narrow escape by one of those masses falling directly behind him.[30]

In 1835, James Douglas's party stopped at Campement du Fusil after travelling through rain and snow. But in 1847, Thomas Lowe's party left Campement d'Orignal in the morning and slept that night at the Grande Batture. The next day, it appears they made their way through Athabasca Pass and stopped at a place he called Mr. Rae's Encampment:

> Cloudy all day, and snowing a little in the afternoon. Much snow in the road all day, on the height of land 2 feet. Made a very long days' march, having encamped at Mr. Rae's Encampment, but it was dark before we reached it.[31]

In 1848, Lowe's party spent the night at Campement d'Orignal, but once again "it was late when we got there." On October 13, a Friday, it "began raining before daylight, and continued so the whole day, but we went on nevertheless. Went on very well in spite of the rain, and encamped at Mr. Roussain's Encampment."[32] For the second time, Lowe's party crossed Athabasca Pass almost without remarking on the place, as on the following day they reached the first batture at the foot of the Grande Côte, on the west side of the Rocky Mountains.

Lowe did not describe his passage through Athabasca Pass, but in 1823 John Work wrote an excellent description of the path that led through Gun Encampment and of Athabasca Pass itself:

> Hard frost in the morning. Proceeded early on our journey sometimes along the river, which got very narrow, & sometimes through points of woods, where the road was frequently very difficult on account of mires and fallen wood. Our course in general nearly Southerly, along a deep valley between high mountains which are topped with snow. . . . In the afternoon we crossed the height of land. This though so named is in the narrow valley which we have been following and is enclosed between high mountains topped with snow that on the left hand or East side is called McGillivray's Rock in honor of Mr. W. McGillivray who was the head man of the NWCos. . . . Between these two mountains are situated three small Lakes all in a line, in the one we first come to the branch of the Elk or Athabasca River which we have been following has its source and is at first very narrow. In the third Lake, the foul or faint hearted river, which empties itself into the Columbia, rises, the Middle Lake empties itself into the third one & when the water is high it also runs into the first one so that in the

season of the high water, both the above rivers may be said to have their rise in this Lake, though they run in opposite directions.[33]

The foul, or Faint Hearted River, was one of many names given to westward-flowing Pacific Creek over the years. The three lakes are the Committee's Punch Bowl, whose rugged landscape, as has been seen, so impressed one Canadien voyageur that he cried out, "God Almighty never made such a place!"[34] In his journals, Aemilius Simpson described his journey west from Gun Encampment to the Committee's Punch Bowl Lakes:

> We commenced our March at 6:30 a.m. & having come thro' a defile over ground intersected by Swamps and small Streams or Brooks, & bearing a stint'd growth of Pines, we arrived at the Committees Punch Bowl, which forms the Source of two small streams running in opposite directions: one to the West, being one of the Sources of the Columbia River, the other to the East, forming one of the Sources of the Athabasca, at present this is only a Small & nearly circular Sheet of Water, having no great depth, but at certain seasons it forms a considerable reservoir.[35]

These three lakes stood nearly 5,700 feet above sea level, some 2,000 feet higher in altitude than Jasper's House, where the express-men had been only a few days earlier. The men may have stopped for their breakfast at this place, as it is almost certain they did not walk straight through. Obviously, a celebration was warranted — was always warranted at any significant height of land. The fur trade had many traditional ceremonies brought to it by its Canadien employees, who imported their Catholic rituals but adapted them to the fur trade, and they likely celebrated a baptism at these lakes, blessing any new voyageurs crossing the height of land for the first time.

As the brigades and expresses crossed the country from Montreal to Hudson Bay and on to the Athabasca District, or the west side of the Rocky Mountains, the Canadiens designated many places where their adapted baptismal ceremony was held. The first was at a sandy point of land on the Ottawa River, where new voyageurs were dunked in the water of the river. Gentlemen were baptised, too, if they were crossing a height of land for the first time.

A voyageur — whether Canadien or Métis — would take great pleasure in this exaggerated ceremony: each gentleman who crossed the height of the Rocky Mountains at Athabasca Pass for the first time almost certainly received a splash of water in his face from a branch dipped in the lakes, and a cheerful warning that he never kiss a voyageur's wife without her permission. When the playful baptism was finished, the voyageurs celebrated by firing their guns into the air.

The fur trade was a mix of cultures. Baptism came from the Catholic Canadiens, and the firing of guns from the First Nations. The shots of rum that followed came, of course, from the senior gentleman, who had carried the alcohol west from Jasper's House for the sole purpose of rewarding his men for their ceremony. This was another tradition of the fur trade.

Sadly, Aemilius Simpson makes no mention of any celebration occurring at the Committee's Punch Bowl Lakes. Instead, he records that about an hour after his party left the lakes,

we commenced our Descent of the Grande Côté, a precipice of enormous Magnitude & which forms a very serious obstacle on the line of communication, and it is only necessity, or an arduous spirit of Enterprise, that could have first induced Man to make it a thorough fare, it has almost a perpendicular descent of about five miles, and occupied us two hours and ten minutes. On arriving at its foot and looking back upon the immense Mountain, that you have just descended, you cannot avoid feeling some degree of amazement at the feat you have performed, and the idea forces itself upon the mind, that this is by no means an agreeable barrier between separated friends. How the poor Horses with their loads succeeded in getting down this immense Hill is most extraordinary. As you descend the Mountain the face of the country assumes quite a new character, the productions now become very different and you are struck with the enormous size of the Trees which cover the face of the country. I measured one on the face of the Hill, whose girth was sixteen feet, and it did not surpass in size many in its immediate neighbourhood, their height in proportion. This was a Pine which with Cedar constitutes the Forest. . . . From the foot of the Hill we pursued our route along a Batture for about 3 to 4 Miles, when we Encampt, having come a distance of about 18 miles, over the most difficult & extraordinary road I certainly ever travelled.[36]

John Work was also impressed by the steepness of the trail, writing, "We came to the top of what is called the big hill, which we descended through a very steep and difficult road in many places toward the top & on top of the hill boggy, and often almost blocked up with fallen wood."[37]

In 1827, Edward Ermatinger's party started from their encampment (possibly Campement du Fusil) a little after 8 a.m. and reached the bottom of the Grande Côte around 4 p.m., without mentioning how long they may have delayed at the Committee's Punch Bowl. "This had certainly been a very labourious [sic] day's march for the horses," he said, "but the road was never better, we had not the least snow on the way."[38]

George Traill Allan was also overwhelmed by the descent:

We descended a very high mountain which occupied us four hours in the descent. It was so very deep that we were obliged to dismount and allow the horses to choose the best and safest track for themselves. . . . On looking from our encampment at the mountains down which we had just descended, it seemed almost increditable [sic] that we could have done so with loaded or even with light horses.[39]

James Douglas's party experienced rain and snow as they travelled what he estimated as a 17-mile distance from Gun Encampment to the bottom of the Big Hill. In 1847, Thomas Lowe experienced little difficulty in coming down the Grande Côte. But in 1848, he noted:

Snowed the whole of last night, and this morning there was upwards of 6 inches of snow on the ground. Brightened up in course of the day, but the melting of the snow rendered the roads miserable. Got to the first Batture at the foot of the Grand[e] Côte.[40]

From the foot of the Rocky Mountains, the men made their way southwest to Boat Encampment. In 1847, Thomas Lowe arrived at

Boat Encampment later than usual because of deep snow in the pass. He discovered artist Paul Kane waiting for him there. In his own journal, Kane wrote of his wait for the arrival of the express:

> We now had nothing to do but to try and pass the time pleasantly as we could under the circumstances, until the arrival of the brigade from the east side of the mountains. The men spent the day principally in gambling, and performing charms which they supposed would hasten the arrival of the brigade, such as erecting crosses, with one of the arms pointing to the direction from which it was expected. They also prepared what they call a "lobstick." For this purpose a high tree is chosen which has thick branches at the top, and all the lower limbs are carefully trimmed off; a smooth surface is then cut on one side of the tree, on which the person in whose honour it has been trimmed is invited to cut his name; this being done, three rounds of blank-charges are fired, and three cheers given, and the spot afterwards bears the name of his encampment.[41]

In 1848, Lowe's journey to Boat Encampment was quick and easy. When he had left the territory in the spring, it had been embroiled in the Cayuse War that broke out after the massacre of missionaries at Waiilatpu Mission in November 1847 (see Chapter 2). Lowe was eager for news of the hostilities. As leader of this incoming Columbia Express, he was responsible for the safety of his men and was reluctant to enter a territory at war. On October 15, Lowe wrote:

> I started ahead this morning for Boat Encampment where I arrived about 3 p.m. . . . About an hour after dark Mr. [Owen Charles] Beardmore & the brigade arrived, except 3 of the laziest who have fallen behind, and can not come up tonight. Mr. [John Lee] Lewes brought up two Boats from Colvile, and there are 7 engaged men and 5 Indians to go back with us.[42]

Lewes had plenty of news for Thomas Lowe, and could assure him that the Cayuse War had settled down enough that the Columbia Express would be able to make its way to Fort Vancouver in safety.

CHAPTER 17

Boat Encampment to Fort Vancouver

§ð

FOR SOME OF THE MEN who reached the west side of the Rocky Mountains, the rockbound Columbia River might stand as a strong symbol of their return home. For those new to the territory, Boat Encampment and the Columbia River served as their introduction to a new life in the Columbia District's fur trade — a life that differed in many ways from that in the east. In the early years, Canadiens had crossed the mountains by the dozens every year to enter the still-traditional fur trade. Later, in the 1840s, some of the men who ventured west were shepherds and agriculturists from England and Scotland, employed to work on the newly established HBC farms at forts Victoria and Nisqually (Tacoma, Washington). Many others were the Métis descendants of earlier Canadiens, who filled the gaps left open now that the Canadiens had found employment in the logging industry that flourished along the St. Lawrence River.

One change these new men immediately noticed was that the rivers on the west side of the Rocky Mountains differed from those on the east. There was little sand along the riverbeds here, only gravel and rocks. It was a harder country, full of steep bluffs or straight-edged mountains that resembled enormous paving stones, or Dalles, which gave the Columbia River rapids their names. These raging rapids challenged the courage of many a man, experienced or not. All must trust their guides and boutes to bring them safely through. But when the guides or boutes failed, accidents happened and men drowned.

In 1848, Thomas Lowe entered the territory with many men new to the fur trade, who had not yet experienced rapids as ferocious as those on the upper Columbia. It had taken his express ten days to make their way upriver from Fort Colvile, it would take only four days to reach the same post on their way downriver. As they began their journey down the Columbia, Lowe noted, "The river is in a fine state, and we encamped a short distance above St. Martins Rapid."[1] But the next day he wrote: "In running the latter [Dalles des Morts] Pierre's boat took in a good deal of water as he had to run straight through the middle of the heavy waves, not being able to put into the eddy on account of the awkwardness of the crew, who were too frightened to do as they were ordered."[2] Luckily, no one died on that occasion.

Another difference was the boat used west of the Rockies. In 1823, John Work arrived at Boat Encampment for the first time, on his way to a new posting in the Columbia District. He described the boats that had always been used on the west side of the mountains:

> Embarked at 9 o'clock, and proceeded down the Columbia River in three boats or kind of wooden canoes, worked by 8 Men each, who row with paddles and not oars. These boats will carry about 55 pieces and are made of a light construction so that 12 men can carry them across the portages.[3]

Three years later, Aemilius Simpson also entered the territory for the first time. Simpson's record of events begins on October 16, 1826:

"Rain during the night, the morning foggy. Our crews were Employed during the early part of the day arranging our Boats and preparing for our voyage down the Columbia River,"[4] while the gentlemen sat around the warm fire. One interesting tradition that might have taken place every year at Boat Encampment was that the men carved new paddles to take them and their boats down the Columbia River. In 1827, Edward Ermatinger wrote of his arrival at Boat Encampment, on October 10:

Started at 7 a.m. and arrived at the end of the Portage about half past 10. Found J[ohn] W[arren] Dease, Esq., and family here — people occupied the remainder of the day making paddles &c.[5]

Simpson's journal continues:

Our arrangements being completed, we wished Mr. Finan MacDonald & those bound across the Mountains farewell,[6] and Embarked at a quarter past Noon, and Commenced our descent of the Columbia, our party being Embarked in three Boats (constructed in imitation of Canoes) including Mr. [John Warren] Deases', and consisting of about 33 hands. We now proceed on our Journey with great rapidity, descending the Stream, at about 7 to 8 miles per hour. In some parts along the Banks a low margin of land extends to the Base of the bounding ridges of Mountains, but generally it is confined by Rocky Cliffs of primitive formation, some of them composed of a similar lime stone with that which constitutes the main mass of the Mountains. The face of the country is thickly cloaked with Wood of a very great growth, principally the Pine & Cedar Tribes.[7]

John Work wrote a good description of the Columbia River north of the Upper Dalles, or Dalles des Morts:

The Columbia all the way we have come is a fine large deep river with high hills on each side several of which are topped with snow. There are a great many strong rapids & the current all the way is very strong. One of the boats being leaky we encamped early a little above what is called the upper dalles.[8]

Simpson's journal continues as his crew passes Dalles des Morts, where he noticed the sturgeon-nosed canoes used by the Sinixt people in this region:

At 7 a.m. we run the Upper Dalles rapids, a very grand shoot, the running of which is attended with considerable Danger, and requires great Skill on the part of the Steersman & Bowsman. The passengers & paper chest are landed at the head of the rapids, a very proper precaution, one of our Boats struck a stone in running the rapids, but fortunately escaped without sustaining any considerable Damage. . . . We saw a few Indians in two very curiously constructed Canoes, in the afternoon we run the 2nd Dalles rapids, our Boats shipping a good deal of Water. The Scenery about these rapids is very fine.[9]

The second Dalles is today's Steamboat Rapid, near Revelstoke. In his journal, John Work described this same section of the river:

In the forepart of the day the current was very strong & the rapids so frequent and so strong that they might be said to be almost one continued rapid. . . . In the morning we passed the upper dalles & towards noon the lesser dalles, these are places where the river is contracted very narrow and the whole body of water rushes with great violence between steep craggy rocks. The boats ran down it very well.[10]

South of Steamboat Rapid, Simpson reported: "At 6 p.m. we Entered the Upper [Arrow] Lake & Encampt upon a low flat at its Entrance, Having come about 80 miles during the Day:

Wednesday 18th. Commenced with rain, which continued until 8 a.m. accompanied with Strong Breeze from the SW, retarding our progress greatly. One of our Boats having fallen out of sight astern we waited her arrival. We passed a few Lake Indians, who were engaged in fishing Salmon, the most miserable looking fish I ever beheld, being in the last stage of existence, after having continued their ascent from the Sea this great distance they become so reduced that they hardly bear any resemblance to what they were, & must prove an indifferent article of food. . . . Noon, fine, but Sharp & Cold,

Thermometer 50°F. At 4:30 p.m. we completed our descent of the Lake when we re-entered the River, but our Boat having again fallen in the rear, we Encampt for the night, so as to allow her come up before dark.

Thursday 19th. This morning Hazy. At 4 a.m. we Embarked when we descended the River for 5 Leagues and then Entered the [Lower] Arrow Lake, which we continued to descend for the remainder of the Day. Noon, fine but cloudy, Thermometer 57°. In the afternoon we had a favourable Breeze from the NE to which we spread our Oil Cloth, and assisted us a good deal. This Lake is generally very narrow for so extensive a Sheet of Water, seldom exceeding two miles.[11]

In Lower Arrow Lake, the voyageurs pointed out a remarkable cliff they called "The Arrow Rock, so named," wrote Simpson, "on account of a round Hole in its face full of arrows, said to have been fired at it by Indians, when practicing the Bow & Arrow before a war excursion."[12] Clerk A.C. Anderson also described Arrow Rock, telling his son that "on arriving at the rock in question the Indian Canoe men all shot arrows at the rock, many of which stuck in the moss, which I believe was considered to be lucky."[13]

Simpson's journal continues as they completed the descent of Lower Arrow Lake, which he estimated to be "about 20 Leagues in extent."[14] Right after they re-entered the Columbia, "McGillivray's [Kootenay] River joins the Main Branch. It is a River of considerable importance & appears little less than the branch we are following."[15] John Work described this river and the country that surrounded it:

McGillivray's is a large river. The hills along the river are not so high as hitherto, the wood is also getting much thinner and of a smaller growth. It is probable that the country a little way from the river is fine plains.[16]

Simpson's journal continues:

At 11:15 we passed the Junction of the Flat head [Pend-d'Oreille] River, another important Stream . . . at 1:30 we ran the Dalles Rapids, a long shoot bounded by steep Rocky Cliffs, & having a remarkable block of Rock rising perpendicular in the bed of the River of considerable height.[17] We arrived at Fort Colvile at 4:30 p.m. We were received here by a number of Indians, the chiefs Mounted on Horses, whom we were obliged to Shake cordially by the hand, in return for this compliment. To a stranger they appear grotesque figures, their faces painted a variety of colour & their leather robes fancifully decorated according to their fashion, giving them a very fantastic air. We found this Post merely in progress, a few Houses only being completed, & no Stockades up for defence.[18]

Aemilius Simpson was visiting the fledgling post two years after his cousin Governor George Simpson had ordered that the new Fort Colvile be built near Kettle Falls. Within a few years, the post would grow into a substantial fort that was surrounded by palisades and neatly fenced fields of grain and potatoes.

Simpson's journal continues:

Sunday 22. Thick fog in the Morning. The Boats and Cargoes having been transported across the Portage to the foot of the falls, we Embarked at 9:45 a.m. & continued our descent of the Columbia. The Kettle Falls are formed by shelving Masses of Rock extending across the Bed of the River, the higher Shelf forms a fall of about fifteen feet, and a second Shelf forms another of about eight feet. The Scenery about these falls is very grand, the rigid & projecting cliffs hanging in fantastic forms over this awful clash of Water, which from the channels being contracted by these projecting Cliffs, the stream urges its way through with such accumulated force that its surface forms immense Whirlpools; on the left of the falls is an Eminence on whose Summit you see a great number of the burial places of the Natives curiously grouped, its face forming a precipice washed by a troubled Stream a branch of the River.[19]

In his 1823 journal, John Work had also described Kettle Falls:

At the kettle fall the river contracts and the whole body of water falls over a ledge of rock, there is an island just at the head of the fall. The country has a fine appearance, fine rising hills covered with tufts of wood, but from the dryness of the season the grass is parched & dry & has a barren appearance.[20]

Between Kettle Falls and the Spokane River, Simpson's party travelled down more sets of rapids. "A few miles below these falls are the Grand [Rickey] Rapids, formed by projecting Masses of Rock obstructing the course of the River."[21] A day later he noted:

We had a Fog in the Morning, which frequently occurs, I observe. We descended about 3 Leagues below the Encampment when we arrived at the Spokan Forks Rapids — a chain of Strong rapids. The passengers Walk across a point on the right, covered with immense blocks of Rock that appear to have been washed here by the force of the Rapids. The view of the Boats running these rapids with the wild character of the Scenery, which was much heightened by the Fog, is rather terrific, they dashed down the rapids as if to an inevitable destruction, and were soon beyond the view of the Spectator, and at the foot of the rapids, without having received further injury than Shipping a good deal of Water. The running of rapids is an operation that requires great Skill and coolness.[22]

Simpson's boatmen had little trouble with these rapids, but not everyone had the same experience. In 1847, Thomas Lowe reported that "in running the [Grand] Rapids two of the boats were broken, and we had to encamp there to have them repaired."[23] In 1849, one of the boats rammed a rock, and its ten-man crew escaped drowning by clambering onto a tiny island in the middle of the river. The remaining men desperately made repairs to the second boat, which had also been damaged in the collision. It took them three full hours to rescue the stranded men from their precarious position.

By this point, gentlemen and voyageurs alike were mentally exhausted by their seven-month-long journey and often worked long days to reach Fort Vancouver. This is clear in Edward Ermatinger's 1827 journal, where he reports that, south of Okanogan House, his men "Put ashore a little above the Marle Banks [Hanford Reach] and took supper. We afterwards started with the intention of drifting all night but the people paddled till 10 p.m. when we considered safest to put ashore till morning, the night being very dark and the River shoal in some places."[24]

Thomas Lowe's 1848 journal confirms this habit. At Upper Arrow Lake the men set up their evening camp halfway down the length of the lake. It rained until past midnight, "when it cleared up, and the moon rose. We then pushed off, and pulled until day light when we found ourselves near the end of the Lake."[25]

The next night they again "pulled all night."[26] Everyone was eager to reach home, so if the moon was bright and the weather good, no one enjoyed a good night's sleep. As a result of the especially long days of river travel and little rest, express journal entries became shorter and shorter. Some contained so little information they barely mentioned the portages over which the men worked their boats.

The voyageurs had their own reason for paddling long hours into the night. After seven months away, they wanted to get home to their wives and children. But they were also all young men, and by this time in as good condition as strong, young men could be. Their hard work and long days were probably part of their private competition, their constant desire to do better than other Columbia Express men who had made this long journey before them, combined with their desire to keep up with their companions.

They challenged each other to work harder, to be better. They teased each other into giving a better performance — "Slow like a Turtle, eh?" Moreover, all but the new men were in familiar territory. The Canadiens who had come from the west side of the Rockies knew every part of this hazardous river.

They understood its dangers and were challenged by them. They could see the end of their journey. They could almost smell the sea, although they were still hundreds of miles away. The Columbia was their home river, and it was carrying them home. And although the newcomers might find the Columbia a harder, rockier river than they were used to, it was still a river and therefore familiar.

— • —

Of all the gentlemen who were keeping journals of their incoming express, only Simpson kept a good record. It seemed that every other gentleman was too exhausted or too eager to reach home to keep up their journals. In 1827, Edward Ermatinger listed the major portages and campsites but gave no other information. In 1831, Allan made no mention of his journey beyond Fort Okanogan. James Douglas's 1835 journal was almost as brief: his narrative ended at Fort Nez Percés. In 1848, Thomas Lowe's record also closed at Fort Nez Percés. Only Aemilius Simpson recorded his express's journey down the Columbia River and through the range of mountains to Fort Vancouver on the lower river. This section of his journal tells of the express's passage through the Little Dalles and other rapids in Nespelem Canyon, and his arrival at Fort Okanogan:

> Tuesday 24th. Fine and clear Weather, having to run a chain of rapids below our Encampment we did not Embark until day light, when we commenced our run of the Rapids, which form a sweeping chain for about 8 Miles. Below these rapids the River follows its course in a very Winding direction for about 3 and a half Leagues, when you arrive at the Junction of the Okinagan River, where we arrived at 9 a.m. We found Messrs. Archibald McDonald, & Armitinga here; who presented a communication from Dr. [John] McLoughlin, directing the brigade to carry a Supply of Salmon, for Walla Walla, but as these fish have not yet arrived from Thompson's River, we will be detained here till then.
>
> Wednesday 25th. A frost thro' the night, followed by fine Weather during the day. Notwithstanding the apparent Sterility of this Spot, Mr. Armitinga has succeeded in rising Potatoes of an excellent quality, on a more fertile spot some distance from the Fort, on an elevated situation where the Soil possesses more moisture than on the lower ground. He has formed a Garden, also, on the Bank of the Okinagan, immediately along side his establishment which produces such Culinary roots as he has had it in his power to try in considerable perfection, the pease came on rapidly & the Cabbages & turnips attained a

large growth, their efforts are praiseworthy and adds much to the comforts of the individuals, as the Potatoes tend to render the Salmon, which forms the chief article of food, a far more palatable and healthy diet. The Okinagan, the Indians that are about this post, appear pretty numerous, tho' a poor looking people, and apparently very inoffensive, as the Weakness of the Post indicates, there being only a Clerk and one man in charge. The Salmon having arrived this evening, we will resume our Journey in the morning.[27]

The man Simpson called "Armatinga" was Francis Ermatinger, younger brother of Edward Ermatinger, whose York Factory Express journals we have read. His current post stood alongside well-used First Nations trails that led north to Kamloops. But it was a lonely place. Never a profitable trading post, Fort Okanogan served as a transfer point for the New Caledonia Brigades that passed through in June and August, on their way to and from Fort Vancouver.

Simpson's journal continues:

Thursday 26th. The morning Showery with Strong Breezes from the Southward but the Weather became fair at 9 a.m. and continued so during the Day. Thermometer at Noon 56°. The face of the Country continues to present the same singular formation, a range of Hills along the River at the Rocky Island Portage, seems somewhat different, the face is columnar but a good deal fractured, giving it the appearance of an immense Pile of Cubical Masses.

Friday 27th. Fine and clear weather, a fresh breeze from the SW. We continue our descent of the River at 4:30 a.m. frequently passing ridges of these columnar faced Hills, at 11 we commenced our run of the Priests Rapids, so called by the Canadian Voyageurs, from the circumstance of an old Indian who constantly visits the Boats, when passing these rapids, who they think resembles one of that Holy order.[28]

Priest's Rapids was named in 1811 by Alexander Ross, an early fur trader. In his book, Ross wrote:

Here a large concourse of Indians met us, and after several friendly harangues [speeches], commenced the usual ceremony of smoking the

pipe of peace: after which they passed the night in dancing and singing. The person who stood foremost in all these introductory ceremonies, was a tall, meagre, middle-aged Indian, who attached himself
very closely to us from the first moment we saw him. He was called
Ha-qui-laugh, which signified doctor, or rather priest. . . . We named
the place, "Priest's Rapid," after him.[29]

Aemilius Simpson's downward river journey continues through desert country south of Priest's Rapids:

Saturday 28th. The morning Showery, we Embarked at 4 a.m., having
descended the River SE about 4 Leagues, we arrived at the confluence
of the Yaccama [Yakima] River, falling in from the Westward. It is to
the confluence of this River they propose removing the Establishment
[Fort Nez Percés]. On descending about 3 leagues further in a SE
course we arrived at the Junction of Lewis & Clarks Branch [Snake
River], the supposed boundary of the United States. . . . About 9 miles
below this Branch the Post of Walla Walla [Fort Nez Percés] is situated on the Left or South Bank of the Columbia, where we arrived at
8 a.m.[30]

This was the second-oldest post in the region, built in the desert
east of the Cascade Mountains in 1818. It was always a dangerous
place, surrounded by strong-minded and powerful peoples who were
not afraid of the HBC men. Sam Black was said to have been too
frightened to go outside the post.

Simpson's journal continues:

This Post is in charge of Mr. [Samuel] Black & tho' small is in a good
state of defence against Indian attack, it is strongly stockaded & has a
bastion on its SW angle, Mounting a few pieces of Artillery. We
found a number of Indians about this Fort of the Nez Percés, Yaccamas
& other Tribes, our Crews carried on a brisk trade of Dogs with them
for the purpose of Eating, they consider the flesh of this Animal
choice food. Orders having been received to send a supply of Horses
to Vancouver, by a detachment of hands from our Brigade, the necessary arrangements will detain us here for the day.

Sunday 29th. Rainy weather. Wind NW. The forenoon was occupied by Sending the Horses across the River, which was a very great caution for these poor animals, some of the younger ones were nearly drowned. 53 Horses & 4 Colts succeeding in crossing, with which Messrs. [James] Birnie & [George] Barnston, with five men, proceeded for Fort Vancouver. We will resume our Journey in the Morning. The Weather continued rainy during the day.[31]

It was common that horses were herded along the Columbia's north bank to Fort Vancouver, as there was no horse-friendly road along the river's south bank. Simpson's journal continues:

Monday 30th. Commenced fair a Strong Breeze from the SW til 7 a.m. We Embarked from Walla Walla, and continued our descent of the Columbia. We fell in with the Horse Brigade at our Breakfast Encampment. Noon, strong Breezes Westerly, Thermometer 57°. The River has expanded considerably being now little short of a Mile. We passed numerous Indians along the Banks of the River, who importuned us very much for Tobacco. At our night's Encampment they collected about us in great numbers, but conducted themselves peaceably, having got Tobacco to Smoke, of which they are passionately fond.

Tuesday 31st. The morning Gloomy, at 5 a.m. we Embarked & pursued our route down the Columbia, altho' it commenced rain which continued during the remainder of the Day. At 2 p.m. we arrived at the Shoots [Chûtes] Falls, where we had to make a Portage of our Boats & Luggage for about a half mile, across a Rocky Point on the North shore, which occupied us two hours. We found about 70 Indians Encampt upon this Portage, who conducted themselves very peaceably, the men upon our guard so as to resist any aggression. We gave the chiefs some Tobacco to have a Smoke when they ranged their Tribes about and indulged in that luxury — making a harangue with their people.[32]

The express-men were beginning their hazardous journey through the Cascade Mountains. The first barrier — the Chûtes — squeezed the Columbia into a rocky passage only 150 paces wide, and the river dropped 20 feet almost immediately, continuing to tumble down rocky rapids as it carved its way through the mountains. The voyageurs avoided these hazards by portaging the boats and loads over the narrow trail along the riverbanks. Simpson's journal continues:

> On leaving the Shore a quantity of Tobacco was thrown among the Crowd, and it was not a little amusing to see the scramble that ensued. At but two miles below the Shoots, we came to the Dalles Rapids, a long & intricate chain rushing with great force through a number of narrow & Crooked Channels, bounded by huge Masses of perpendicular Rock, the faces very much fractured. . . .[33]

The voyageurs normally ran the boats through The Dalles, where the river continued its downhill tumble between perpendicular rock walls. If the water was low enough, they might pause at the two-mile mark to pick up the gentlemen who had wisely walked across the portage. Simpson's journal continues:

> At 6:30 p.m. We Encampt about 3 Leagues below the Dalles, when we were visited by a number of Indians — who got the usual donation of Tobacco, and behaved themselves peaceably.
>   Wednesday [November] 1st. With the exception of one short bend our average course has been West[er]ly, as we approach the Cascades more to the SW. From below the Dalles the Current has diminished in Strength. The Cascades are a chain of strong rapids or falls, presenting a broken & foaming surface from their commencement to their foot. . . . At the Head of the Cascades stand a few Small Islands richly Wooded & two Indian villages, these combined objects forming a very picturesque appearance. . . . As we descend, the River becomes skirted by Hills which attain a greater elevation as we continue our descent, until at the Cascades they are nearly two thousand feet, & from a country free from Wood, we arrive in one richly cloathed with Forest.[34]

Once west of the Cascades Portage, the express-men had passed through the Cascade Mountain range and were in the lower Columbia River, following its course westward to Fort Vancouver. They were almost home. Simpson's journal continues:

> For about a League below the Cascades there is a very strong current with rapids. The River branches off into several channels formed by Islands; for about 6 Leagues below the Cascades the River is bounded by a range of High Hills densely Wooded, their faces in some places being perpendicular with pretty cascades descending some hundred feet. [This is the Columbia Gorge.]
>
> We breakfasted at the Prairie de Tea [Prairie du Thé], a few miles above Johnsons Island, from here the Banks of the River become low & continue so to the Fort. . . . At 1:40 p.m. We arrived at Fort Vancouver, our place of destination, having Made the Journey from York Factory in three months and nineteen days, a distance which I estimate by our route of Two thousand eight hundred and seventeen miles, the whole of which is by Water communication, except the Assiniboine & Rocky Mountain portages.[35]

— • —

Thomas Lowe brought in his Columbia Express party in 1847, and although he saw the changes that were happening on the lower Columbia River, he naturally did not realize what would be the result of the sickness that was infecting the First Nations people close by the Waillatpu Mission. On November 14, his party reached Fort Nez Percés, where "we found the Measles very prevalent, the Indians were dying in great numbers. Delivered 4 bags flour for the [Waiilatpu] Mission, and left 2 bags flour, and 1 keg Biscuit for the use of the express next spring. [Edouard] Crete whom we brought from Okanagan was left here."[36]

Lowe's party was delayed by wind, but set off at midday on November 15. Two days later they were at the Chûtes and "succeeded in getting the boats and pieces across with our eight men & only about a dozen Indians, most of them being sick."[37] The express reached Fort Vancouver on November 20, where Lowe found all was well. "The Fort fired a salute of 7 guns. The measles now raging much in the upper country have not yet reached this. Mr. [John] Work is here. . . . The men got their Regale in the evening."[38]

As noted in Chapter 2, the measles that raged around Fort Nez Percés that fall changed the course of the history in the HBC's Columbia District and New Caledonia. Thousands of First Nations people died as the disease spread up and down the brigade trails, reaching as far north as Fort Alexandria, on the Fraser River. For the HBC men, however, the most immediate changes were to the outgoing route of the 1848 express. Because of the massacre of the missionaries at Waiilatpu Mission, and the Cayuse War that resulted from that massacre, Thomas Lowe's party avoided the wide open Shawpatin Road, used by the express for a decade or more. Instead he travelled to Fort Okanagan, following the Columbia River north to the overland land route through the Grande Coulée.

In 1849, John Charles made his way outbound to Fort Colvile via the Shawpatin Road with no trouble at all. There are no journals for expresses of later years, but also no record of any particular difficulties in the existing reports sent to Governor George Simpson. It is likely the Shawpatin Road continued to be used in safety.

But the York Factory Express continued to undergo change. Over the decade of the 1830s, the Canadiens still in the territory grew too old for the hard work of the express, and younger Métis men took their place. By the 1840s, there were probably more mixed-blood men than Canadiens in the Columbia District, and by the late 1840s even they became hard to find, as many succumbed to the measles or abandoned the fur trade for the California goldfields, where many died. First Nations men began to fill the gaps left by men who had disappeared, and the express continued to make its way over the mountains to Hudson Bay for a few more years.

We Are Still Here

ᘒᘓ

JOHN CHARLES'S JOURNAL ended when he reached Edmonton House, but he travelled over the portage to Fort Assiniboine and passed through Jasper's House. Two days later, the Columbia Express arrived at Moose Encampment on the Athabasca River. Sir Edward Poore, a British tourist who joined the express at Edmonton House, told the story of Charles's death in a letter to his mother:

> In crossing the Mountain portage a most melancholy accident happened [to] the gent in charge, a very agreeable person by the name of Charles. One even[ing] after camp a raven came and lit on a tree close by. F[ranklin] took his rifle and missed it. . . . "No, stop" said Charles "let us all have a shot for a shilling a piece the best to win." There was an oldish man of the name of Young who had an American rifle. I had warned him as being a very dangerous one and apt to go off. C[harles] said to him come out and bring your old rifle.[1]

Edward Poore had earlier inspected Young's gun and found it unsafe. What followed proved that the gun was as dangerous as the English adventurer claimed. As Alexander Young carried it from the tent, "the rifle went off and shot poor Charles in the right breast."[2] John Charles collapsed onto the edge of the campfire. His shocked men extinguished the fire, but there was nothing they could do for the man, and he died two hours later in excruciating pain. Just before he died, he sat up and, looking wildly around, said clearly, "That was well done, Mr. Young."[3]

His men buried him at Moose Encampment, in secluded pine woods alongside the trail. They covered his grave with stones and built a small log house over it to prevent animals from digging up the body. Such was the culture of the fur trade that passenger Frederick Lewes, son of a chief factor but not an employee of the Company, was asked to take charge of the express, bringing it down the Columbia River to Fort Colvile.

Charles's express arrived at Fort Vancouver on November 19. A shocked Peter Skene Ogden reported that "the expression made use of by the unfortunate Mr. Charles after receiving the shot has not been satisfactorily explained to me and leaves an unpleasant impression on my mind, nor did Mr. Young in my presence evince any feeling of regret."[4] Alexander Young owed the Company six months' labour, but he disappeared from fur trade records almost immediately. The Company may have made it clear his services were not wanted.

— • —

Young's attitude toward the HBC men and their French and Métis employees was typical of the Americans who, in the 1840s, came by the thousands to settle in the Oregon Territory. Many Americans learned to hate the British who had opened up the territory almost forty years earlier, and who had brought in the thousands of Canadien and Métis men who now settled there. The fur trade changed rapidly over the next few years as the newly created Washington Territory fell into a state of almost constant war between the Americans and First Nations peoples who lived in the interior.

This had its effect on some gentlemen of the fur trade, who anticipated the HBC's decline and moved on — if they lived long enough. Lieutenant Aemilius Simpson, for example, did not survive for many years after he arrived at Fort Vancouver. He captained the ships that helped build the lower Fraser River post of Fort Langley in 1827 and the first Northwest Coast post, Fort Simpson, in spring 1831. On that voyage he sickened and died of liver disease, and his body was buried outside the gates of the post.

Edward Ermatinger left the fur trade at the end of his contract in 1828, returning to Canada where he became a banker and a merchant. Although he left the fur trade behind, he kept in close touch with the many friends he had made over the years. He also saved the voyageurs' songs he had collected, and probably played them many times over in the years that followed.

George Traill Allan foresaw the future and retired from the fur trade in 1850, becoming a commission merchant in partnership with Archibald McKinlay and Thomas Lowe. They formed the firm of Allan, McKinlay, and Lowe at Oregon City, where they supplied the new American settlers with goods. In 1861, a crippled Allan moved to James Birnie's house in Cathlamet, where he died in 1890. His grave is in the Cathlamet Pioneer cemetery.

James Douglas did not move on, but became chief factor and a member of the Board of Management at Fort Vancouver, close to the mouth of the Columbia. In 1849, he moved north to take charge of Fort Victoria, on southern Vancouver Island. He became the second governor of the Colony of Vancouver's Island, and the first governor of the Colony of British Columbia in November 1858. He was knighted by the Queen in 1863 prior to his retirement in the following year. He died in Victoria in 1877.

Thomas Lowe retired from the fur trade in 1849, going into partnership with Archibald McKinlay and George Traill Allan. He expanded his business to San Francisco, where he became the HBC's eyes and ears in that area. By 1862, he had moved north to the fledgling town of Victoria, in the Colony of Vancouver's Island, where he became a commission merchant, selling products he brought in from San Francisco. He sold, among other things, French wines and cigars. In 1872, he returned to Scotland, where he died at the ripe old age of eighty-eight.

And so ended the fur trade careers of the gentlemen who led out the York Factory Express.

It might appear that the tragedy which caused the death of John Charles would put an end to the York Factory Express as well, but it did not. William Sinclair led out the Express in 1850 and 1851, leaving Fort Vancouver in late March, as usual. In 1850, his express returned in November, also as usual, but the 1851 Columbia Express was delayed by extraordinarily wet weather and high waters on the North Saskatchewan, returning to Fort Vancouver a week and a half later than was normal.

In 1852, apprentice clerk Henry Hetling, who had been in the Columbia District only two years, led the express. It was a little late leaving Fort Vancouver, and as it passed through Fort Colvile in April, Angus McDonald reported it was later than usual, but earlier than the previous year. By early November, Fort Vancouver's temporary chief factor, John Ballenden, was keeping a sharp eye out for the express boats' arrival. He was not disappointed.

In 1853, Ballenden went out with the express, with clerk Robert Miles in charge. By this time, Fort Victoria had become the final stop, and Miles returned there, via Fort Vancouver, on December 26, 1853. Miles reported some difficulties: four men had deserted at the Grand Rapids, and one man (an English cooper) remained in the Saskatchewan District because his wife was ill.

In 1854, Henry Shuttleworth's express left Fort Vancouver. In the autumn, when the returning Columbia men were expected at Boat Encampment, the Fort Colvile men travelled upriver to await Shuttleworth's arrival, as they always did. Through no fault of their own, the incoming Columbia Express men were delayed. The Iroquois in charge of the small party at Boat Encampment grew frightened of the advancing winter and abandoned the camp in the boat that was supposed to carry the express-men home. Shuttleworth and his men arrived at the meeting place four days later and, finding no boat or provisions left for them, returned to Jasper's House with the horses. His guides remained behind, and when Angus McDonald sent a second boat upriver to Boat Encampment, his men found them there.

In 1855, the governor of the HBC sent specific instructions that the Fort Vancouver gentlemen were not to send an express over the mountains that year.[5] No one remembered to tell the gentleman in charge of New Caledonia. From Fort St. James, Donald Manson sent a boat to Tête Jaune Cache to pick up the new recruits, and was disappointed when no one arrived.

And so the York Factory Express died, although the Saskatchewan Brigades ran to York Factory for many more years. The express was replaced by a steamship service that ran up and down the coast between the Columbia River and Panama, where a new railway carried mail and passengers across the isthmus and were picked up by ships on the east coast.

The death of the York Factory Express also meant the death of Fort Assiniboine, which was closed down, its meadows reabsorbed by the bush. Fort Vancouver itself was taken over by the United States Government in 1860, and the gentlemen who still remained moved north to Fort Victoria. The Athabasca Portage continued to be used by the men of Jasper's House and those of Lesser Slave Lake, but it was rerouted to higher ground in the 1850s. In 1877, the Athabasca Landing trail followed a different path north from Edmonton to the new community of Athabasca Landing, and this later trail is the one that thousands of gold miners followed to the Klondike mines.

The York Factory Express remains an important part of the history of the territory west of the Rocky Mountains, and it played a part in the life of every man who worked west of the mountains. For twenty-eight consecutive years, the men left Fort Vancouver and travelled across the continent to Hudson Bay and back. Although on occasion the Columbia gentlemen were a little late for the annual meeting, the men themselves made it to York Factory at a remarkably consistent date, and always returned in time to cross the Rocky Mountains before deep snow blocked the passes. This was a huge accomplishment and was largely due to the character of the Canadien and Iroquois men who rowed the boats in the early years, and the Métis and First Nations men who later replaced them.

With the death of the York Factory Express, the men residing in the Columbia District must have felt the loss of a major part of their lives, their identity, and their culture. However, by the 1840s, loss was part of their lives. Many of the Canadiens and Métis who remained in the territory had already grown too old for the hard work of paddling the express boats upriver. Others had abandoned the fur trade, although they never entirely cut themselves off from their connection with the Hudson's Bay Company. A large number left Oregon Territory for the California goldfields of 1849, where more than a few of them died. Others settled on farms in the Willamette Valley and elsewhere, or worked the new goldfields near Fort Colvile or the Kamloops post in British territory.

Those who remained near Fort Vancouver and the other posts in the territory established their own communities, where they lived in harmony with people of other races and religions. They kept their traditions for a while. Many of the early settlers may not have needed to learn a language other than French, but later Canadiens did. They adapted.

For a while they hunted to feed themselves, as their French and Indigenous ancestors had done. They kept their Catholic religion alive, both in the white communities and the First Nations communities where many of them settled. They respected their elders, but they were also now the elders and earned the respect of others, who were younger than them. They taught the younger generations their old skills, until the old skills were of no use.

They lived an easier life on their scattered plots of land, but they also worked hard to build their farms and their businesses. They married and had children, and their children married and had children who gradually forgot their Canadien and Métis ancestry. Even their names disappeared, to a degree, as the spelling was changed to simplified American spellings, and their French way of speaking was muted.

There was good reason for them to forget their past. In the years after the West was populated by colonists who came in from England or from the eastern United States, the descendants of the fur trade employees learned to be silent. Prejudice against the Canadien and the Métis was strong in the new immigrants, and almost everyone faced that racism in one form or another. The fur trade descendants put their Indigenous past behind them and did not talk of it. If they mentioned it, they learned there were those who would hate them forever for their mixed-blood. Their history and culture did not matter to those who hated "the Indians."

But for the most part, the descendants of the Canadiens and Métis west of the Rocky Mountains have not forgotten our past. We tolerated the occasional prejudice that others expressed, although its unfairness angered us. We did not put our stories aside forever. Many of us who live today, who have Canadien and Indigenous blood, saw and heard how our parents and grandparents were treated by the descendants of the colonists who came from England and the United States to settle our country, making it a copy of their old world. We learned to remain quiet and to allow ourselves to be absorbed into whichever community we felt most comfortable in.

But recently there has been a revival of interest in the history of the fur trade even among academics, and descendants of these people are now claiming their heritage — our heritage. The history of the Métis, in the communities west of the Rocky Mountains, is everyone's history. Today, hopefully, we can mix in both communities without prejudice, and claim our share of the history of the territory west of the Rocky Mountains. We are here. We are still here.

NOTES

PROLOGUE: York Factory Express (pp. 1–10)

1 His lime kiln was not at modern-day Lime Bay, in Victoria, B.C., but at the end of Admirals Road near the Songhees Reserve.

2 Although the French pronounce the word "may-tiss," the Métis say "may-tea."

CHAPTER 1: The First York Factory Express Journeys (pp. 11–23)

1 John McLeod would continue the re-construction of Norway House on Mossy Point, and would also build the new Norway House at the Jack River fisheries.

2 John McLeod's original journal was written in pencil in two notebooks, with many of the notations out of order, and some written upside down. Most of his journal was written during torrential downpours. His son, Malcolm McLeod, transcribed the journal many years later, and a copy of his transcription has been stored in the British Columbia Archives for almost a century. As Malcolm had no familiarity with the words of the trade, I have corrected some errors of transcription and have arranged the notes in chronological order. This was not a major rearrangement, but the record that follows is not an exact copy of the original journal, nor of the transcription.

3 "John McLeod Journal, March 20–April 27, 1826," Malcolm McLeod Papers, pp. 67–68 (transcript), A/B/40/M22.2A, British Columbia Archives (henceforward BCA).

4 McLeod, pp. 69–70.

5 McLeod, pp. 72–73.

6 McLeod, pp. 74–76.

7 McLeod, p. 60.

8 "William Connolly's Journal of the Brigade from New Caledonia to Fort

Vancouver and Return, 5 May to 23 September 1826," fo.1, B.188/a/8, Hudson's Bay Company Archives (henceforward HBCA).

9 Aemilius Simpson, "Journal of a Voyage Across the Continent of North America in 1826," fo. 34, B.223/a/3, HBCA. Chief Trader James McMillan had explored this pass in 1825.

10 Valemount Historic Society, *Yellowhead Pass and Its People* (D.W. Friesen & Sons, 1984), p. 2.

11 Valemount Historic Society, *Yellowhead Pass and Its People*, p. 2.

12 "Edward Ermatinger's York Factory Express Journal, Being a Record of Journeys Made Between Fort Vancouver and Hudson Bay in the Years 1827–1828," with an introduction by Judge C.O. Ermatinger and notes by Judge C.O. Ermatinger and James White, FRSC (Ottawa: Royal Society of Canada, 1912), p. 82. Online at Peel's Prairie Provinces, University of Alberta Libraries, www.peel.library.ualberta.ca/bibliography (search for "Edward Ermatinger"). With this download comes part of David Douglas's journal of his crossing of the Athabasca Pass with Ermatinger's Express. Henceforward "Edward Ermatinger's York Factory Express Journal (1827)."

13 George McDougall to John McLeod, March 8, 1828, Journal and Correspondence of John McLeod, fo. 106, A/B/40/M22K, BCA.

14 James Douglas to Governor George Simpson, March 12, 1849, D.5/24, fo. 428, HBCA. Douglas recommended that John Charles be promoted to apprentice clerk and said that the class of postmaster should be discontinued in the Columbia District.

CHAPTER 2: Fort Vancouver to Fort Nez Percés (pp. 24–43)

1 "Edward Ermatinger's York Factory Express Journal (1827)," p. 70.

2 Regales were a treat of rum (in this case) or meat and potatoes as a reward for hard work.

3 Charles Wilkes (Richard E. Moore, ed.), *Life in Oregon Country Before the Emigration* (Ashland: Oregon Book Society, 1975), p. 146. Tracking is the practice of pulling the boat upriver with ropes tied to harnesses worn by the men. Boats are tracked when the river is too deep for poling or too fast for rowing.

4 Aemilius Simpson, "Journal of a Voyage Across the Continent of North America in 1826," fo. 49. A league was equal to three French miles,

which are slightly longer than English miles, and was approximately the distance a man could walk in an hour.

5 The Bonneville Dam now stands where the Cascades used to be.

6 "Edward Ermatinger's York Factory Express Journal (1827)," p. 71.

7 According to the editor of Ermatinger's journals, Cape Horn appears to be near Rowena Point, and not at Wind Mountain to the west.

8 Phoca Rock, in the Columbia Gorge, west of the Cascades, was named by Lewis and Clark for the many seals they found there.

9 Aemilius Simpson, "Journal of a Voyage Across the Continent of North America in 1826," fo. 47.

10 "Edward Ermatinger's York Factory Express Journal (1827)," p. 72. Ouvré came to the Columbia District in 1811. In 1827, he was on his way to Fort Nez Percés from Fort Vancouver, where he was generally employed. In later years, he worked at Fort Nisqually.

11 In fur trade parlance, a slave was a First Nations man rescued from the Indian slave trade that flourished up and down the coast.

12 "Edward Ermatinger's York Factory Express Journal (1827)," p. 72.

13 Ermatinger, p. 72.

14 Ermatinger, p 72.

15 Umatilla Rapids was about 288 miles from the mouth of the Columbia River, and 180 from Fort Vancouver.

16 "Edward Ermatinger's York Factory Express Journal (1827)," p. 73.

17 "Clinker-built" meant that the planks running down the sides of the boats overlapped each other. The boats on the west side of the Rockies differed from the carvel-constructed York Boats on the Saskatchewan River.

18 Charles Wilkes, *Life in Oregon Country Before the Emigration*, p. 147.

19 James Robert Anderson, "Notes and Comments on Early Days and Events in British Columbia, Washington and Oregon" (unpublished transcript in author's possession), p. 140.

20 Donald Manson, then employed at Fort Langley, had delivered dispatches to Fort Vancouver.

21 "Edward Ermatinger's York Factory Express Journal (1828)," pp. 112–13.

22 Ermatinger, p. 114.

23 Ermatinger, p. 114.

24 Ermatinger, p. 114. John Days' River was named for a member of W.P. Hunt's overland expedition of 1810–12.

25 James Douglas, "Private Papers: Diary of a Journey from Fort Vancouver in 1835," p. 5 (transcript), B/20/1858, BCA.

26 Montreal had both express and brigades, but the Saskatchewan Brigades, which the York Factory Express men would join, were that district's combined express and brigade.

27 James Douglas, "Diary of a Journey from Fort Vancouver in 1835," pp. 5–7.

28 John Kirk Townsend, *Narrative of a Journey Across the Rocky Mountains to the Columbia River* (Corvallis: Oregon State University Press, 1999), p. 178.

29 James Douglas, "Diary of a Journey from Fort Vancouver in 1835," p. 8.

30 John Kirk Townsend, *Narrative of a Journey Across the Rocky Mountains to the Columbia River*, p. 179.

31 James Douglas, "Diary of a Journey from Fort Vancouver in 1835," pp. 8–9.

32 Douglas, pp. 11–12.

33 Boisterous younger brother of Edward Ermatinger, whose journals from 1827 and 1828 are included here.

34 George Traill Allan, "Journal of a Voyage from Fort Vancouver, Columbia, to York Factory, Hudson's Bay, 1841," p. 1 (transcript), A/B/40/AL5.3A, BCA.

35 William Henry McNeil to Governor George Simpson, September 1, 1847, D.5/20, fo. 172, HBCA.

36 Thomas Lowe, "Journal of a Trip from Vancouver to York Factory per York Factory Express, Spring 1847 (March 24), by Thomas Lowe, in charge of party," A/B/20.4/L95, BCA. "Pieces" were wrapped or packaged bundles of trade goods or supplies, provisions, tobacco, and guns.

37 Lowe (March 27, 1847).

38 Lowe (March 28, 1847).

39 Lowe (March 30–April 1, 1847).

40 Lowe (November 14, 1847).

41 Peter Skene Ogden to Governor George Simpson, March 12, 1848, D.5/21, fo. 436, HBCA.

42 The *Mary Dare* was an HBC ship that worked on the Pacific Coast from 1846 to 1854.

43 By 1848, Roman Catholic priest and missionary Modeste Demers was bishop of Vancouver's Island. He was travelling to Europe to raise funds for his new mission.

44 Thomas Lowe, "Journal of a Trip from Vancouver to York Factory, Spring 1847 (March 20, 1848).

45 Lowe (March 21, 1848). Portage Neuve, and the old portage upriver, are probably the "bad rapid" shown on some early maps of the lower Columbia, west of the Cascades. They caused trouble to anyone going upriver, but coming downriver the HBC men paddled through it.

46 Lowe (March 24, 1848).

47 Lowe (March 25, 1848).

48 Lowe (March 29, 1848).

49 Lowe (March 30, 1848).

50 John Charles, "Journal of the Columbia Express Party, March 20–September 20, 1849 (March 22–23)," (transcript), A/B/20.4/C38A, BCA. Mr. Menetrez was a Jesuit missionary named Menetre.

51 This is a reference to the Board of Management at Fort Vancouver, which consisted of chief factors Peter Skene Ogden, James Douglas, and John Work.

52 John Charles, "Journal of the Columbia Express Party, 1849," (March 25).

CHAPTER 3: Fort Nez Percés to Fort Colvile (pp. 44–59)

1 Priest's Rapid was 397 miles from the Pacific Ocean and 290 miles from Fort Vancouver.

2 "Edward Ermatinger's York Factory Express Journal (1827)," p. 72.

3 Ermatinger, p. 72.

4 As mentioned in the prologue, George McDougall led four men out via the Rocky Mountain Portage in spring 1827. James McDougall had come in by this portage for the first time in October 1826. It was abandoned as an outgoing express route in 1828 but used every year in the fall as the incoming route.

5 "Edward Ermatinger's York Factory Express Journal (1827)," p. 73. According to Gabriel Franchère, Priest's Rapid was named by John Stuart, who in 1811 saw a First Nations man performing ceremonies that appeared to imitate Catholic rituals.

6 Ermatinger, p. 73.

7 Ermatinger, p. 74.

8 Ermatinger, p. 74.

9 Traditionally, the early voyageurs left Montreal for the interior on May 6 every year.

10 Fur traders often called Fort Nez Percés Walla Walla, as it stood on or near the Walla Walla River. The muskets and accessories were probably left for the men of the brigades who would be coming downriver from Kamloops and New Caledonia in early June.

11 "Edward Ermatinger's York Factory Express Journal (1828)," p. 115.

12 Ermatinger, p. 115.

13 Ermatinger, p. 116.

14 Ermatinger, p. 116.

15 Ermatinger, p. 116.

16 Ermatinger, p. 117. John Warren Dease was at Norway House to meet Governor George Simpson in June 1828, and he spent the summer there.

17 James Douglas, "Diary of a Journey from Fort Vancouver in 1835," pp. 12–13.

18 There are badgers here, but also groundhogs and prairie dogs.

19 George Traill Allan, "Journal of a Voyage from Fort Vancouver, Columbia, to York Factory, Hudson's Bay, 1841," pp. 2–4.

20 Allan, p. 6.

21 David Finlay was the son of a female descendant of famed fur trader and explorer Jacques Raphael Finlay and of visiting botanist David Douglas.

22 Thomas Lowe, "Journal of a Trip from Vancouver to York Factory, Spring 1847," (April 2–6).

23 Lowe (April 7–8, 1847).

24 Lowe (April 10, 1847).

25 Alexander Dumond was a retired employee of the fur trade who settled near Fort Colvile.

26 Thomas Lowe, "Journal of a Trip from Vancouver to York Factory, Spring 1847," (April 12).

27 Marineau was introduced in the prologue. Michel Ogden, son of Peter Skene Ogden, was a long-time employee in the New Caledonia District.

28 Thomas Lowe, "Journal of a Trip from Vancouver to York Factory, 1848," (April 1–3).

29 Lowe (April 5, 1848).

30 Lowe (April 6–8, 1848).

31 Alexander Caulfield Anderson, *Handbook and Map to the Gold Region of*

Frazer's and Thompson's Rivers (San Francisco: J.J. Le Count, 1858), p. 13. The Grande Coulée was formed during the last Ice Age when the waters of a huge lake covering Montana burst its glacier dam and carved deep valleys into the basalt rock of central Washington. Today it is underwater, behind the Grand Coulee Dam.

32 Thomas Lowe, "Journal of a Trip from Vancouver to York Factory, 1848," (April 10–12).

33 Lowe (April 13, 1848).

34 John Charles, "Journal of the Columbia Express Party, 1849," (March 30–April 1).

35 Charles (April 2–4).

36 Charles (April 5–6).

37 Aemilius Simpson, "Journal of a Voyage Across the Continent of North America in 1826," fo. 37.

CHAPTER 4: Fort Colvile to Boat Encampment (pp. 60–72)

1 George Traill Allan, "Journal of a Voyage from Fort Vancouver, Columbia, to York Factory, Hudson's Bay, 1841," pp. 7–8.

2 "Edward Ermatinger's York Factory Express Journal (1827)," p. 75.

3 Ermatinger, p. 76.

4 *Pas d'ours* are bear-paw snowshoes.

5 At the top of Upper Arrow Lake, they are 785 miles from Fort Vancouver.

6 "Edward Ermatinger's York Factory Express Journal (1827)," pp. 76–77.

7 "Douglas' Journey to Hudson's Bay," published in *Companion to the Botanical Magazine*, Vol. II, edited by Sir W.J. Hooker (London: Edward Couchman, 1826), pp. 134–35. Sourced at Biodiversity Heritage Library, online at www.biodiversitylibrary.org, the world's largest open access digital library for biodiversity literature and archives. Another version of this journal is included in "Edward Ermatinger's York Factory Express Journal," Peel's Prairie, see Chapter 1, Note 12.

8 "Edward Ermatinger's York Factory Express Journal (1827)," p. 77.

9 Ermatinger, p. 77.

10 Ermatinger, p. 77.

11 Ermatinger, p. 77. The rapid below Les Dalles des Morts was known as Priest Rapid, on the Columbia River north of Downie Creek, 51 degrees, 118 mins, SE.

12 Les Dalles des Morts or Death Rapid was on the Columbia River north of today's Revelstoke, B.C.

13 "Edward Ermatinger's York Factory Express Journal (1827)," pp. 77–78.

14 Rapides Croches may be Gordon Rapid, on the Columbia River 15 miles north of Goldstream River on modern maps. In these journals, this word Croche(s) could have meant Crooked, Quavering, or Cross, and at various times meant any one of the three words.

15 "Edward Ermatinger's York Factory Express Journal (1827)," p. 78.

16 Ermatinger, 78.

17 James Douglas, "Diary of a Journey from Fort Vancouver in 1835," pp. 14–15.

18 Douglas, pp. 16–17. Chief Trader Francis Heron, then in charge of Fort Colvile, travelled out with the express to begin a four-year-long furlough in Europe.

19 Thomas Lowe, "Journal of a Trip from Vancouver to York Factory, Spring 1847," (April 22). Dease's Encampment was almost certainly named for John Warren Dease, who was chief trader in this district and died in 1830.

20 Lowe (April 26, 1847).

21 Lowe (April 27, 1847).

22 James Douglas, "Diary of a Journey from Fort Vancouver in 1835," p. 16.

23 Thomas Lowe, "Journal of a Trip from Vancouver to York Factory, Spring 1847," (April 28).

24 Lowe (April 29–30, 1847).

25 Alexander Caulfield Anderson, Map, "Sketch of the Upper Columbia, Fort Colvile to Jasper's House," CM/13662B, BCA.

26 Thomas Lowe, "Journal of a Trip from Vancouver to York Factory, Spring 1847," (May 2).

27 A cassette that probably belonged to Pierre Chrysologue Pambrun is three feet long by seventeen inches wide and sixteen inches deep.

28 Alexander Caulfield Anderson, Map, "Sketch of the Upper Columbia, Fort Colvile to Jasper's House."

29 Thomas Lowe, "Journal of a Trip from Vancouver to York Factory, 1848," (April 24).

30 Lowe (April 28, 1848).

31 Lowe (April 29, 1848).

32 Lowe (May 1–4, 1848). Capot Blanc was a First Nations man who lived

at Cranberry Lake, on the headwaters of Fraser River, and who visited Boat Encampment, Jasper's House, and Kamloops.

33 John Charles, "Journal of the Columbia Express Party, 1849," (April 23–May 2).

34 Charles (May 4).

CHAPTER 5: Boat Encampment to Jasper's House (pp. 73–84)

1 George Traill Allan, "Journal of a Voyage from Fort Vancouver, Columbia, to York Factory, Hudson's Bay, 1841," pp. 9–10. (The apostrophe in Hudson's Bay was common usage at this time).

2 Allan, p. 12.

3 Allan, p. 12.

4 "Douglas' Journey to Hudson's Bay," p. 135.

5 George Traill Allan, "Journal of a Voyage from Fort Vancouver, Columbia, to York Factory, Hudson's Bay, 1841," pp. 12–14.

6 National Gallery of Canada, Russell J. Harper, ed., *Paul Kane's Frontier* (Toronto: University of Toronto Press, 1971), p. 88.

7 George Traill Allan, "Journal of a Voyage from Fort Vancouver, Columbia, to York Factory, Hudson's Bay, 1841," p. 14.

8 Allan, p. 14.

9 Allan, p. 15.

10 Allan, p. 15. Quizzing, or asking teasing questions, appears to have the meaning that is closest to the way this word is used.

11 John Work, "Journal, July 18 to October 25, 1823, York Factory to Spokane House," p. 35 (transcript), A/B/40/W89.1A, BCA.

12 Ross Cox, *Adventures on the Columbia River* (New York: J. & J. Harper, 1832), p. 248.

13 While it is not true that the Committee's Punch Bowl Lake was the source of the Columbia River, the waters of the Committee's Punch Bowl Lake flowed west at high water, following Jeffrey Creek and Wood River into the Columbia at Boat Encampment. Most of the York Factory Express men considered the Wood River a continuation of the Columbia.

14 George Traill Allan, "Journal of a Voyage from Fort Vancouver, Columbia, to York Factory, Hudson's Bay, 1841," p. 16.

15 Allan, p. 16.

16 Allan, pp. 19–20. The "afore said goose" refers to the meal the horse-keeper had prepared for him on his arrival at Campement d'Orignal.

17 Allan, pp. 22–23. This comment is based on the legend that Richard the Lion-Heart dined with Robin Hood and his men, including Friar Tuck, in Sherwood Forest.

18 Frederick Merk, *Fur Trade and Empire: George Simpson's Journals* (Cambridge, Harvard UP, 1931), p. 145.

19 Thomas Lowe, "Journal of a Trip from Vancouver to York Factory, Spring 1847," (May 2).

20 Lowe (May 3–8, 1847).

21 John Charles, "Journal of the Columbia Express Party, 1849," (May 9).

CHAPTER 6: Jasper's House to Edmonton House (pp. 85–100)

 1 Aemilius Simpson, "Journal of a Voyage Across the Continent of North America in 1826," fo. 31. Simpson says the distance is 285 miles, although it is only 185.

 2 "David Douglas' Journey to Hudson's Bay," p. 137.

 3 James Douglas, "Diary of a journey from Fort Vancouver in 1835," p. 18. By 26 current, he meant the 26th of April, which was the current month.

 4 Douglas, pp. 18–19.

 5 Douglas, p. 20.

 6 "Edward Ermatinger's York Factory Express Journal (1827)," footnote, p. 82.

 7 John Work, "Journal, July 18 to October 25, 1823, York Factory to Spokane House," p. 17. Work travelled west via the old NWC route in one of the early canoe brigades that preceded the Columbia District's York Factory Express.

 8 George Traill Allan, "Journal of a Voyage from Fort Vancouver, Columbia, to York Factory, Hudson's Bay, 1841," pp. 23–24.

 9 "David Douglas' Journey to Hudson's Bay," p. 138.

10 Aemilius Simpson, "Journal of a Voyage Across the Continent of North America in 1826," fo. 25.

11 "Edward Ermatinger's York Factory Express Journal (1827)," p. 84.

12 Terry Pettus, "Frolic at Fort Nisqually," *Beaver Magazine*, Summer 1961, p. 11.

13 "Edward Ermatinger's York Factory Express Journal (1827)," pp. 84–85.

14 Ermatinger, pp. 85–86.

15 Ermatinger, p. 120.

16 James Douglas, "Diary of a Journey from Fort Vancouver in 1835," pp. 20–21.

17 Douglas, p. 21.

18 Mark Anderako, *Historic Trails of Alberta* (Edmonton: Lone Pine Publishing, 1985), pp. 105–11.

19 John Charles, "Journal of the Columbia Express Party, 1849," (May 20–25).

20 Augustus Richard Peers, "Journal 1842–52," p. 122, Transcript, E/B/P34, BCA.

21 Dorothy L. Boggis, "York Boat Coming," *Beaver Magazine*, June 1954, p. 50.

CHAPTER 7: Edmonton House to Carlton House (pp. 101–112)

1 George Traill Allan, "Journal of a Voyage from Fort Vancouver, Columbia, to York Factory, Hudson's Bay, 1841," p. 29.

2 Castoreum is a rank-smelling, oily, yellowish secretion from the beaver's castor glands, used by the beaver to scent-mark its territory. In the 1840s, castoreum had value as a medicine to treat headache, fever, and hysteria.

3 James Douglas, "Diary of a Journey from Fort Vancouver in 1835," p. 22.

4 Douglas, p. 22.

5 Aemilius Simpson, "Journal of a Voyage Across the Continent of North America in 1826," fo. 16. His "cattle" were bison.

6 Simpson, fo. 13.

7 George McDougall, introduced in Chapter 1, was not officially part of this brigade. He was travelling only as far as Carlton House, where he would spend the summer. He will rejoin the express in Chapter 12.

8 "Edward Ermatinger's York Factory Express Journal, 1827," p. 86.

9 Another Vermilion Creek was north of Edmonton, and is called Redwater Creek today. This Saskatchewan river is still called the Vermilion. Neither of these forts is the same as the one of the same name on the Peace River, established by the NWC in 1788.

10 "Edward Ermatinger's York Factory Express Journal, 1827," p. 86.

11 Ermatinger, pp. 87–88. A bison's speed on land is 35 to 40 miles an hour, and they are very agile.

12 The medical man Ermatinger expected to find at Carlton House was Dr. John Richardson, a member of Sir John Franklin's Arctic land

expedition of 1825–27. In 1825, his party mapped most of the shoreline of Great Bear Lake, and in 1827 the Arctic Ocean shoreline between the Mackenzie and Coppermine rivers. When that work was done, Richardson made an amazing overland journey to the Saskatchewan River to study the spring bird migration.

13 "Edward Ermatinger's York Factory Express Journal (1828)," p. 121. The dog was probably part of their provisions.

14 The Circus Indians were probably Sarcee, who spoke Athapascan. According to Douglas, they were not Woodland Cree, Gros Ventres (Fall), Blood, Peigan, or Blackfoot, and they spoke a language that differed from the Woodland Cree that the fur traders knew.

15 James Douglas, "Diary of a Journey from Fort Vancouver in 1835," p. 24.

16 Thomas Lowe, "Journal of a Trip from Vancouver to York Factory, 1848," (June 2).

17 John Charles, "Journal of the Columbia Express Party, 1849," (May 29).

18 Thomas Lowe, "Journal of a Trip from Vancouver to York Factory, 1848," (June 4).

19 John Work, "Journal, July 18 to October 25, 1823, York Factory to Spokane House," p. 9. Without exception, the fur traders spelled pemmican "Pemican." The flour would have been mixed with the pemmican and onions to make a stew-like meal the voyageurs called rubaboo.

20 George Traill Allan, "Journal of a Voyage from Fort Vancouver, Columbia, to York Factory, Hudson's Bay, 1841," p. 29.

21 James Douglas, "Diary of a Journey from Fort Vancouver in 1835," pp. 38–39.

22 Douglas, 23–24.

23 John Charles, "Journal of the Columbia Express Party, 1849," (June 1).

24 George Traill Allan, "Journal of a Voyage from Fort Vancouver, Columbia, to York Factory, Hudson's Bay, 1841," p. 30. This was actually the third location of Carlton House; earlier posts were on the Saskatchewan and the Assiniboine Rivers.

25 Aemilius Simpson, "Journal of a Voyage Across the Continent of North America in 1826," fo. 14.

CHAPTER 8: Carlton House to Norway House (pp. 113–126)

1 "Edward Ermatinger's York Factory Express Journals (1827)," p. 89.

2 Laudanum was a dangerous cocktail of opium, codeine, and alcohol.

3 James G. MacGregor, *Blankets and Beads: A History of the Saskatchewan River* (Edmonton: Institute of Applied Art, no date), pp. 105–6.

4 John Charles, "Journal of the Columbia Express Party, 1849," (June 5–8).

5 Thomas Lowe, "Journal of a Trip from Vancouver to York Factory, Spring 1847," (June 2–4).

6 Alexander Caulfield Anderson, "British Columbia," draft unpublished manuscript, pp. 27–28, mss. 559, vol. 2, folder 8, BCA.

7 Thomas Lowe, "Journal of a Trip from Vancouver to York Factory, Spring 1847," (June 4–7).

8 Lowe (June 7–8, 1847).

9 Lowe (June 8, 1847).

10 Lowe (June 9, 1847).

11 Lowe (June 10–13, 1847).

12 Augustus Richard Peers, "Journal, 1842–52," p. 124.

13 Thomas Lowe, "Journal of a Voyage to York Factory, Spring 1847," (June 14–15).

14 Lowe (June 16–20, 1847).

15 Augustus Richard Peers, "Journal, 1842–52," p. 118.

16 Pine Island might be today's Selkirk Island, and little Stoney Island might be Eagle Island, according to the editors of Ermatinger's published journals.

17 "Edward Ermatinger's York Factory Express Journal (1828)," pp. 122–23.

18 John Charles, "Journal of the Columbia Express Party, 1849," (June 14–15).

19 Charles (June 20–21).

20 Charles (June 22).

21 Thomas Lowe, "Journal of a Trip from Vancouver to York Factory, Spring 1847," (June 22).

22 Lowe (June 24, 1847).

23 Thomas Lowe, "Journal of a Trip from Vancouver to York Factory, 1848," (June 20).

24 John Charles, "Journal of the Columbia Express Party, 1849," (June 27).

CHAPTER 9: Norway House to York Factory (pp. 127–143)

1 Alexander Caulfield Anderson, *Notes on North-Western America* (Montreal: Mitchell & Wilson, 1876), p. 11.

2 John Birkbeck Nevins, *A Narrative of Two Voyages to Hudson's Bay: With Traditions of the North American Indians* (London: Society for Promoting Christian Knowledge, 1847), p. 81. Found online at www.canadiana.org.

3 John Charles, "Journal of the Columbia Express Party, 1849," (June 28–29).

4 Charles (June 30–July 3, 1849).

5 Augustus Richard Peers, "Journal, 1842–52," p. 59.

6 Robert Michael Ballantyne, *Hudson's Bay: Or, Every-day Life in the Wilds of North America, during Six Years' Residence in the Territory of the Hon. Hudson's Bay Company* (Boston: Phillips, Sampson and Co., 1859), p. 126.

7 Augustus Richard Peers, "Journal, 1842–52," pp. 36–37. The Ten Fathom Hole was some fifteen miles from York Factory.

8 Thomas Lowe, "Journal of a Trip from Vancouver to York Factory, 1848," (Sept. 7).

9 John Charles, "Journal of the Columbia Express Party, 1849," (July 15).

10 Augustus Richard Peers, "Journal, 1842–52," p. 56.

11 George Traill Allan, "Journal of a Voyage from Fort Vancouver, Columbia, to York Factory, Hudson's Bay, 1841," p. 44.

12 Thomas Lowe, "Journal of a Trip from Vancouver to York Factory, Spring 1847," (July 1–10).

13 Thomas Lowe, "Journal of a Trip from Vancouver to York Factory, 1848," (July 3).

14 John E. Foster, "Paulet Paul: Métis or House Indian Folk-Hero?" (*Manitoba History*, Number 9, Spring 1985). Article online at http://www.mhs.mb.ca/docs/mb_history/09/pauletpaul.shtml.

15 Augustus Richard Peers, "Journal, 1842–52," p. 63.

16 Peers, p. 43.

17 Alexander Caulfield Anderson, "History of the Northwest Coast," mss. 559, box 2, file 3, p. 27 (TS, B.A. McKelvie version), BCA.

18 Augustus Richard Peers, "Journal, 1842–52," p. 43.

CHAPTER 10: York Factory to Norway House (pp. 144–157)

1 In 1824–25, Governor George Simpson travelled to the Columbia District by an experimental northern route that eventually brought him to the Athabasca River and Fort Assiniboine. John Rowand travelled to Edmonton House via the North Saskatchewan and crossed over to the Athabasca River to meet Governor Simpson. When Simpson finally

arrived at Fort Assiniboine, he found Rowand had given up the wait and returned to Edmonton House. This convinced Simpson that the North Saskatchewan route was better and faster, and he ordered that a good road be cut over the portage in winter and spring 1824–25. In April 1825, the governor rode over the new trail on his return to Edmonton House from the Columbia. He decided that the threat of Indian attack along the North Saskatchewan route could be averted by combining the Saskatchewan brigades with the spring canoe brigades from the Columbia District, which would increase manpower in the boats enough to ensure the brigades could travel downriver in safety. Since 1826 was the first year the York Factory Express travelled out by the new route over the Athabasca Portage to Edmonton House, it was Aemilius Simpson's duty to report to Governor Simpson on the success of the new experiment.

2 James Douglas, "Diary of a Journey from Fort Vancouver in 1835," p. 28.

3 Thomas Lowe, "Journal of a Trip from Vancouver to York Factory, 1848," (July 14).

4 Aemilius Simpson, "Journal of a Voyage Across the Continent of North America in 1826," fo. 3.

5 Simpson, fo. 3.

6 Obsolete word meaning "causeway," although the editors of "Lt. Aemilius Simpson's Survey from York Factory to Fort Vancouver, 1826," explain this is a standard Scottish word for cobbled street (13).

7 Aemilius Simpson, "Journal of a Voyage Across the Continent of North America in 1826," fo. 3.

8 Simpson, fo. 4.

9 Simpson, fo. 4.

10 Simpson, fo. 5.

11 Simpson, fo. 5.

12 Simpson, fo. 5.

13 Simpson, fo. 5.

14 John Franklin was knighted in 1829.

15 Aemilius Simpson, "Journal of a Voyage Across the Continent of North America in 1826," fo. 5.

16 Simpson, fo. 5. Simpson refers to Robert Hood, the artist who accompanied John Franklin's expedition to the Arctic by land in 1819–21. He was murdered by one of the expedition's voyageurs on October 20, 1821.

17 Simpson, fo. 6.

18 Quoted in "Lt. Aemilius Simpson's Survey from York Factory to Fort Vancouver, 1826," p. 10, note.

19 Augustus Richard Peers, "Journal, 1842–52," p. 108.

20 John Charles, "Journal of the Columbia Express Party, 1849," (August 1).

21 Charles (August 2–5).

22 Aemilius Simpson, "Journal of a Voyage Across the Continent of North America in 1826," fo. 6.

23 Also called the Sea Carrying Place, the east channel of the Nelson River was known as the Sea River. By "Monton," Charles might have meant Montagne (mountain), as in the last rapid on the mountain.

24 John Charles, "Journal of the Columbia Express Party, 1849," (August 6–7).

25 Charles John Griffin to Governor George Simpson, February 27, 1850, D.5/27, fo. 367, HBCA.

26 Thomas Lowe, "Journals Kept at Fort Vancouver, Columbia River, 1843–1850," p. 61, E/A.L95A, Transcript, BCA.

27 Lowe, p. 65. Although Tayentas died of apparent lung disease, the measles might have indirectly caused his death. Measles destroys the immune system and allows other diseases, such as tuberculosis, to take over.

CHAPTER 11: Norway House to Cumberland House (pp. 158–168)

1 James Douglas, "Diary of a Journey from Fort Vancouver in 1835," p. 31.

2 Augustus Richard Peers, "Journal, 1842–52," p. 128.

3 Fort Edmonton Post Journal 1832, entry for September 20, 1832. B.60/a/27, fo. 15, HBCA.

4 "Edward Ermatinger's York Factory Express Journal (1827)," p. 97.

5 Alexander Caulfield Anderson, *Notes on North-Western America*, p. 11.

6 Augustus Richard Peers, "Journal, 1842–52," p. 136.

7 "Edward Ermatinger's York Factory Express Journal (1827)," p. 98.

8 Thomas Lowe, "Journal of a Trip from Vancouver to York Factory, Spring 1847," (August 7–8).

9 Lowe (August 9, 1847).

10 Lowe (August 12–13, 1847).

11 The Poire is what is now known as serviceberry or saskatoon berry (*Amelanchier alnifolia*).

12 Mountain barometers were mercury barometers used to determine elevation above a known base level.

13 A reference to Red Rock Rapids, where Xavier Sylvestre drowned twenty-two years later, in 1848.

14 Aemilius Simpson, "Journal of a Voyage Across the Continent of North America in 1826," fo. 8.

15 Thomas Lowe, "Journal of a Trip from Vancouver to York Factory, Spring 1847," (August 14).

16 Thomas Lowe, "Journal of a Trip from Vancouver to York Factory, 1848," (August 9).

17 Thomas Lowe, "Journal of a Trip from Vancouver to York Factory, Spring 1847," (August 15–17).

18 Lowe (August 19–20, 1847).

19 As mentioned in Chapter 8, the Saskatchewan River's estuary began at Thoburn Rapids (Tobin Lake) and ran 120 miles to Cedar Lake.

20 John Work, "Journal, July 18 to October 25, 1823, York Factory to Spokane House," p. 4.

21 Thomas Lowe, "Journal of a Trip from Vancouver to York Factory, Spring 1847," (August 21–22).

22 Aemilius Simpson, "Journal of a Voyage Across the Continent of North America in 1826," fo. 10.

23 James Douglas, "Diary of a Journey from Fort Vancouver in 1835," p. 34.

24 Thomas Lowe, "Journal of a Trip from Vancouver to York Factory, 1848," (August 15).

CHAPTER 12: Cumberland House to Carlton House (pp. 169–182)

1 Aemilius Simpson, "Journal of a Voyage Across the Continent of North America in 1826," fo. 11.

2 "Edward Ermatinger's York Factory Express Journal (1827)," p. 99.

3 George McDougall to John McLeod, March 8, 1828, "Journal and Correspondence of John McLeod Senior," Malcolm McLeod Papers, p. 106 (Transcript), A/B/40/M22K, BCA.

4 "Edward Ermatinger's York Factory Express Journal (1827)," pp. 99–100.

5 Aemilius Simpson, "Journal of a Voyage Across the Continent of North America in 1826," fo. 7.

6 "Edward Ermatinger's York Factory Express Journal (1827)," pp. 100–1. Probably Blackfoot and Sarcee, who got along well with each other.

7 Aemilius Simpson, "Journal of a Voyage Across the Continent of North America in 1826," fo. 13.

8 George Traill Allan, "Journal of a Voyage from Fort Vancouver, Columbia, to York Factory, Hudson's Bay, 1841," p. 30.

9 Probably Bigstone River.

10 Zig Zag Creek, near Mosquito Point, now part of the Torch River because of changes in the flow of the river.

11 James Douglas, "Diary of a Journey from Fort Vancouver in 1835," pp. 34–35.

12 Douglas, pp. 35–36.

13 Douglas, p. 36.

14 Augustus Richard Peers, "Journal, 1842–52," pp. 134–35.

15 James Douglas, "Diary of a Journey from Fort Vancouver in 1835," p. 36.

16 Douglas, p. 37.

17 This Sturgeon River was six miles north of modern-day Prince Albert, Saskatchewan.

18 James Douglas, "Diary of a Journey from Fort Vancouver in 1835," pp. 37–38.

19 Augustus Richard Peers, "Journal 1842–52," p. 129.

20 James Douglas, "Diary of a Journey from Fort Vancouver in 1835," p. 38.

21 In 1805, Nor'Wester F.A. Larocque traded with a Rocky Mountain tribe he called the Crerokas, who were probably the Sarcee.

22 James Douglas, "Diary of a Journey from Fort Vancouver in 1835," pp. 22–23.

23 John Charles, "Journal of the Columbia Express Party, 1849," (August 22–31).

24 George Traill Allan, "Journey of a Voyage from Norway House to Fort Vancouver, Columbia River, 1831," p. 20.

25 John Charles, "Journal of the Columbia Express Party, 1849," (September 1).

CHAPTER 13: Carlton House to Fort Pitt (pp. 183–191)

1 Aemilius Simpson, "Journal of a Voyage Across the Continent of North America in 1826," fo. 14–15. These deer were probably mule deer.

2 Simpson, fo. 15–16.

3 Simpson, fo. 17.

4 Simpson, fo. 17.

5 Simpson, fo. 17.

6 Simpson, fo. 18.

7 Simpson, fo. 22.

8 George Traill Allan, "Journal of a Voyage from Norway House to Fort Vancouver, Columbia River, 1831," pp. 20–21.

9 Allan, p. 22.

10 James Douglas, "Diary of a Journey from Fort Vancouver in 1835," p. 38.

11 Douglas, p. 39.

12 According to Philip Turnour's Hudson House entry of April 25, 1779, Geboch was the man who brought the news of the attack on Peter Pangman's post. E.E. Rich, ed., *Cumberland and Hudson House Journals, 1775–82, First Series, 1775–79* (London: Hudson's Bay Record Society), 331n.

13 James Douglas, "Diary of a Journey from Fort Vancouver in 1835," p. 40.

14 The NWC's Pine Island post was sometimes called Fort de L'Isle, although the real Fort de L'Isle was farther west along the river, in Alberta.

15 John Charles, "Journal of the Columbia Express Party, 1849," (September 2).

16 Charles (September 4–6).

17 Charles (September 7).

CHAPTER 14: Fort Pitt to Edmonton House (pp. 192–203)

1 Aemilius Simpson, "Journal of a Voyage Across the Continent of North America in 1826," fo. 20.

2 Simpson, fo. 20.

3 Simpson, fo. 20.

4 James Douglas, "Diary of a Journey from Fort Vancouver in 1835," p. 41.

5 Aemilius Simpson, "Journal of a Voyage Across the Continent of North America in 1826," fo. 20.

6 Simpson, fo. 20.

7 There is an overland portage from Moose Lake, in the North Saskatchewan watershed, to Lac la Biche, in the Athabasca River watershed.

8 Aemilius Simpson, "Journal of a Voyage Across the Continent of North America in 1826," fo. 20.

9 Simpson, fo. 20.

10 "Edward Ermatinger's York Factory Express Journal (1827)," p. 102. The editors of the journal identify "the Old Fort" as Fort George.

11 James Douglas, "Diary of a Journey from Fort Vancouver in 1835," p. 41.

12 Douglas, p. 41.

13 Aemilius Simpson, "Journal of a Voyage Across the Continent of North America in 1826," fo. 20.

14 "Edward Ermatinger's York Factory Express Journal (1827)," p. 102.

15 James Douglas, "Diary of a Journey from Fort Vancouver in 1835," p. 41.

16 Douglas, pp. 41–42.

17 Aemilius Simpson, "Journal of a Voyage Across the Continent of North America in 1826," fo. 21.

18 Trente-Un was a seventeenth-century three-card game; bouilotte was a later derivative of this game that had a 20-card pack with the Jack of Clubs as a wildcard. Poque was a fifteenth-century five-card game played with thirty-two cards, which involved knocking on the table and which eventually gave poker its name. Faro is a seventeenth-century French gambling game played between a banker and several players with one deck of cards.

19 Aemilius Simpson, "Journal of a Voyage Across the Continent of North America in 1826," fo. 21.

20 James Douglas, "Diary of a Journey from Fort Vancouver in 1835," p. 42.

21 "Edward Ermatinger's York Factory Express Journal (1827)," p. 102.

22 Aemilius Simpson, "Journal of a Voyage Across the Continent of North America in 1826," fo. 21.

23 James Douglas, "Diary of a Journey from Fort Vancouver in 1835," p. 42.

24 Aemilius Simpson, "Journal of a Voyage Across the Continent of North America in 1826," fo. 21.

25 Now Victoria Settlement, Alberta.

26 Aemilius Simpson," Journal of a Voyage Across the Continent of North America in 1826," fo. 21.

27 Simpson, fo. 22.

28 Simpson, fo. 22.

29 Simpson, fo. 23.

30 George Traill Allan, "Journal of a Voyage from Norway House to Fort Vancouver, Columbia River, 1831," pp. 22–23.

31 James Douglas, "Diary of a Journey from Fort Vancouver in 1835," p. 41.

32 Thomas Lowe, "Journal of a Trip from Vancouver to York Factory, Spring 1847," (September 16).

33 Thomas Lowe, "Journal of a Trip from Vancouver to York Factory, 1848," (September 7).

34 John Charles, "Journal of the Columbia Express Party, 1849," (September 14).

35 Charles (September 20).

36 Aemilius Simpson, "Journal of a Voyage Across the Continent of North America in 1826," fo. 23. The Red Deer were elk. Earlier in Chapter 7, it is explained that George Traill Allan had described the fort that later replaced this one.

37 Simpson, fo. 23.

CHAPTER 15: Edmonton House to Jasper's House (pp. 204–216)

1 Simpson, fo. 24. Chief Factor John Stuart was going to his new posting at Lesser Slave Lake. Chief Trader Joseph McGillivray was entering New Caledonia, and clerk George Barnston was going to Fort Vancouver to assist Simpson with his surveys.

2 Simpson, fo. 24.

3 Simpson, fo. 24.

4 Simpson, fo. 24.

5 Simpson, fo. 24.

6 Cruche, or Pitcher.

7 Aemilius Simpson, "Journal of a Voyage Across the Continent of North America in 1826," fo. 25.

8 Simpson, fo. 25.

9 Simpson, fo. 25.

10 Simpson, fo. 25.

11 Simpson, fo. 25.

12 Simpson, fo. 24–25.

13 George Traill Allan, "Journal of a Voyage from Norway House to Fort Vancouver, Columbia River, 1831," pp. 23–24.

14 Travelling with this incoming Columbia Express were Archibald McKinlay and John McIntosh with his family who, while travelling via Leather Pass into New Caledonia, would survive a snowstorm that endangered everyone's lives. See Nancy Marguerite Anderson, *The*

Pathfinder: A.C. Anderson's Journeys in the West (Victoria: Heritage House, 2011), pp. 53–56.

15 James Douglas, "Diary of a Journey from Fort Vancouver in 1835," pp. 42–43.

16 "Edward Ermatinger's York Factory Express Journal, 1827," pp. 85 & 104.

17 James Douglas, "Diary of a Journey from Fort Vancouver in 1835," pp. 43–44.

18 Aemilius Simpson, "Journal of a Voyage Across the Continent of North America in 1826," fo. 27.

19 Governor George Simpson to Board of Management, June 24, 1848, D.4/69, fo. 778, HBCA.

20 James Douglas, "Diary of a Journey from Fort Vancouver in 1835," p. 44.

21 Possibly Five Mile Island. Compass Point might be the sharp corner in the river west of Fort Assiniboine, where paddlers come close to making a 360-degree turn to the east before again turning southwest.

22 James Douglas, "Diary of a Journey from Fort Vancouver in 1835," p. 44.

23 John Work, "Journal July 19 to October 25, 1823, York Factory to Spokane House," p. 27.

24 Aemilius Simpson, "Journal of a Voyage Across the Continent of North America in 1826," fo. 28.

25 George Traill Allan, "Journal of a Voyage from Norway House to Fort Vancouver, Columbia River, 1831," p. 24.

26 This is the mysterious Norman Smith who is mentioned in the prologue. Once west of the mountains he disappeared, although he might have been at Kamloops or Fort Colvile.

27 There is a LaCrosse Rapids farther upriver, where two men drowned. Also called Rapids des Morts by some. This island might also bear a cross, hence the name.

28 They are now at Whitecourt, Alberta, which stands at the junction of the McLeod River and the Athabasca.

29 Thomas Lowe, "Journal of a Trip from Vancouver to York Factory, 1848," (September 23–27).

30 Lowe (September 23–October 1, 1848).

31 Lowe (October 2, 1848).

32 Lowe (October 3–5, 1848).

33 Alexander Caulfield Anderson, "History of the Northwest Coast," p. 144.

34 Kenneth R. Lister, *Paul Kane, The Artist: Wilderness to Studio* (Toronto: Royal Ontario Museum Press, 2010), p. 96.

35 George Traill Allan, "Journal of a Voyage from Norway House to Fort Vancouver, Columbia River, 1831," p. 24.

36 Aemilius Simpson, "Journal of a Voyage Across the Continent of North America in 1826," fo. 31.

37 Thomas Lowe, "Journal of a Trip from Vancouver to York Factory, 1848," (October 6–7).

38 Lowe (October 8–9, 1848).

39 Jacques Cardinalle lived here, as did Antoine Auger, Dick Coulen, Courtipatte, La Plante, Louis the Iroquois, Thomas and Little Thomas, Morrigieu, and Bourdignon. Jaco Finlay might have spent time here and two of his children never left the valley.

40 Aemilius Simpson, "Journal of a Voyage Across the Continent of North America in 1826," fo. 33.

CHAPTER 16: Jasper's House to Boat Encampment (pp. 217–231)

1 Miette's Rock was sometimes called Millet's Rock, and it appears a Canadien man named Millet might have worked at Jasper's House in its early years. Bonhomme Miette was employed at Jasper's House a few years later.

2 Thomas Lowe, "Journal of a Trip from Vancouver to York Factory, Spring 1847," (October 21).

3 Thomas Lowe, "Journal of a Trip from Vancouver to York Factory, 1848," (October 10).

4 John Work, "Journal, July 18 to October 25, 1823, York Factory to Spokane House," p. 31.

5 Aemilius Simpson, "Journal of a Voyage Across the Continent of North America in 1826," fo. 33.

6 John Work, "Journal, July 18 to October 25, 1823, York Factory to Spokane House," p. 31.

7 "Edward Ermatinger's York Factory Express Journal (1827)," p. 108.

8 Ross Cox, *Adventures on the Columbia River*, pp. 253–54.

9 Aemilius Simpson, "Journal of a Voyage Across the Continent of North

America in 1826," fo. 32. Miette's Rock has changed over the years. Its massive nose was blasted away when the railway went through the valley.

10 Simpson, fo. 34.

11 Simpson, fo. 34.

12 Simpson, fo. 34.

13 "Edward Ermatinger's York Factory Express Journal (1827)," p. 108.

14 Ermatinger, p. 109. George McDougall was returning to New Caledonia with James McDougall's wife and family, who had been left at Carlton House in 1826.

15 James Douglas, "Diary of a Journey from Fort Vancouver in 1835," p. 47.

16 A.C. Anderson wrote that both Rocher du Bon Homme and Rivière Bon Homme were named for Bonhomme Miette.

17 James Douglas, "Diary of a Journey from Fort Vancouver in 1835," p. 47.

18 The man in charge of the New Caledonia men at Jasper's House that year was clerk Alexander Caulfield Anderson. He had already waited for the Express boats for ten days. The story of the misadventures of his return journey to Fort St. James is told in *The Pathfinder: A.C. Anderson's Journeys in the West*.

19 Campement des Vaches, now known as Buffalo Prairie, was about halfway between the junction of the Miette River and the mouth of Whirlpool River to the south. It was on the west bank of the Athabasca River.

20 Aemilius Simpson, "Journal of a Voyage Across the Continent of North America in 1826," fo. 35.

21 Simpson, fo. 35.

22 John Work, "Journal, July 18 to October 25, 1823, York Factory to Spokane House," p. 34.

23 "Edward Ermatinger's York Factory Express Journal (1827)," p. 109.

24 George Traill Allan, "Journal of a Voyage from Norway House to Fort Vancouver, Columbia River, 1831," p. 25.

25 Aemilius Simpson, "Journal of a Voyage Across the Continent of North America in 1826," fo. 35.

26 James Douglas, "Diary of a Journey from Fort Vancouver in 1835," p. 47.

27 Thomas Lowe, "Journal of a Trip from Vancouver to York Factory, 1848," (October 11).

28 Aemilius Simpson, "Journal of a Voyage Across the Continent of North America in 1826," fo. 36.

29 "Edward Ermatinger's York Factory Express Journal (1827)," p. 109.

30 George Traill Allan, "Journal of a Voyage from Norway House to Fort Vancouver, Columbia River, 1831," pp. 25–26.

31 Thomas Lowe, "Journal of a Trip from Vancouver to York Factory, Spring 1847," (October 26). Because snow covered the Pacific Creek valley until late spring, there were few campsites here that were not waterlogged. Lowe called it the swamp.

32 Thomas Lowe, "Journal of a Trip from Vancouver to York Factory, 1848," (October 13).

33 John Work, "Journal, July 18 to October 25, 1823, York Factory to Spokane House," pp. 35–36.

34 Ross Cox, *Adventures on the Columbia River*, p. 248.

35 Aemilius Simpson, "Journal of a Voyage Across the Continent of North America in 1826," fo. 36. His pines were *Pinus banksiana*, or Jack pine.

36 Simpson, fo. 37.

37 John Work, "Journal, July 18 to October 25, 1823, York Factory to Spokane House," p. 36.

38 "Edward Ermatinger's York Factory Express Journal (1827)," p. 109.

39 George Traill Allan, "Journal of a Voyage from Norway House to Fort Vancouver, Columbia River, 1831," p. 26.

40 Thomas Lowe, "Journal of a Trip from Vancouver to York Factory, 1848," (October 14).

41 National Gallery of Canada, Russell J. Harper, ed., *Paul Kane's Frontier*, pp. 129–30.

42 Thomas Lowe, "Journal of a Trip from Vancouver to York Factory, 1848," (October 15).

CHAPTER 17: Boat Encampment to Fort Vancouver (pp. 232–246)

1 Thomas Lowe, "Journal of a Trip from Vancouver to York Factory, 1848," (October 16).

2 Lowe (October 17, 1848). The deaths that gave Dalles des Morts (Death Rapids) its fearsome name were not caused by drowning. In 1817, seven NWC men making their way south from Boat Encampment lost canoes and provisions to the rapids. One by one they died of starvation (and cannibalism) in the woods. Only one man survived long enough to be rescued by the First Nations people and returned to Spokane House.

3 John Work, "Journal, July 18 to October 25, 1823, York Factory to Spokane House," p. 38.

4 Aemilius Simpson, "Journal of a Voyage Across the Continent of North America in 1826," fo. 39.

5 "Edward Ermatinger's York Factory Express Journal (1827)," p. 110.

6 Finan McDonald was retiring, and he and his family were heading to Edmonton House for the winter. In 1827, they joined Edward Ermatinger's outgoing York Factory Express, when Finan McDonald was attacked by the Bison (see Chapter 7). The journals of Aemilius Simpson and Edward Ermatinger provide prime examples of otherwise unrecorded women and children travelling in the York Factory Express boats.

7 Aemilius Simpson, "Journal of a Voyage Across the Continent of North America in 1826," fo. 39.

8 John Work, "Journal, July 18 to October 25, 1823, York Factory to Spokane House," pp. 38–39.

9 Aemilius Simpson, "Journal of a Voyage Across the Continent of North America in 1826," fo. 39.

10 John Work, "Journal, July 18 to October 25, 1823, York Factory to Spokane House," p. 39.

11 Aemilius Simpson, "Journal of a Voyage Across the Continent of North America in 1826," fo. 40.

12 Simpson, fo. 40.

13 James Robert Anderson, "Indian Tribes of North America," unpublished manuscript, mss. 1912, box 16, file 1, p. 23, BCA.

14 Aemilius Simpson, "Journal of a Voyage Across the Continent of North America in 1826," fo. 40.

15 Simpson, fo. 40.

16 John Work, "Journal, July 18 to October 25, 1823, York Factory to Spokane House," p. 42.

17 The Dalles Rapids is the second of three Little Dalles on the Columbia, the southernmost being just east of Fort Okanogan in Nespelem Canyon, and the northernmost being Steamboat Rapid, near Revelstoke, B.C.

18 Aemilius Simpson, "Journal of a Voyage Across the Continent of North America in 1826," fo. 41.

19 Simpson, fo. 42.

20 John Work, "Journal, July 18 to October 25, 1823, York Factory to Spokane House," p. 43.

21 Aemilius Simpson, "Journal of a Voyage Across the Continent of North America in 1826," fo. 42.

22 Simpson, fo. 43.

23 Thomas Lowe, "Journal of a Trip from Vancouver to York Factory, Spring 1847," (November 7).

24 "Edward Ermatinger's York Factory Express Journal (1827)," p. 112.

25 Thomas Lowe, "Journal of a Trip from Vancouver to York Factory, 1848," (October 18).

26 Lowe (October 19, 1848).

27 Aemilius Simpson, "Journal of a Voyage Across the Continent of North America in 1826," fo. 43–44.

28 Simpson, fo. 45.

29 Alexander Ross, *Adventures of the First Settlers on the Oregon or Columbia River: Being a Narrative of the Expedition fitted out by John Jacob Astor*, (London: Smith, Elder & Co., 1849), p. 134.

30 Aemilius Simpson, "Journal of a Voyage Across the Continent of North America in 1826," fo. 45–46.

31 Simpson, fo. 46–47.

32 Simpson, fo. 47.

33 Simpson, fo. 47.

34 Simpson, fo. 48–49.

35 Simpson, fo. 49–50.

36 Thomas Lowe, "Journal of a Trip from Vancouver to York Factory, Spring 1847," (November 14).

37 Lowe (November 17, 1847).

38 Lowe (November 20, 1847).

EPILOGUE: We Are Still Here (pp. 247–253)

1 Sir Edward Poore to Lady Agnes Poore, November 19, 1849, Poore Family Papers 1915/251, Wiltshire & Swindown Archives. Another tourist named Franklin travelled with him.

2 Poore.

3 Poore.

4 Peter Skene Ogden to Governor and Council, March 19, 1850, B.223/b/39, fo. 32, HBCA.

5 Dugald McTavish to Governor George Simpson, April 4, 1855, B.223/b/41, fo. 74, HBCA.

LIST OF WORKS CONSULTED

Campbell, Marjorie Wilkins, *The Saskatchewan* (Toronto: Clarke, Irwin & Company, 1950).

Johnson, Dennis F., *York Boats of the Hudson's Bay Company: Canada's Inland Armada* (Calgary: Fifth House, 2006).

Kemp, H.S.M., Northern Trader: *The Last Days of the Fur Trade* (Regina: University of Regina Press, 2014).

Kostash, Myrna, *Reading the River: A Traveller's Companion to the North Saskatchewan River* (Regina: Coteau Books, 2005).

Layman, William D., *River of Memory: The Everlasting Columbia* (Vancouver: UBC Press, 2006).

MacLaren, I.S., Michael Payne & Peter J. Murphy, PearlAnn Reichwein, Lisa McDermott, C.J. Nisbet, Jack, *The Mapmaker's Eye: David Thompson on the Columbia Plateau* (Pullman, WA.: Washington State University Press, 2005).

Payne, Michael, *The Most Respectable Place in the Territory: Everyday Life in Hudson's Bay Company Service, York Factory, 1788 to 1870* (Ottawa: National Historic Parks and Sites, Canadian Parks Service, Environment Canada, 1989).

Podruchny, Carolyn, *Making the Voyageur World: Travelers and Traders in the North American Fur Trade* (Toronto: University of Toronto Press, 2006).

Sanford, Emerson & Janice Sanford Beck, *Life of the Trail 6: Historic Hikes to Athabasca Pass, Fortress Lake & Tonquin Valley* (Victoria: Rocky Mountain Books, 2011).

Silversides, Brock, *Fort de Prairies: The Story of Fort Edmonton* (Surrey: Heritage House Publishing, 2005).

Taylor, Gabrielle Zezulka-Mailloux, Zac Robinson & Eric Higgs, *Culturing Wilderness in Jasper National Park: Studies in Two Centuries of Human History in the Upper Athabasca River Watershed* (Edmonton: University of Alberta Press, 2007).

ABOUT THE AUTHOR

Nancy Marguerite Anderson fell into the stories of the pre-gold rush history of the territory west of the Rocky Mountains when she researched her great-grandfather's writings. Her first book, The *Pathfinder*, told the story of Alexander Caulfield Anderson's life in the Hudson's Bay Company west of the Rockies, and of his experiences in the early colonial history of British Columbia. Many of these stories are told on Nancy's blog on her website. To her surprise, when Nancy wrote *The York Factory Express*, she discovered that her great-grandfather, James Birnie, travelled out, and in, with the first York Factory Express. The stories told in this book are his stories, but they are also the stories of all of our Hudson's Bay Company gentlemen and voyageurs, many of whom travelled in the Saskatchewan Brigades and the York Factory Express. Visit Nancy Marguerite Anderson on her website at www.nancymargueriteanderson.com.

INDEX